EDWARD A. ARMSTRONG, a retired priest of the Church of England, was born October 3, 1900, in Belfast, where he received his B.A. from Queens' University. He received his M.A. from Leeds University and an Honorary M.A. from Cambridge University. He is married and has two sons. Father Armstrong served as curate in various parishes in England and in China and has traveled to the Middle East, Africa, North and South America and the Arctic. He is an authority on folklore and ornithology.

Father Armstrong has contributed to the *Classical Review*, *Archaeology*, *Folklore* and the *Encyclopedia of Man, Myth and Magic*. He broadcasts on the B.B.C. and has published several books.

THE GOSPEL PARABLES

THE
GOSPEL PARABLES

by

EDWARD A. ARMSTRONG

SHEED AND WARD : NEW YORK

Library of Congress Catalogue Card Number 69-16989

Manufactured in the United States of America

CONTENTS

CONTENTS

CHAPTER IV WORK AND WAGES

CHAPTER V LOST AND FOUND, FATHER AND SON

INTRODUCTION

A woman searching for a lost coin, a man tending another by the roadside, a father welcoming his son—such incidents have never been unusual; and yet brief accounts in simple language of these and other commonplace events have enriched the imaginations of generation after generation, and inspired ordinary men and women to lives of heroic self-sacrifice. Were we not aware of the background of these stories this would seem unaccountable—and naturally so, for the tales cannot be understood apart from the Teller, and the Teller is revealed in the tales. To folk of all kinds, simple and learned, the educated Westerner and people in New Guinea just emerging from the Stone Age, the parables are a vehicle of truth, moral and spiritual, for they reveal not only the path of virtue but also the truth as it is in Jesus. The imagination of the small child is illuminated by mind-pictures drawn from the parables; hard-pressed folk are sustained in the trials of life by their teaching; and scholars have found profundities in them calling forth all their resources of learning and insight. We gain new inspiration and perceive deeper implications as we ponder on them. All who come asking, 'Sir, we should like to see Jesus' (Jn. xii. 21) may meet Him in the stories He told.[1]

While it is true that the parables, or at least many of them, have a plain, direct message for all who humbly and prayerfully seek enlightenment, yet their apparent simplicity can be misleading. Early in Christian history scholars, convinced that much more lay beneath the surface than met the eye, brought to them interpretations and presuppositions which led to distortions of their meaning. Rightly divining that they were intended to arouse the imagination they interpreted them as if it need never draw rein.[2] Thus for

7

Augustine the traveller who fell among thieves is Adam, fallen man, Jerusalem signifies the heavenly city, the thieves are the devil and his angels who stripped man of his immortality, the setting of the injured man on the beast represents belief in the Incarnation, the inn stands for the Church, the Samaritan for Christ, the innkeeper for St. Paul, the two pence for the two principles of love—and so forth.[3] Such commentators did not always agree with one another; for each enjoyed fitting his own whimsical notions into the parables. Origen, who preceded Augustine by a century and a half, considered the two pence to represent the Father and the Son. In spite of protests from John Chrysostom (347–407), Theodore of Mopsuestia (350–428) and other scholars of Antioch, such allegorizing interpretations prevailed down the centuries with only an occasional dissenting voice. Archbishop Trench's best-seller, *Notes on the Parables* (1841), continued the tradition, and its influence is still apparent in the interpretations sometimes heard from English pulpits today. On the Continent the authority of St. Thomas Aquinas has served to justify the time-worn allegorizations.[4]

The wind of criticism which was to overthrow this ancient tradition began to blow about a century ago. Its gusts, which emanated from Holland and Germany, did not seriously ruffle the theological scene in this country for a considerable time, mainly because the works of the pioneers were not translated into English— nor have they yet been.[5] The critics contended that allegory is absent from the parables. This conclusion has been shown to be too sweeping; but the new approach enabled much unfruitful interpretation to be discarded. The abandonment of preconceptions concerning the Gospel parables led to an intensive study of rabbinic literature, which contains many parables, practically all recorded later than the first century A.D.[6] At the same time new methods of studying the Gospels as a whole were being developed—source criticism, form criticism, linguistic analysis and, recently, the scrutiny of newly discovered material, such as the Dead Sea Scrolls and the Coptic sayings, rather inappropriately called the Gospel of Thomas. Much attention has been directed to the period when the material in the Gospels was being transmitted orally in Aramaic. As a result of such studies we can now look behind the Gospels and envisage the Evangelists compiling their records from the stream of oral and written tradition. Although the scene inevitably becomes more obscure as we try to peer still further into the past we can glimpse the small but growing churches of the eastern Mediterranean collecting reminiscences of Jesus and records of His sayings with a view to their use in worship, for instruction and for the defence of the faith.[7]

Thus we are able to perceive how some parables have come to be recorded in more than one version and we can detect, or at least suspect, the existence of passages where the Evangelists or their sources have selected, arranged, emphasized, interpolated material or coloured the tradition. We see that during the period of oral transmission, when importance was attached to aids to memory, and again when the Gospels were compiled, material with some connecting theme was grouped in paragraphs, as is apparent to the attentive reader. The Evangelists were little concerned with chronology, and not at all with such details as our Lord's appearance. His coming and His message were all-important.

Owing to the inadequacy of our information on the sequence of the parables in our Lord's teaching, little attention will here be paid to the order in which they have come down to us. As we try to recover the original setting of the parables in our Lord's ministry we must not only bear in mind those who first heard them and how they were most likely to have understood them but also make allowance for the views, interests and aspirations of the first and second generation Christians who transmitted and influenced the tradition. We shall see, however, that to ascertain to whom some of the parables were first addressed is more difficult than has sometimes been supposed.

It is also important to take into account the tendencies in our own time which may influence our evaluation of the parables. Modern New Testament scholarship tends to be dominated by source- and form-criticism. It is proper that these techniques should be given due weight, but some writers, notably Bultmann and his followers, plunge so deep into literary criticism and existential interpretation that the reader, looking up from their pages, finds himself wondering why the Gospels, after all these centuries, still claim such attention if they are so much the product of accretion and the crystallization of tradition as these scholars suggest. It is very difficult to believe that tiny groups of Christians, including few educated people, could have influenced the record to this extent. When allowance has been made for sound scholarly opinion and some extraneous matter has been pruned away the parables carry their own authentication.

The cogency of the evidence for the reliable memorizing of our Lord's sayings needs to be stressed. It is easy for us, saturated in a literary culture, to underestimate the rôle of the memorizing of teaching in less literate societies. There still survive, even in Western communities, story-tellers who, evening after evening, can relate in word-perfect form extensive ancient tales.[8] In India Vedic doctrines were transmitted orally for a thousand years without material alteration, and in China and the Moslem world immense importance was attached to memorized knowledge. Many unlettered peoples have retained in their myths records of events which occurred centuries earlier. In Judaism the committal of teaching to memory received great emphasis. Of one of his disciples a rabbi remarked: 'He is like a well-plastered cistern that loses not a drop'—perhaps a backhanded compliment! 'From birth to death the Jew was subjected to an endless succession of signs and symbols, ceaselessly exhorting him "to remember".' That which had been learned by reading was considered inferior to knowledge acquired orally.[9] The rabbis framed their instructions in rhythmic sentences, thus rendering memorizing easier, and some of our Lord's sayings and parables such as The Foxes' Dens and the Birds' Nests (Mt. viii. 20; Lk. ix. 58) and The Sheep and the Goats (The Great Assize) (Mt. xxv. 31–46) are seen to be in poetic form when translated back into Aramaic—and poetry facilitates memorizing.[10]

In the Early Church, as in rabbinic Judaism, there was bias

against written sources and in favour of oral teaching. Papias, Bishop of Hierapolos, writing in the first half of the second century preferred oral to written tradition when it was available. 'I supposed,' he commented, 'that things out of books did not profit me so much as the utterances of a voice which liveth and abideth.' Irenaeus, later that century, attached special importance to what he had heard from a certain presbyter who had heard it from those who had seen the apostles.[11] Despite the vicissitudes to which the tradition was subjected and the modifications, presently to be considered, which it received during transmission, we may be sure that in the parables we hear the voice of Jesus.

It is easy to misunderstand the nature of Gospel parables if we accept naïvely the Sunday-school definition—earthly stories with a heavenly meaning. They are much more than that. Indeed, they are sparks from that fire which our Lord brought to the earth (Lk. xii. 49)—the message of One who was 'a prophet . . . and more than a prophet' (Mt. xi. 9; Lk. vii. 16). C. W. F. Smith comments: 'In the parables Jesus appears as no Eastern sage or objective moralist, but as the Initiator of God's new age and the Agent of His purpose. He is not the kindly advocate of brotherly love, but the revealer of the dreadful love of God and the awe of the divine mercy.' C. F. D. Moule speaks of careful study of the parables giving us back 'this arresting and terrifying picture of the "Strong Son of God" '.[12] We are told that the crowd 'listened eagerly' (Mk. xii. 38) and 'the people were astonished at His doctrine; for He taught as One having authority, and not as the scribes' (Mt. vii. 29; Mk. i. 22). 'What new teaching is this?' they asked. His 'I say unto you' (Mt. vi. 29, xviii. 22, xxi. 31; Mk. xiii. 27) transcended traditional teaching. (Until the finding of the Dead Sea Scrolls the 'Amen, Amen' preceeding His sayings was considered to be unique, constituting a claim to special authority.) Käsemann remarks that His 'I say unto you' embodies a claim to authority rivalling and challenging that of Moses.[13] His teaching that God might be addressed as *Abba*, Father, was a departure from all previous Jewish practice. No Jew before had ventured to approach the Almighty with the child's familiar form of address. As Jeremias has stressed, with the use of *Abba* 'we are confronted with something new and unheard of which breaks through the limits of Judaism'.[14]

Similar startling teaching is embodied in Jesus' statement that 'whoever does not accept the Kingdom of God like a child will never enter it' (Mk. x. 15). His attitude to the Temple authorities showed that He set His teaching above theirs. His claims, such as entitlement to forgive sins, to transcend the Sabbath laws and to cast out evil spirits by the Spirit of God, went far beyond those of any rabbi. His followers were convinced that He had 'the words of eternal life' (Jn. vi. 68).

The seeker after Christian truth has ever had to interpret the words by the Person and the Person by His words. The people said, 'No man ever spoke as this man speaks' (Jn. vii. 46); and, although His words come to us echoing down the centuries, His claims are clear. He confronts us with a choice, indeed, with a series of challenges—to alert ourselves to God's approach to us whether in our experience of life, or in the reading of the Gospels or in the worship and teaching of the Church. As Nygren points out: 'Only if God comes to meet us can we possibly come to Him.' The interpretation of the parables will depend on whether they are regarded as demonstrational or revelational, but we shall miss their impact if we do not find in them more than the demonstrational. The revelational 'takes its starting point in the religious life itself'.[15] Being revelational the parables point beyond themselves to a realm of higher than earthly values and to One who claims more than a hearing—our utmost devotion. Here are 'the lively oracles of God', here is wisdom from on High delivered by Him in whom 'the complete being of the Godhead dwells embodied' and in whom we are 'brought to completion' if our lives be lived 'in union with Him' (Col. ii. 9 f). In reading the parables we must never forget that in telling them Jesus was making Himself, as well as His message, known to men.

The parable as an art form and vehicle for teaching reaches its highest perfection in the parables of Jesus. They have a quality beyond those of the rabbis and the compositions of other times and peoples. A Jewish scholar has written: 'Close comparison of the Gospel parables with the most similar of the rabbinic nearly always reveals dissimilarity within the similarity ... Fiebig is clearly right when he claims the Gospel parables are marked by characteristic features which testify to an original and exalted personality in their authorship.'[16] Another scholar, studying the parables of Jesus in the light of contemporary parabolic teaching, has said of them, 'The Gospel parables are revealed as supremely beautiful examples of an established art.'[17]

The beginnings of the art may be traced far back in Israel's history. The outstanding example is the story of the poor man's ewe lamb by which Nathan led David to convict himself of his crime (II Sam. xii. 1–4). There are also fables in the Old Testament, a class of story in which animals, plants or inanimate objects act out of character, as in the story of The Trees seeking a King (Judges ix. 7 ff.) and The Thistle which taunted the Cedar (II Kings xiv. 9). These are of a pattern common among folk-tales.

The Hebrew word māshāl which was translated into Greek as parabólē could be used for a proverb, aphorism or even oracle, though, of the list given by Manson only Ezek. xvii. 3–10 and xxiv. 3–5 are described as māshāl.[18] Some Old Testament stories are allegorical rather than symbolic, such as Ezekiel's account of the eagles and the trees (p. 53). Our Lord used a number of these forms of speech, ranging from the quotation of accepted maxims to example stories and illustrative narratives. In the Old Testament, too, we find figurative forms of expression varying from metaphors and proverbs to narrative tales. Here 'parable' will be regarded as an inclusive term covering a number of these.

What follows in this Introduction does not constitute a general survey of parabolic teaching, for that would require much more space than is available, but a brief review of a few considerations which may explain the writer's approach and opinions in regard to some vexed questions so that the reader may attach what value he thinks fit to views expressed which differ to some extent from such great authorities as C. H. Dodd and J. Jeremias. Only with reluctance has the writer diverged from the opinions of these and other scholars, to whom, as will be apparent, he is deeply indebted.

In recent years strenuous efforts have been made to identify the original settings of the parables. If we could be certain in what circumstances and to what audience our Lord first uttered each one we would have a useful key to their meaning, but in many instances the Evangelists themselves were uncertain of the actual setting of a parable and therefore fitted it into their narratives where they considered most appropriate—often in connexion with related sayings or apposite situations. The problem which beset the Evangelists is evident when we try to determine those to whom The Wicked Vinedressers (Mt. xxi. 33–41; Mk. xii. 1–9; Lk. xx. 9–16) was addressed. They are variously said to have been the chief priests, scribes and elders (Mk. xi. 27), the chief priests and elders (Mt. xxi. 23), chief priests and Pharisees (Mt. xxi. 45), the crowd (Lk. xx. 9) or scribes and chief priests (Lk. xx. 19). Jeremias (pp. 41 f.), who points out these anomalies, goes on to argue that 'parables which were originally addressed to opponents or to the crowd have in many cases been applied by the primitive Church to the Christian community'. But undoubtedly some sayings which referred to others have been transferred to the Pharisees, e.g. Lk. xvi. 14–15, which applies rather to the Sadducees, whose luxurious living was notorious.[19]

We must here discuss briefly the extent to which the parables were directed against the Pharisees, as our estimate of the nature of parabolic teaching may be influenced by our views on this matter. A. T. Cadoux, challenging the assumption that the parables are simple, edifying, illustrative stories, asserted: 'In its most characteristic use the parable is a weapon of attack or defence.'[20]

This has been endorsed by later writers. Jeremias states (p. 21): 'For the greater part, though not exclusively, the parables are weapons of warfare' and (p. 124): 'The parables which have as their theme the gospel in its narrower sense are, apparently without exception addressed, not to the poor, but to Christ's opponents. . . . They are controversial weapons against the critics and foes of the gospel.' The concept of the parables as weapons has been useful in depreciating jejune interpretations and emphasizing the urgency with which this teaching was presented, but the metaphor has been pushed so far as almost to suggest that much of our Lord's teaching consisted of a stream of diatribes against the religious leaders in general and the Pharisees in particular.

The priestly leaders during the period preceding the fall of Jerusalem were selfish and irresponsible and we may therefore infer with plausibility that their behaviour some decades earlier was unworthy and open to criticism.[21] Certainly the claims of Jesus offended the Jewish leaders. Their animosity was manifested during His ministry and is abundantly evident in the events of Passion Week. But this is no reason for assuming that the teaching of Jesus was continuously and predominantly against them during His ministry, which may have lasted several years. It must be remembered that those who collected the traditions, and the Evangelists themselves, were antagonistic to the Jewish religious leaders and this may have led them to emphasize and exaggerate the controversial aspects of His message. Thus some critics, through not making sufficient allowance for this tendency, have laid undue stress upon the polemical element in our Lord's teaching. It is impossible here to set out fully the grounds for being doubtful about their treatment of the scribes and Pharisees, but commentators, including some who accept the view that much of our Lord's teaching was polemical, are in many cases prepared to allow that this aspect of His teaching has been over-emphasized by the Evangelists.[22]

It is significant that source Q, concerning which there is some disagreement, but which is generally considered to be the second source, apart from Mark, used by Matthew and Luke, has extremely little polemical material and records no arguments with scribes or Pharisees, though it contains one denunciation of Pharisaism (Lk. xi. 37–41; 42–52; cf. Mt. xxiii. *passim*).

In spite of the bias against the religious leaders in the Gospels

B

they also contain evidence of a sympathetic attitude on the part of the Pharisees (Lk. xiv. 15, xxiii. 51; Jn. iii. 1 f., vii. 50 f., ix. 16. Cf. Mk. xii. 28–34 for a friendly relationship with a scribe). Luke (xiii. 31) records that Pharisees warned Jesus that Herod was plotting to kill Him. There is a tendency to think of the Pharisees as a great body of scholars. In fact, they are believed to have numbered about six thousand and apart from a few theologians to have been a mixed group of craftsmen, traders and so forth.[23]

If allowance is made for this colouring of the record by the Evangelists we shall be less disposed to interpret parables as being weapons aimed at the scribes and Pharisees. While due attention should be paid to the skilful efforts of scholars, such as Jeremias, to detect instances in which the setting of parables may have been altered, we must bear in mind, firstly, that most of the parables reached the Evangelists without information concerning their original setting, and, secondly, that, as we have noted, it has been too readily assumed that many parables were directed as polemics at one particular group of people. Those who handled the traditions in the first century strove to locate them in precise settings and if twentieth-century scholars, bent on detecting definite settings for these traditions find them in the records this is what we should expect, as the Evangelists, seeking suitable contexts, placed them where they are in the Gospels.

Critics have stressed the limited and particular application of parables to such an extent that their profounder religious and ethical lessons may sometimes have been obscured or neglected. Dodd (p. 146) rules out 'any interpretation of the parables which gives them a general application' and insists upon 'their intense particularity as comments upon an historical situation'. He admits that, like any serious work of art, they have significance beyond the original occasion, but fails to give weight to the consideration that such works of art were not limited by their particularity on their first presentation. Particularity there may be, but not mere particularity. A portrait by Rembrandt was never just a likeness; and when Dante likens Beatrice's glance to the look of a mother gazing on her delirious child he enlists memories, associations and feelings which load the simple illustration with immense power.[24]

Jeremias (p. 169) remarks of the parables which he regards as concerned with the impending crisis (The Sulking Children, The Fig Tree, The Discarded Salt and others): 'It is not their purpose to propound moral precepts, but to shock into realization of its danger a nation rushing upon its own destruction, and more especially its leaders, the theologians and priests. But above all they are a call to repentance.' Yes, indeed, but a call to repentance cannot be dissociated from a proclamation of moral precepts.

The Gospel parables may be divided into two main categories: Those which depict a type of character to be copied or avoided and those which illustrate some principle of God's rule. In both principles are called to our attention. No warning in the Gospels is without a moral background. Significantly, among the versions of the story which we know best in the form of the parable of The Rich Man and Lazarus none more definitely concentrates on the moral aspect than the story as told by Jesus (pp. 108–116).[25]

Apart from these considerations Jesus may have repeated His teaching on different occasions to different groups which, in taking them to heart, might apply them to their own circumstances. Manson remarks that 'in the first century A.D. in Palestine the only way to publish great thoughts was to go on repeating them in talk or sermons'. . . . Great teachers constantly repeat themselves.' Jeremias quotes this last remark with approval. He comments: 'Jesus was never tired of expressing the central ideas of His message in constantly changing images.'[26]

Dodd points out how significant is one form of this repetitiveness. Certain themes, such as fulfilment and judgement, appear again and again in the Gospels, sometimes as parables and sometimes illustrated or presented in other ways. Thus the teaching is driven home by variety of appeal.[27]

Concentration on identifying the original audience has tended to focus attention on the concept of parables as devices for rebutting erroneous opinions; but they are primarily positive teaching about

God and the Good News concerning His relationship to men. The titles by which some of the parables are generally known indicate that the human actors, with their frailties, have caught the imagination more readily than the truths taught about God. The behaviour of the men in The Labourers in the Vineyard is not central to the story but a background to illustrate the magnanimity of the Generous Employer (pp. 125–128). The spendthrift youth is not the most important figure in the parable of The Prodigal Son. Both the sons are important, but the central figure is the welcoming father (pp. 169–177). In contemplating the Pharisee and the Publican neither the self-righteousness of the Pharisee nor the self-depreciation of the Publican is primary; the parable is about God's forgiveness and what men are in His sight. In the parables the sins of men, whether Pharisees or not, are illustrated to render more vivid God's righteousness and man's responsibility as a child of God to live in His image. 'Why be jealous because I am kind?' asks the employer in the parable of The Labourers in the Vineyard (Mt. xx. 15). But we tend to concentrate our attention on the human sins and failings rather than on spiritual truths about God in the parables. Contrast is of their essence; but the fundamental comparison is between what God is and requires and what men do. The strand in human character which inclines men to criticize each other rather than see themselves as they might appear before the throne of God has biased the interpretation of the parables.

These considerations must be set against the arguments which have been, and are, current, against generalizing the parables. 'Of the total number of parables, two-fifths . . . are so embedded in their historical situation or their references so limited and particular that they hardly permit of an additional interpretation or application having to do either with the promulgation of precepts or modes of ethical conduct, or describing the conditions of human existence or what is valid for all.'[28]

The assumption underlying this point of view, which is shared by a number of scholars, seems to be that a parable, as uttered by Jesus, was, very often, an *ad hoc* illustration, comparison or admonition, exclusively limited in its reference to a particular historical occasion and special circumstances. This presupposes, firstly, a narrow concept of the nature and function of a parable, secondly, a restrictive view of the wisdom and insight of our Lord, and thirdly, as suggested a little earlier, hearers with sluggish imaginations. If it be argued that we must distinguish between those parables which can, and those which cannot, be generalized, we must insist that people listening to a master of parabolic teaching would seldom or never accept any parable he uttered as applicable only to a specific situation.

Apart from the difficulty, or impossibility, of limiting the significance of a parable to that which it had in its original setting, when, with perhaps a few exceptions, this cannot be ascertained with any certainty,[29] there are cogent reasons in the very nature of parabolic teaching for a more generous attitude. He who tells parables is asking others to share and extend his intuitions rather than arguing. Jerome realized something of this when he commented: 'The marrow of a parable is different from the promise of its surface, and like as gold is sought for in the earth, the kernel in a nut and the hidden fruit in the prickly covering of chestnuts, so in parables we must search more deeply after the divine meaning.'[30] Now, however, with the insights scholarship has given us, we would add that there must be an appreciation of the chestnut's setting in its covering and of its origin as a culminating outgrowth of the tree if we are to understand its nature and interpret its significance. But to suppose that a parable's application could be limited to its primary setting is to misconceive the nature of a parable. Teaching of this kind is based on the mind's alacrity in making comparisons and generalizations; and the *raison d'être* of a parable is to alert the mind and to stimulate or tease it into associative activity. The degree of such activity may vary immensely, though generally, so far as the nature of such Gospel parables is concerned, some form of personal challenge or involvement with the situation depicted is required. 'What if this were I?' 'Is the Kingdom of God really like this?' 'Where do I stand?'

Statements vary immensely in their power to arouse the imagination and generate associations and personal response. We recognize 'A stitch in time saves nine' as by no means relevant only to needlework, and we are entranced by the magic of a phrase such as Milton's reference to the nightingale's song: 'Silence was pleased.' Our Lord's hearers would no more suppose the proverb, 'Where the corpse is there the vultures will gather' (Mt. xxiv. 28; Lk. xvii. 37), to be a statement of purely ornithological interest than any of us would imagine, 'There is never smoke without fire' to be a mere statement of fact. Any teacher using parables extensively assumes that his audience will accept imaginatively what he says. Ripples of radiating reference are initiated and, although the immediate application may be restricted, the potential ramifications are unlimited.[31] Many proverbs owe their pithiness to the individual's ability to grasp a familiar statement's relevance to a novel situation. Humour, too, calls on the mind to perceive a relationship where it had not been obvious before. A joke bridges the distance between two points, hitherto apparently unrelated. It pleases by its novelty and the element of incongruity. Parables occupy an intermediate position between proverbial wisdom and wit. This is particularly true of those Gospel parables which contain an unexpected twist (pp. 65, 83, 126, 137, 165). They have kinship with poetry and humour. Whether the hearer or reader is presented with the simplest forms of figurative speech, elaborate parable, analogy or poetry, an imaginative leap, small or great, is required. The mind is stimulated to make comparisons between disparate things, seeking out points of resemblance, as in, 'Ye are the salt of the earth' or the comparison between the action of leaven and the coming of the Kingdom of God. Unexpectedness adds to the aesthetic pleasure. Poets sometimes achieve it by the transposition of imagery, as in Edith Sitwell's:

> What would these ghosts do, if the truths they know,
> That were served up like snow-cold jewelled fruits
> And the unfeathered airs of lutes
> Could be their guests in cold reality?[32]

Or Denis Devlin's:

> The fireflies of your gentle thoughts through
> my gnarled thorntree nerves
> Smile through my eyelids soothing as a
> shaded lamp.[33]

A parable is an artistic creation initiating associative activities which, up to a point, have a life of their own. In using parables any teacher is necessarily accepting this quality in them, though the capacity of any particular parable in this respect varies immensely.

Not to generalize a parable is like visiting a church as an historical and architectural monument without realizing its symbolism, such as the progress from font to altar as representing the Christian's advance in life and devotion, though, of course, in studying parables we must always do our best to determine the original significance and application. In teaching we should make these clear. We should also point out those parables which seem to have had special relevance to the situation which called them forth. Then nobody need be misled by the extension of meaning given to parables. They demand to be regarded like leaven in dough or as a store from which a householder may produce things new and old (Mt. xiii. 52).

As Christian history enshrines nearly two thousand years of meditation on the Gospels and because the outlook of the Church and individual Christians is coloured by centuries of assimilation and interpretation of the parables, which constitute about one-third of the material in the Synoptics, we must constantly bear in mind the artificiality of assessing them as isolated stories or even as confined within their Gospel contexts. As we have noted, much has justifiably been made of the importance of identifying their original 'setting in life', but ever since their first utterance they have had a 'setting in life' within the Church and every generation has been enriched by contemporary interpretations of them, including insights into the way in which they complement and qualify each other—an aspect of parabolic teaching not dwelt on in these pages, but which must be given full weight.

An entomologist whose knowledge of a butterfly extended no further than acquaintance with what he could discover under the microscope would gain a very inadequate conception of it as a living creature. If we neglect or underestimate the life of a parable, moulding thought and conduct, our interpretation of it will be limited or distorted. When dealing with parables as teaching and literature we must not forget that our ultimate concern is to know God through them. Although, in what follows, brevity compels concentration on the teaching of Jesus in the parables it is clear that it cannot be understood apart from knowledge of the Teacher and the life of the Society inspired by His teaching. 'We know that you are a teacher sent by God' (Jn. iii. 2), said Nicodemus, and we, inheritors of the Christian centuries on whom the light of the knowledge of God in Jesus Christ has shined, are able to interpret the parables by all that the Church has transmitted to us and the Holy Spirit has granted us of revelation and insight. A parable cannot be comprehended until it is assimilated, translated into Christian character and authenticates itself in life.

At this point we may ask, To what extent did our Lord use parables to conceal His meaning, as some of the statements in the Gospels suggest (Mk. iv. 10 ff.; Mt. xiii. 34 f.; Lk. viii. 9 f.; Jn. xvi. 25)? The crucial verses are Mk. iv. 11 f.: 'To those who are outside everything comes by way of parables, so that (as Scripture says) they may look and look, but see nothing; they may hear and hear, but understand nothing; otherwise they might turn to God and be forgiven.' This passage, which probably inspired the Oxford Dictionary's definition of a parable as an 'enigmatical saying', has been interpreted in different ways by commentators, though it would be hard to find any authority who regarded it as a verbatim record. Cranfield (p. 61) thinks the statement should be understood in the light of God's action in the person, words and works of Jesus as setting forth a secret or mystery. Dodd (pp. 13–15) considers that the conception of parables being allegorical mystifications could have arisen only in a non-Jewish environment. The suggestion of mystery indicates, at the very least, the colouring of the passages by later ideas, such as appear in Paul's epistles. Several scholars, including Taylor (pp. 256–258) and Jeremias (pp. 13–19), believe that Mk. iv. 11 f. may not apply to the parables but to Jesus' teaching as a whole. It was originally a sad recognition that only His close followers understood the nature of His call. There were many to whom Isaiah's words (vi. 9) were applicable: 'Hear ye, indeed, but understand not; and see ye, indeed, but perceive not.' Black points out that in Lk. viii. 10 'we get a contrast between the crowds without, who, while they see and hear, neither perceive nor understand, and the disciples, those within, who see with their eyes and understand, and are blessed on that account'. With reference to its authenticity as a saying of our Lord he remarks: 'It is most unlikely that He was in any way responsible for the grim adaptation of it which we find in Mark.'[34] We must bear in mind the conviction, held by the early Christians and derived from Jewish beliefs, that God willed the salvation of some and the condemnation of others. Jeremias (p. 98) thinks that Jesus, after polemical utterances, gave deeper instruction to 'the narrower circle of the disciples', but the significance of polemics is usually evident. Another explanation of the saying is that what our Lord said was misunderstood because of His use of a Hebrew idiom by which the consequence of an action was expressed as if it has been its purpose. The view has also been put forward that the Evangelists' convictions concerning the 'Messianic secret' influenced their outlook on our Lord's teaching.[35] Possibly Jesus set forth some of His teaching in a form which required a sympathetic hearing if its full import were to be understood by slow-witted hearers who may have been puzzled by pithy sayings. Certainly, on some occasions He aimed to surprise and intrigue His audience. Since there is more than meets the eye in a parable there is some excuse for the supposition that the interpretation is not always open to all. Also, there is an affinity with some Old Testament parables and even riddles. When Ezekiel told the parable of The Forest Fire (Ezek. xx. 45–49) it was found to be so obscure that he was commissioned to explain it.[36] But, in interpreting the parables we must assume that, with perhaps a rare exception, Jesus delivered them in such a way as to drive home His message clearly and vigorously. Undoubtedly Mk. iv. 11 f. should not be regarded as applying to the parables in general. In view of the urgency of our Lord's message, 'quick and powerful and sharper than any two-edged sword, piercing even to the dividing asunder of soul and spirit' (Heb. iv. 12), it is unthinkable that He framed His teaching in terms designed to baffle His hearers.

Several factors induced the Evangelists to believe that He spoke in mystifying terms. As at least many parables reached them without context their significance was not clearly apparent so they surmised that they were intended not merely to intrigue but to puzzle. They also found it unaccountable that His proclamation of truth should have been rejected and sought an explanation in the supposition that some of it must have been designed to conceal its meaning from the multitude. As a parable calls for comparison and recognition of its application it is possible for there to be an interval of non-recognition, usually momentary, such that when recognition occurs, the significance strikes home with special force. David was obtuse enough to fail to perceive Nathan's parable to be an indictment of his lust and connivance at murder until the prophet said, 'Thou art the man.' But this story, designed to illustrate the extent to which pride and lust blind the soul is rather different in character from the Gospel parables. It belongs to a special group of stories, with many examples among the folk-tales of various peoples, in which unpalatable truths are revealed to exalted personages in ambiguous terms and by privileged individuals, such as bards or court jesters.

The 'life' of the Gospel parables must be viewed as involving three phases, Firstly, the parable as it was uttered by Jesus; secondly, the interpretation by the early Church of the version in which it was known, as indicated by its treatment in the New Testament; and thirdly, its expository treatment in subsequent ages, including bringing it into relationship with contemporary problems, as preachers have sought to do throughout the Christian centuries, using modes of thought varying from the allegorizing favoured in the past to the existentialist treatment of recent times. The present writer's view has already been indicated: It is desirable, having grasped, so far as we may, the original point of a parable, to follow out its wider associations and applications so that it speaks as it was intended to do, to the heart.

Many of the parables are concerned with the Kingdom of God. In *Parables of the Kingdom* Dodd discusses thirty in detail.[37] Thus some comments on our Lord's teaching about the Kingdom cannot be avoided, although this topic has been so much discussed ever since the publication of Schweitzer's *Quest of the Historical Jesus* that any brief summary must be inadequate. It is now widely agreed that in Jesus' proclamation of the Kingdom the emphasis was on the wonderful works of God, rather than on any human activity, on the initiative of God rather than the cooperation of man.[38] The Kingdom is the direct, regnant power of God intervening in men's affairs. Many now hold that the conception long current of the Kingdom as the outcome of man's striving, through the power of God, to establish faith, piety, righteous dealing and neighbourliness on earth was generated from the original proclamation, but was not implicit in it. Discussion has centred on the question whether the Kingdom proclaimed by Jesus was present or future. Did He anticipate an imminent in-breaking of the Kingdom or did He teach that its fulfilment might be delayed until after His death? Schweitzer's extreme view that He expected the Kingdom before His death now receives little support. Dodd urges that Jesus proclaimed its in-coming as taking place in His ministry. He writes (p. 141) of 'the Kingdom of God in process of realization' and in a later work, calls his view 'inaugurated eschatology'.[39] Jeremias' point of view (p. 230) is fairly close to Dodd's. The latter believes that the Kingdom proclaimed by our Lord was in process of actualization in His mission and ministry. The translation of the crucial saying, Lk. xvii. 20, adopted by the New English Bible is: 'You cannot tell by observation when the Kingdom of God comes. There will be no saying, "Look, here it is!" or "there it is!" for in fact the Kingdom of God is among you.' Dodd has revised his opinion of its meaning and accepts the suggestion that the final words should be interpreted 'within your reach' or 'within your grasp'.[40]

Perrin, in a review of the history of the discussion, holds that the Kingdom was proclaimed as both present and future and that there was thus a 'tension' in this respect in our Lord's teaching.[41] Whatever uncertainties may remain on this matter it is clear that in the parables the Kingdom of God is represented as being manifested in Jesus' mission.

Among the arguments put forward in favour of the view that the coming of the Kingdom lay in the future is that the ethical teaching of our Lord shows little sign of being framed for a situation in which the End was regarded as imminent. Much has been written on these lines. Here it will be sufficient to point out that this view is supported by the themes of a number of parables. There is in them no hint that shortly there will be no employers or employed, no roads or robbers, no erring sons, no fields to be sown and reaped. This can hardly be because ethical principles remain valid 'though the skies fall'.

Another consideration has not received the attention it deserves. Our Lord's attitude to nature is not that of one who expected the imminent dissolution of the world order. The sympathy with nature which He expressed is unsurpassed and probably unparalleled in antiquity. H. B. Swete wrote of the parables: 'The intimate knowledge which they show of nature and of man is not less unique than their beauty.'[42] Greek curiosity concerning nature needs no emphasis and Virgil stands out as the Latin poet who took pleasure in nature, but compassionate interest in the natural world, such as is prominent in the Gospels, is very rare in the literature of Greece and Rome. In the Old Testament we find hints of concern for the welfare of animals, admonitions to spare the parent bird when a nest is raided and to treat draught animals with consideration (Deut. xxii. 6, 10, xxv. 4), but these may indicate self-interest and an eye to conservation and good husbandry more than compassion. Pleasure in nature as a setting for love is represented in

the Song of Solomon. The outstanding expression of divine compassion for the animal creation to be found in the Old Testament is
the conclusion of the book of Jonah (iv. 11): 'And should not I spare
Nineveh, that great city, wherein are more than sixscore thousand
persons that cannot discern between their right hand and their left
hand; and also much cattle?'[43]

More than sixty years ago Paul Fiebig remarked, commenting on the rabbinic parables, that 'in comparison with the Synoptic
parables, it strikes one that the processes of Nature—sowing and
harvest, flowering and fruitage, were taken little account of'.[44] This
is fair comment, though it somewhat overstates the case, as some
Jewish scholars have shown.[45] Illustrations from the natural world
came so readily to our Lord's lips that to read the Gospels is to be
transported to anemone-strewn hillsides and sheep-cropped pastures,
to cornfields, vineyards and plantations of fruit trees. In imagination
we see the swooping vultures, the sparrows on the rooftops, the
raiding birds descending on the newly-sown fields, the camel
ambling along the narrow street, the fox sneaking in the gloaming
back to its den and the wolves prowling from the woods in search of
prey. We find assurance of God's care for us, as Jesus did, in His
provision of food for the raven and raiment for the wild flowers.

> He spoke of grass and wind and rain,
> And fig trees and fair weather;
> And made it His delight to bring
> Heaven and earth together.

Imagery drawn from nature appears in our Lord's teaching when
worldliness and spirituality are contrasted, as in The Birds of the
Air and The Flowers of the Field, The Moth and the Rust, and
The Camel and The Needle's Eye. His reference to The Foxes'
Dens and The Birds' Nests (Mt. viii. 20; Lk. ix. 58) expresses with
poetic poignancy the loneliness which was His lot and which so
many of His followers have, in some measure, known.[46]

Mourning compassionately over Jerusalem the image which
sprang to His mind was that of a hen sheltering her chicks as from

a bird of prey (Mt. xxiii. 37; Lk. xiii. 34). Again, when malice and innocence were contrasted the imagery was taken from the animal world: wolves and sheep (Lk. x. 3), serpents and doves (Mt. x. 16), serpent and fish (Mt. vii. 10). In reminding His hearers that they were of more value than many sparrows and that not a sparrow falls to the ground without its being noticed by the Heavenly Father (Mt. x. 29–31; Lk. xii. 6 f.), He implied that sparrows were not of negligible value in God's sight; so also with the Flowers of the Field, because they wither and are burnt up does not mean that God does not value their beauty. Their lives, like man's life, are ephemeral, but all have a place in the divine compassion. Perhaps we may even detect a solicitude for plant life in the gardener's concern for the Barren Fig Tree (Lk. xiii. 6–9). When Jesus sought a simile expressing the contrary of John the Baptist's robust character He found it in nature—'a reed-bed swept by the wind' (Mt. xi. 7; Lk. vii. 24). Likewise, in an image from nature he summed up the predatory, crafty character of Herod Antipas—'that jackal' (Lk. xiii. 32).[47]

John Oman wrote: 'Jesus was no ascetic. He was full of the joy of life and He cherished all that was beautiful in Nature and human nature.' Countering the picture of Christ's ministry conjured up by some scholars as 'one succession of excited expectations and enthusiastic endeavours' anticipating the End' he remarked: 'All His teaching speaks of leisure not only of itself and from the world but even from His ministry. To teach the parables at all meant leisure. He noticed the flowers and the sky and the farmer at work and the children at play.'[48] His message 'quick and powerful' indeed, was proclaimed in language pervaded by the tranquillity of nature imagery, reflecting interludes of quiet apartness in the wilderness (Mt. xiv. 13, 23; Mk. vi. 31; Lk. ix. 28)—a place of great beauty, bright with flowers in spring, and, at all seasons, bathed in flaming glory at dawn and dusk. The shepherd, sower and vinedresser in their dealing with nature were, in His eyes, in touch with God, and for Him their labours imaged God's care for His own:

The Sower flinging seed on loam and rock;
The darnel in the wheat; the mustard-tree
That hath its seed so little, and its boughs
Wide-spreading; and the wandering sheep; and nets
Shot in the wimpled waters—drawing forth
Great fish and small:—these, and a hundred such,
Seen by us daily, yet never seen aright,
Were pictures for Him from the page of life,
Teaching by parable.[49]

Jesus indeed spoke as One quietly surveying the scenes around Him, but they are scenes of activity. The parables are full of busy people. When the unemployed are mentioned it is with compassion (Mt. xx. 16). The idle rich are condemned (Lk. xvi. 19–31).

Many down the centuries have been preoccupied with the imminent dissolution of the cosmos and the End of all things, but those who have done so have seldom shown a compassionate interest in nature. Acceptance and enjoyment of the regularity and beauty of the natural scene, not simply as an intellectual conviction or scientific postulate, but as a profoundly experienced reality, inhibits inclinations to dwell on catastrophic interference with the natural order. The thoughts of the lover of nature do not move along such lines. Whatever pronouncements Jesus made concerning crisis and judgement there is below the surface of His message a ground swell of reliance on natural and ethical law which finds clear expression in His teaching. Dodd remarks (p. 91), 'This sense of the divineness of the natural order is the major premise of all the parables.'

Although regard for nature as manifesting the divine was lamentably neglected during long periods of the Church's history innumerable Christians throughout the centuries have been led to perceive natural order and beauty as sacramental and have thus found in them special joy. Dante expresses this appreciative delight in the knowledge that everything belonging to the natural order which is loved for God's sake expresses His glory:

> And through the garden of the world I rove,
> Enamoured of its leaves in measure solely
> As God the Gardener nurtures them above.[50]

We have seen that the attitude of the early Church to the Jewish religious leaders has coloured the Gospel accounts of our Lord's teaching. There is also good reason to believe that most of the reported sayings in the Gospels concerning portents and catastrophes, such as those in Mk. xiii. and Mt. xxiv. and xxv., are additions inserted in the course of the transmission of Gospel material.[51]

Account should also be taken of the possibility that at least some of a number of sayings regarded as forecasting future calamities, such as The Weather Signs (Mt. xvi. 1–4; Lk. xii. 54–56), The Defendant (Mt. v. 25 f.; Lk. xii. 58 f.) and The Barren Fig Tree (Lk. xiii. 6–9) referred, not to cosmic catastrophe, but to the future conflict with Rome which Jesus considered probable or even inevitable.[52]

The early Church's expectations of an imminent Second Advent and Day of the Lord (II Thess. i. 6–10) modified the Gospel record. Our views on these matters must influence our opinions in regard to the extent to which the parables of the Kingdom, especially those concerned with nature and natural processes presuppose an imminent End.

The point of view of those who deny that Jesus proclaimed the Kingdom of God as a growing reality is represented by B. T. D. Smith who states (p. 120): 'The Kingdom which He preached does not grow—it comes; and its coming does not depend upon its acceptance by the world but upon the will of God.' Yet, in connexion with The Mustard Seed, he quotes a rabbinic parable comparing the growth of a scholar's reputation with the growth of a seed. The sprout 'continues to shoot up'. Dodd has a chapter entitled 'Parables of Growth', but he and Jeremias consider them to be concerned with present harvest rather than future development.

Dodd remarks (p. 40), 'Jesus proclaimed that the Kingdom of God, the hope of many generations, had at last come. It is not merely imminent, it is here.' Accordingly the 'parables of growth' must be regarded as parables of harvest: 'But, look, I tell you, look around on the fields; they are already white, ripe for harvest' (Jn. iv. 35–38. Cf. Mt. ix. 37 f.; Lk. x. 1–2). The emphasis is on the 'putting in of the sickle'. Dodd claims that his interpretation, by considering growth to be in the past up to the time of the mission of Jesus 'does justice to the emphasis laid on the processes of growth'. We shall presently comment further on this interpretation, but it is difficult to believe that country folk, hearing these parables, would understand them thus. As Jeremias points out (pp. 225 f.) the introduction to parables such as The Sower and The Net means 'it is the case with the Kingdom of God as with . . .' not the seed or the net, but what happens in the story. If our Lord had intended to lay the stress on the harvest to the extent that writers, such as Dodd, believe, these parables would surely have been framed differently. For instance, 'The Kingdom of God is as when the reaper at last goes into the harvest field. . . . The Kingdom of God is as when the leaven in the dough has completed its activity. . . . The Kingdom of God is as when a bush having reached maturity, the birds flock to the branches'. Jeremias (p. 227), laying rather less stress than Dodd on the harvest having arrived with the preaching of Jesus, comments on The Tares and The Net: 'The field must be left to ripen in patience, the net must be cast widely, and everything else left to God in faith, until His hour comes.' But the implications are not only that the Kingdom must be awaited but also that man has a task before him as a fisher of men. He has work to do. In short, man has some responsibility for the initiation of the Kingdom. Jeremias (p. 78) notes that according to Colossians i. 6 and Acts vi. 7, xii. 24, xvii. 20 the 'word' grows.[53]

These expressions, together with the Evangelists' additions to the parables, show that from very early times interpretations envisaging future growth were accepted. It is a bold assumption that such a tradition of interpretation, which may well go back to a time when some of those who heard Jesus speak were still alive, is mistaken. That so much implying growth was faithfully transmitted in the parables during the period when the early Church was dominated by apocalyptic hopes and expected a sudden, imminent Second Advent (Parousia) is a testimony to their authenticity. Whatever our view we should remember that, as many scholars have pointed out, the date of the Kingdom of God was not, for Jesus, a vital concern.

In our Lord's teaching there was, as we have noted, tension between the present and the future. The parables show that He laid stress alike on the urgency of decision and preparedness and on the necessity for patience and hope. All human life involves this tension and its reconciliation. This means that however our Lord's eschatological utterances may be interpreted, the traditional concept of the Kingdom as extending and growing is justified, whether the development be thought of, as is implicit in some of His teaching, in terms of rapid transformation in the individual or society, or, as a slower process of maturation through the sunshine of God's grace. The Seed Growing Secretly (or Spontaneously) and The Hidden Treasure alike mirror life and man's spiritual predicament, for God makes Himself known and fulfils His purpose by means of the expected as well as the unpredictable.

CHAPTER I

PARABLES FROM NATURE

Natural Law and Spiritual Truth

THE SOWER

Mk. iv. 3–9; Mt. xiii. 3–9; Lk. viii. 5–8.

ANTICIPATION AND WARNING

Many young people today know little of sights, sounds and scents which meant much to their forefathers. The industrial revolution changed the conditions of life and work in the towns; but the agricultural revolution has transformed rhythms of activity in the countryside which had scarcely been altered since the Bronze Age. The beautiful, though laborious, rituals of the fields, the sower casting his handfuls of grain as he strides across the land, the ploughman steering straight furrows behind the plodding horse, the creaking waggon bearing the harvest homewards are now only matters of hearsay. Each year there are fewer who can cherish in their memory the hiss of the scythe in the lush grass, the pungent smell at the door of the smithy or the pulse of the cow's teat in the hand as the milk spurts and gurgles into the pail. Even our language betrays the trend towards depersonalization and the inroads of mechanization. Plans sometimes 'go out of gear', and a man's inmost motivations are described as 'what makes him tick'. Committees discuss 'mechanisms' for dealing with situations rather than 'procedures'. We read of the work of the government or party 'machine'. In these days some of the details in the parables cannot speak with

33

such immediacy as formerly they did, but incidental allusions in them may yet have value in directing our attention to simple things and encouraging the quality of mind such contemplation evokes.

It has been customary for commentators to point out that we must not picture the Palestinian farmer acting like a European farmer, first ploughing and then sowing his field. They tell us that in Palestine the field was first sown and then ploughed. Authoritative as these statements seemed to be one could not help wondering why such a peculiar and wasteful procedure should be adopted. According to the parable the birds were ready enough to pick up what fell 'along the footpath', but would they not descend in flocks on the exposed grain on the unploughed field? A recent article by an agriculturist has shown that the theologians' explanation was based on generalizations resting on inadequate observations made during the last century in the Holy Land.[1]

There is evidence that farming practice was more efficient in New Testament times than after the Saracen and Turkish occupations of the country. Two thousand years ago the farmer tilled his land before sowing the grain as farmers all over the world do today. He followed the procedure recommended much earlier by Jeremiah (iv. 3): 'Break up your fallow ground and sow not among thorns.'

It has also been assumed that the sower scattered his seed on the path trodden across the unploughed field, but this is questionable. In some years, at least, seed grain was very precious and the sower would not carelessly expose it to the birds and scorching sun. But he could not avoid some seed falling on the path alongside the field and among the thistles and other weeds which fringed it.

Commentators have also misinterpreted the statements concerning the yield. The emphasis is not on the bulk yield but on the increase yielded by individual seeds. A yield of 'a hundredfold' from an uncrowded bushy plant with many sprouts would not be fantastic, as some writers have argued. Indeed, Varro mentions seed bearing a hundredfold in fields near Gadara on the slopes of Mount Gilead.[2]

This interpretation of the parable in terms of practical farming suggests that attention was meant to be directed to the seeds and what happened to them. The significance of this will be apparent presently when we consider the extent to which leading scholars, intent on interpreting the parables eschatologically, have stressed the importance of the harvest rather than the sowing. This parable, like The Seed Growing Secretly (The Patient Husbandman) and The Mustard Seed, is about the growth of individual seeds. The little crowd listening to Jesus knew that the stone-strewn field could look unpromising; but if they ploughed in faith and sowed in hope, then, in spite of shallow soil, weeds, birds and 'the worm' mentioned in the Coptic sayings attributed to Thomas, they might look forward to piled-up threshing floors and well-stocked barns. They would perceive that in a parable 'sowing' stood for teaching (IV Ezra ix. 31) and accept the hope held forth of a superabundant harvest of souls.

Simple as this story appears to be there is disagreement as to its original meaning. Divergencies spring from differences of opinion concerning where the emphasis is to be laid. Is the Kingdom of God like the germinating seed, an inward, transforming, creative principle, like the process of growth or like the harvest? Is it, as some writers assume, about the soils rather than the seed? This is doubtful. When Jesus told the parable was He calling on His hearers to pay attention to His teaching or emphasizing how great would be the success of His mission? It might be assumed that we need go no farther than the explanation appended in the Gospels, but many scholars consider this to be an editorial addition. Vincent Taylor (p. 251) accepts it as a reference to the amazing harvest, but points out that it does not suggest a speedy in-breaking of the Kingdom. Other authorities reject it because nothing is said of the opposition of scribes and Pharisees in making Jesus' work unfruitful; but this view will not appeal to those unconvinced that Pharisees are to be found lurking in every bush of the Gospel. On general grounds it is objected that no master of parabolic teaching would explain his parables, any more than a wit would explain his witticisms. Against this is the possibility that a teacher might explain ambiguities to his disciples. There are, however, a number of other objections to the genuineness of the explanation. For example, allegorization such as is found here is unusual in the Gospel parables. Also, some scholars have pointed out that in contrast to the language of the parable itself, which bears evidence of translation from Aramaic, the explanation contains non-Hebraic words. However, as Moule, Cranfield and others have shown, the linguistic objections have been exaggerated.[3] Moreover, there are inconsistencies as, for instance, in Mk. v. where in verse 14 the seed is said to be the 'word' (a technical term coined by the early Church), whereas in verses 16, 18 and 20 it is identified with the hearers. Perhaps one further point should not be pressed, but it may be noted that while the birds in The Sower are said to represent the devil, in The Mustard Seed the birds lodging in the fronds of the bush stand for those attracted to the Kingdom (pp. 53 f.). The identification of the birds as satanic powers would seem to be added allegorization.

It is improbable that the explanation as we have it was uttered by Jesus, but He realized and emphasized that the cares of this world and the deceitfulness of riches led men to reject His message (Mt. vi. 24–34; Mk. x. 23 ff.; Lk. xii. 13–21, 33 f., xvi. 19–31). If, indeed, we have here, as is probable, a reflection of conditions in the Church when the difficulties of converting others and establishing them in the faith were evident, we see that the Church was not finding its task easier than its Master had done.

The parable depicts eternal truth concerning human nature. If, as has been suggested, it marks the point when, according to Mark, Jesus turned from teaching in the synagogue to teaching in the Galilean countryside, it may, perhaps, represent His determination to proceed in spite of set-backs.[4] At all events we may note that Mark must have placed The Sower and the other four accompanying parables where we find them in this chapter as a reassurance that, despite the criticism and opposition to our Lord described in the preceding chapters, the progress of the Kingdom of God could not be halted.

Dodd and Jeremias, in accordance with their eschatological views, are agreed that the emphasis is on the bumper harvest which, through the mission of Jesus, awaits the prompt reaper. Accordingly the message is that in spite of opposition and apathy the harvest is ripe. Harvest traditionally symbolizes the Last Judgement preceding the New Age (Isa. ix. 3; Joel iii. 13), thus hearers bearing in mind this inner meaning might be reminded of God's concern for Israel in the past, and think of growth in terms of past history as well as represented by the ministry of Jesus. But would they naturally interpret the harvest described as definitive? The parable as it stands does not suggest that the final harvest is imminent. Nor does it say whether the period to harvest will be long or short. It proclaims that through the activities of Jesus forces are at work which will lead to an abundant crop in God's good time. We should bear in mind that in Jewish apocalyptic the harvest stood for divine intervention, but, with Jesus, man's efforts are also required.[5]

Undoubtedly the emphasis on the magnificent yield was intended to give encouragement. Cheer up! Never doubt that in spite of wastage and adverse conditions success will come. But it is plain that most of the parable is concerned with the situations which precede maturity. A Palestinian countryman could not hear it narrated without picturing the events in stages—the bare ground—newly-sown seed pounced on by birds—seedlings in the shallow skin of limey soil sending up green shoots, soon to be scorched by the sun—sturdy shafts pushing forth, but being strangled after some weeks by the weeds; finally, flourishing ranks of tall stems loaded with grain. We are shown all the stages from seed to full corn in the ear. The picture is not only of the harvest but also of the developments whereby God brings His purpose to fruition despite man's frailties. Hearers are warned to consider seriously what their response is to be; but the failures fade into insignificance compared with the superabundant harvest. We rejoice in hope because God's purpose cannot be thwarted. Nor is development to be thought of as occurring only in the past; for no Palestinian countryman could forget God's promise: 'While the earth remaineth, seedtime and harvest . . . shall not cease' (Gen. viii. 22).[6]

In applying the parable to our own circumstances it is most reasonable, in spite of arguments to the contrary, to hold that a parable such as this may be double-edged or dual-pointed. It conveys warning and encouragement. The narrative dealing with the sowing and growth of the seed is a warning against hard-heartedness and flippancy; the culmination is a message of hope and encouragement. The Sower reflects experience of life, and especially of the religious life, the disappointments as well as the joyous hopes of our Lord and of His followers in Galilee and of the faithful throughout the centuries. The stony ground, weeds and raiding birds which belong so naturally to the scene may be allegorized in Matthew's explanation, but they make vivid to any hearer or reader the difficulties and vexations in store for any teacher. Failure is often more obvious than success, especially in the earlier phases of any enterprise, as the farmer knows when he observes the birds bearing down on his seeded fields or sees the weeds outgrow the grain: 'For just as the husbandman sows much seed upon the ground and plants a multitude of plants, and yet not all which were sown shall be saved in due season, nor shall all that were planted take root, so also they that are sown in the world shall not all be saved' (IV Ezra viii. 41). Fishermen, too, know disappointment. They sometimes toil all night and take nothing (Lk. v. 5). Nevertheless, in spite of failures farmer and fisherman, not least the fisher of souls, can look forward to ultimate success, for the overruling power of God is at work. Ever since the time when the parable was first told in Galilee the stony-hearted and shallow-minded have rejected the Gospel, and prickly folk have resented its intrusion; but those gathered in have found joy in the Holy Spirit. In our day mental superficialities resulting from being assailed daily with trivial and sensational words and pictures hinder the Gospel from taking root; but, on the other hand, the Church is able to make use of modern mass-communication techniques, one of which is appropriately named after the procedure of The Sower—broadcasting.

THE GRAIN OF WHEAT

John xii. 24

CONTINUITY OF GROWTH

The Grain of Wheat is one of seven miniature parables in St. John's Gospel, pointed out by Dodd, the others being The Pains of Childbirth (xvi. 21), The Benighted Traveller (xi. 9–10), The Slave and Son (viii. 35), The Shepherd, the Thief and the Doorkeeper (x. 1–5), The Bridegroom and Bridegroom's Friend (iii. 29) and The Apprentice Son (v. 19–20a). These parables are believed to come from the same reservoir of tradition as the parables of the other Gospels, but bear evidence of not being derived from them; so they form an important addition to the parabolic tradition.[7]

In the parable of The Grain of Wheat there is recognition of the natural law of continuity. The famine-stricken farmer will not eat his seed grain until he is near the point of death; for he knows that if he does not maintain the sequence of sowing seed in the earth to 'die' and thus receive new life, he and other members of the community cannot continue to live. It also illustrates the natural law of transformation from lower to higher life. From early times nature has been interpreted as speaking in acted parables.[8] From the ball of dung the beetle emerges—life from the dust in the thought of the ancient Egyptians for whom the scarab was a sacred symbol. In due course the egg-shell cracks and releases the living chick. The seed buried in the damp earth decays into life. As an illustration of life from death the dying and reviving seed is mentioned in the Talmud and in I Clem. xxiv. 4 f. In biological terms the less complex gives place to the more highly organized with its greater capacity for sensitivity. Death is the gate to life—so nobly proclaimed by St. Paul in I Corinthians xv.

In accordance with typical Semitic usage the description leaps from the death of the grain to the contrast—its fruitfulness—leaving us to supply the idea of resurrection. Thus in growth parables ideas

which are implicit prove to be of great importance. Development
and transformation are taken for granted.

There was a phase towards the close of our Lord's ministry when
opposition had mounted to such an extent that it must have been
apparent to Him that He and His followers were risking death. To
those who wondered whether He were the Messiah He gave this
answer. Through His death would come the promised fulfilment.[9]

It is a short step in thought from the soil generating growth,
spontaneously and 'secretly' (Mk. iv. 27 f.) (p. 50)—you know
not how—to the idea of death leading to resurrection; and from the
triumphal rural harvest-home to the Heavenly Harvest and Banquet.
These concepts dovetail into one another and are reflected in our
hymns and prayers. No Cross, no Crown. When Jesus called men
to leave all and follow Him there was no suggestion that following
at a distance would be good enough. Full commitment was and is
demanded. The way of sacrifice and suffering, of attainment
through tribulation and effort, is the way of salvation. 'Dying we
still live on; disciplined by suffering, we are not done to death; in
our sorrows we have always cause for joy, poor ourselves we bring
wealth to many; penniless we own the world' (II Cor. vi. 10).

THE TARES

OR

THE WEEDS IN THE GRAIN

Mt. xiii. 24–30

PATIENCE AND JUDGEMENT

In common with a number of other parables, such as The Two
Builders (Lk. vi. 47–49; Mt. vii. 24–27), The Hidden Treasure
(Mt. xiii. 44), The Prodigal Son (Lk. xv. 11–32), The Good
Samaritan (Lk. x. 30–37), The Dishonest Steward (Lk. xvi. 1–8)

and The Importunate Neighbour (Lk. xi. 5–8) this story may have been inspired by a recent episode. Instances of malicious weed-sowing have occasionally been reported and the theme appears in folk-tales. One such tale describes the sowing by an enemy of a species of reed in a neighbour's garden; the weed grew so exuberantly that even the olive trees died. There is a rabbinic story with some affinities with the parable: Eleazar b. Simon (c. A.D. 180) served the Roman government by catching thieves. When rebuked by Rabbi Joshua b. Qarha he excused his conduct by explaining, 'I am only weeding the vineyard.' Whereupon Rabbi Joshua retorted, 'Let the Lord of the vineyard come and weed out his thorns.'[10] Apparently it was sometimes the practice to root out poisonous darnel (*Lolium temulentum*) from the growing crop. The field might be worked over more than once.[11]

It has been suggested that this parable might be an adaptation of The Patient Husbandman (The Seed Growing Secretly) (p. 46) elaborated through memories of what had followed John the Baptist's mission; but its teaching is closer to that of The Net near to which it is placed by Matthew. Jesus may have had in mind critics of His teaching who said: 'You talk about the Kingdom of God being in our midst, but the world seems to be in a sorry state. Oppression and cruelty are rife, bandits and thieves roam the countryside. We see plenty of malicious people in our midst rather than the Kingdom. Some of your own followers are far from perfect.'

As darnel in its early stages of growth is not easily distinguished from wheat, so in any community good and bad people are not identifiable at a glance, still less are the good and bad in individuals readily separable. None of us is completely a Pharisee or a Publican. Milton wrote in *Areopagitica*: 'Good and evil grow up in the field of this world almost inseparably.' Scrutiny revealed to the workers on the farm that there were weeds in the crop, but to detect and eliminate the individual plants would have been an immensely laborious task. The roots of the darnel interlace with those of the wheat, so that to disturb the darnel would be to displace the wheat.

Time is needed, and not only time; for we are not dealing merely with what is temporal. We must not trust in our unaided ability but recognize that in some matters, having done what we can, we must leave the rest to God. In the light of eternity and of the purging fires of judgement the secrets of all hearts will be disclosed.

The allegorizing explanation appended to the parable (vv. 36–43) is too contrived to be original. Apart from other considerations it misses the point of the story, the necessity for patience. And it is saturated with expressions typical of Matthew. As we shall see its most interesting aspect is the light it throws on the outlook of the early Church. In the parable itself the emphasis is on avoiding precipitate action in weeding the field. It also stresses God's Judgement, though it does not emphasize the immediate imminence of this Judgement, as some have suggested. Dodd (pp. 138 f.) admits that here the harvest has not yet actually begun but concludes: 'It does not seem necessary to suppose that the judgement is treated as a new event in the future.' According to him the Judgement is already taking place although the parable places the harvest in the future. He refers to John iv. 35–38, interpreting this passage as showing that the disciples were sent to reap, not to sow. Jeremias (pp. 78–151) supports this, remarking that it was not characteristic of Jesus to refer to preaching as sowing. This cannot easily be reconciled with the teaching of The Sower. However this may be, the plain meaning of the parable is that the world, with evil and good inextricably entangled, proceeds towards the consummation when God, not man, will put in the sickle. All must be fulfilled according to His plan and men will be judged according to the response they have given. The darnel, unlike the thorns in the parable of The Sower, cannot strangle or choke the crop, but neither can the wheat eradicate the darnel, although, in so far as there is a good crop, it is able to overcome it. The situation will be dealt with adequately in due course. Jesus, commenting on the disgruntled Pharisees, told His disciples: 'Any plant which is not of my heavenly Father's planting will be rooted up. Leave them alone;

they are blind guides, and if one blind man guides another they will both fall into the ditch' (Mt. xv. 13 f.). St. Paul wrote: 'Pass no premature judgement; wait until the Lord comes. For He will bring to light what darkness hides, and disclose men's inward motives; then will be the time for each to receive from God the praise which he deserves' (I Cor. iv. 5). As in The Sower, we survey the sequence from seed to sickle, perceiving that God's hand is ever over His creation for good, but that man must learn patience. This is, indeed, the lesson that nature has to teach all who would learn her secrets.[12]

Matthew, in his explanation, applies the parable to the Church of his time. There were sinners and saints in its congregations and people were saying, 'Without so-and-so, how much easier the Christian life would be and how much more effective the Church's witness! Should not those who disgrace the community be expelled? Their presence proclaims the activity of the devil.' That the Church should continue to harbour sinners and traitors in spite of their mischief-making was only comprehensible on the long view—that judgement lies with God. Throughout the centuries Christians, aware of the wickedness around them and of the frailty of their brethren, have found solace in this conviction.

The deplorable state of the crop was not due to the farmer's neglect. Here is encouragement for the Christian who might blame himself for evils in the world which he is unable to eradicate. The more ardent our longing for the rule of righteousness, the more we need to temper our zeal with patience. There is a type of reformer who has to learn that God is not in such a hurry as he.

From the wider point of view The Tares is concerned with the problem of evil. Its pervasiveness is apparent to all. The form and timing of the Judgement on it, whether pictured parabolically as its being cast into the bonfire or baking oven, or as being eliminated in some other way, is secondary in comparison with the assurance that God is working out His purpose. St. Paul expressed this same assurance by means of different imagery: 'Then comes the end,

when He delivers up the kingdom to God the Father, after abolish-
ing every kind of domination, authority and power. For He is
destined to reign until God has put all enemies under His feet'
(I Cor. xv. 24–26).

THE NET

Mt. xiii. 47–50

GATHERING AND SORTING

The two parables, The Tares and The Net (The Seine Net or
Drag Net), both deal with the problem of the intermingling of good
and evil, the righteous and the unrighteous. Here, too, Matthew
has apparently added comments (vv. 49 f.), evidently designed to be
a warning that there will be a day of reckoning for unworthy
members of the Church. We need not accept the minatory phrase
foretelling weeping and gnashing of teeth (cf. viii. 12; xiii. 42;
xxii. 13; xxiv. 51; xxv. 30) as having been uttered by Jesus any
more than we need regard as an authentic detail the reference to
destruction by fire which seems to have been taken over incongruously from the earlier parable. The introductory formula—'It
is so with the Kingdom of God as with . . .' resembles the introduction to The Tares. The Kingdom is compared, not to a net but
to the catching of fish in a net. People gathered into the Kingdom
are of all kinds, some better than others. As outcasts crowded
round to listen to Jesus, critics wondered why he accepted and
welcomed them. They thought it unseemly that He should be seen
associating with publicans and sinners. But He reiterated that His
mission was to such people (Mt. ix. 13; Mk. ii. 17; Lk. v. 32).
Many are invited but few are chosen (Mt. xxii. 14). So far the
parable might be regarded as an explanation of His mission.

Some scholars, such as Manson, assuming that The Net has been
amplified to apply to a situation in which it was all too evident that

the Church included bad Christians as well as good, suggest that the original parable consisted only of verse 47, all the rest being Matthaean embroidery. According to this view the Evangelist has approximated it to The Tares.[13]

The parable may also be interpreted as a picture of missionary activity in which the net is spread wide to include as many as possible; all sorts and conditions of men are gathered in, as in the parable of The Wedding Feast. As our Lord called on the disciples to be 'fishers of men' (Mk. i. 17) the idea of gathering is certainly involved, but unless we accept Manson's drastic pruning of the parable the emphasis on selection is more important.[14] As the unpalatable or ritually unclean (Lev. ii. 9 ff.) aquatic organisms are eliminated from the fisherman's catch so the unrighteous will be segregated from the righteous.[15] Those who have seen a pile of grotesque creatures rejected by longshore fishermen will realize the vividness of this message. The word 'bad' used in the Authorized Version to describe the discarded fish is more accurately rendered 'unusable'; in xii. 33 it is applied to unwholesome fruit. The phrase 'when it was full' parallels the delay until harvest in The Tares. The Final Judgement is not yet. However, as it seems improbable that vv. 49 f. belong to the parable, doubt has been expressed concerning its application to the Final Judgement. Dodd (pp. 140 f.) points out that Jesus repeatedly made it quite clear that the gathering together of His followers involved a process of selection. Those without sufficient resolution, devotion or pertinacity were eliminated or eliminated themselves (Mk. x. 17–22; Lk. ix. 57–62).

The point made by some scholars that the selection is made by the fishermen and that the fish do not eliminate themselves is academic, for where human beings are concerned, choice, whether or not to follow Jesus and accept His teaching, is inevitably involved. The parallel must not be pushed too far. Fish cannot choose to enter a net as men make decisions. But here we are primarily concerned with God's Judgement when man's activities will be assessed by the standard of absolute righteousness.

The parable sounds a note of warning as well as of assurance. You ask why wickedness should be widespread and God's justice tardy? See these men sitting by the shore sorting out and throwing away the noxious and inedible creatures; they are also carefully selecting the wholesome fish. God will judge righteously, but most certainly He will care for His own.[16]

THE SEED GROWING SECRETLY
(SPONTANEOUSLY)

OR

THE PATIENT HUSBANDMAN

Mk. iv. 26–29

PATIENCE AND PURPOSE

Some commentators with strongly eschatological views, from Johannes Weiss onwards, convinced that the parables of growth were not meant to stress the thought of growth, have claimed that they should be called Contrast Parables.[17] The Patient Husbandman, together with The Sower, The Mustard Seed and The Leaven have been placed in this category because in them the beginning and the end are contrasted. But a considerable number of other parables also embody contrast. For example, The Rich Man and Lazarus is a study in contrasts. Jeremias (pp. 151 f.) considers that these growth parables were designed to teach: 'The corn is ripe, the sickle is thrust in, the joyful cry rings out, "the harvest has come".' Accordingly the emphasis is on harvesting, not on growth, apart from the growth necessarily preceding harvest. Dodd (pp. 132 f.) even more definitely regards these as harvest parables. He paraphrases The Seed Growing Secretly in these terms: 'Can you not see that the long history of God's dealing with His people has reached its climax? After the work of the Baptist

only one thing remains: Put ye in the sickle for the harvest is ripe.'
Here Dodd is following Schweitzer.[18] Not everyone would accept
this narrowing of the sowing to the mission of John.

In seeking to identify the life-setting of the parables in our Lord's
ministry scholars are apt to forget that they were told to country-
folk, fishermen and farmers, in a rural community. Even rich
Sadducees had their large farms and so were not alienated from the
land as are most modern theologians. We must ask, in regard to
parables, and especially nature parables, what they conveyed to
simple country people. Would it occur to them that the message of
this parable was the imminence of the End? If it had been our
Lord's aim to drive this message home by means of a parable and
to emphasize the climax of maturity as forcibly as possible, would
He have clothed His meaning in such obscurity that only after
nearly two millennia have scholars realized His intention? Why did
He frame it so that it could be so readily misunderstood? To the
plain man the stress seems to be at least as much on the growth
which takes place independent of man as on the harvesting opera-
tions of the farmer, though man, as sower or reaper, is shown as by
no means inactive at critical times. (Matthew's reference to the
angel reapers in his explanation of The Tares is his own contribution.) Except for the final sentence the emphasis is wholly on
growth, and some commentators suspect that this verse, which is
quoted from Joel iii. 13, may be an addition.[19]

Life as the farmer knows it is a continuous rhythm. At harvest
he knows that he is not only gathering grain for present use but also
garnering seed for future sowing. The acceptance of such a cycle,
past, present and future, so vividly depicted in the parable, is in the
farmer's bones. Harvest is a climax, but it also looks forward to the
future. The urgency of in-gathering does not rule out provision
for future sowing and harvests. Jeremias (p. 149) exaggerates the
difference between our outlook and that of our forefathers when he
remarks that 'modern man passing through the ploughed field
thinks in terms of what is going on beneath the soil and envisages
a biological development whereas the countryman of the Bible sees

miracle upon miracle, nothing less than resurrection from the dead'. Hence he holds that the words 'first the blade, then the ear, then the full grain in the ear' do not imply the thought of development as we understand it. But even with us our scientific outlook need not preclude acceptance of the poetic analogy of the resurrected seed (Jn. xii. 24; I Cor. xv. 20 ff.). A man can be scientific without being incapable of experience of the numinous or suffering deprivation of sensitivity to the beauty and mystery at the heart of nature. Nor was the countryman of the Bible unimpressed by the evidence of slow development to maturity. For him the miracle did not consist only in the end-product, whether harvest or the birth of a child, but included the process. Ecclesiastes (xi. 5) asked: 'Dost thou know how the child groweth in the womb of her that is with child?' In a parable in IV Ezra (v. 46–49), which answers the question why Judgement should be delayed, we read: 'Just as the young child does not bring forth, nor she that is aged any more, so have I also disposed of the world which I have created by definite periods of time.' The writer's point is that the Judgement will come when conditions are right, orderly and natural, but in making this state-ment he implies a sequence in cosmic development as in the con-ception, growth and birth of a child. (Cf. also IV Ezra iv. 25–40, vii. 74, viii. 41.)[20]

The concept of organic development is clearly set forth in Enoch (i. 2–5), where it is stated that 'the stars follow their appointed order, the seasons follow in sequence, the trees bud and bear fruit accord-ing to the seasons . . . according as God has ordained so it is done'.[21] Such passages, with their recognition of order, process, sequence and growth show full awareness of the concept of development.

Because the people of the first century were without our grasp of evolutionary development it does not follow that they were not thoroughly conversant with organic development. Writing in that century Clement of Rome used an illustration comparable with the parable: 'Ye fools, compare yourselves unto a tree; take a vine. First it sheddeth its leaves, then a shoot cometh, then a leaf, then a flower, and after these things a berry, then a full ripe grape. Ye see that in a little time the fruit of the tree attaineth unto mellow-ness. Of a truth quickly and suddenly shall His will be accom-plished, the scripture also bearing witness to it, saying: "He shall come quickly and shall not tarry; and the Lord shall come suddenly into His temple, even the Holy One, whom ye expect" ' (I Clem. xxiii. 4; cf. II Clem. xi. 2 f.; Mal. iii. 1). Thus Clement dwells on development, and then, influenced by the eschatological expectation of his time, switches somewhat incongruously to the thought of God's sudden intervention. The Evangelists were also subject to these pressures and frequently interpreted the traditions they re-ceived, including the parables, with such ideas in mind.[22]

They found precedents in the Old Testament for regarding the harvest and vintage as symbolizing the Final Judgement.[23] Such imagery was readily assumed to be an illustration of the prelude to the End. First-generation Christians living at a time of apocalyptic expectations, tended to find in it support for such hopes and fears to the exclusion of the thought of gradual development.

As we have seen (p. 26) it is now widely agreed that the Kingdom announced by Jesus was both present and future, and therefore His message stressed both growth and harvest. Growth and harvesting go on continuously. This is a law both of natural life and of the spiritual life. Birth, growth, death, resurrection and rebirth—these form a sequence of ideas without which neither the teaching of our Lord nor its elaboration in the New Testament can be rightly understood. According to the most reasonable interpretation of the teaching of Jesus about the Kingdom He expected a period of growth even though it might be short. This justifies the traditional interpretation of the parables of the Kingdom as a picture of growth in the world of men through the power of God in their midst leading on to the final fulfilment at the End.

In The Sower we have viewed the vicissitudes of the crop at various stages, and in The Tares we are given a picture of the farmer and his men keeping an eye on the fields and considering what further work is necessary; but in this parable the seed, once sown, is pictured as owing nothing to the farmer. It grows while he is asleep. The rôle of the soil is rather different from that which it performs in The Sower. We are told that it brings forth of itself—spontaneously—and eventually, 'as soon as the crop is ripe' the reaper puts in the sickle. A power outside man's control or comprehension brings about this wonderful development. The givenness of the process is stressed; all is 'under God'. As He ordains the sequence—rain, growth, bread—so His word 'prospers in the thing whereto He sent it' (Isa. lxv. 10–11). This emphasis on spontaneity is central to the picture and is crucial for its interpretation. The parable suffers by being analysed into fragments; it needs to be taken as a whole and understood in the sense in which it must have appealed to Jewish rustics or others familiar with the countryside. Although nothing much seems to be happening, the miracle of growth is taking place—God's purpose is being gloriously fulfilled. Man must learn to wait upon God; he must have faith in His prevailing purpose. The farmer cannot improve the crop by staying awake at night and fretting lest it grow too slowly. As William Watson wrote in his poem 'To one expounding unpopular truth':

> The sower soweth seed on vale and hill,
> And long the folded life waits to be born,
> Yet hath it never slept, nor once been still,
> And clouds and suns have served it night and morn.
> The winds are of its secret council sworn,
> And Time and nurturing silence work its will.

Impatience, both political and religious, was rife in the first century. Economic distress and oppression led to lawlessness, revolutionary ardour and apocalyptic expectations. Our Lord found it necessary to curb the enthusiasms of excitable men such as Simon the Zealot, as well as to encourage hope in the despondent. Accordingly some parables counsel preparedness, others patience. Here it is the need for patience that is stressed, and the lesson is echoed in James v. 7 f.: 'Be patient, my brothers, until the Lord comes. The farmer looking for the precious crop his land may yield can only wait in patience until the winter and spring rains have fallen. You too must be patient . . .' and Clement (I Clem. xxiii. 3, 4), at the end of the century still counselled patience to those with too ardent apocalyptic hopes who were saying: 'These things we did hear in the days of our fathers also, and behold we have grown old and none of these things hath befallen us. Ye fools, compare yourselves unto a tree; take a vine. First it sheddeth its leaves, then a shoot cometh, then a leaf, then a flower, and after these a sour berry, then a full ripe grape.'

In the time of our Lord people who expected the Kingdom to appear in sudden, terrible power found it difficult to believe in its coming in the person of an itinerating village carpenter who taught men to learn the profoundest truths about God from the grain germinating in their fields. And still today there are sects of people who expect the imminent Return of our Lord; they need to learn the lesson of patient waiting. It is not for the disciples of Jesus to know times and seasons. For most of us, however, the call for patience takes a different form. We dedicate ourselves to working for the Kingdom and this involves laborious sowing and reaping in the sweat of our brows—harvesting is not all jubilation but a back-breaking chore in the scorching sun. We would be less prone to anxiety and despondency if we could make our own the patience of the farmer in the parable who is prepared to wait.

> And not by eastern windows only
> When daylight comes, comes in the light,
> In front the sun climbs slow, how slowly,
> But westward, look, the land is bright.
>> Arthur Hugh Clough

THE MUSTARD SEED
Mt. xiii. 31 f.; Mk. iv. 30–32; Lk. xiii. 18 f.

ENLARGEMENT AND SHELTER

This parable and the other two seed parables in Mk. iv is pre-Marcan, as Jeremias (pp. 93 f.) points out. It appears in the 'Gospel' of Thomas as well as the three Synoptics. Mark's special emphasis on the extreme smallness of the seed reflects tradition which exaggerated its tininess. The expression, 'Small as a mustard seed' was proverbial (Mt. xvii. 20; Lk. xvii. 15).[24] According to the Koran: 'God will bring both good and evil to light, even if they are no bigger than a mustard seed', and Sir Richard Burton commented on the expression 'the size of a mustard grain' as signifying among the Arabs a very small object. The comparison is with other larger seeds sown by the farmer, such as lentils, gourds and cereals. As in so many parables there is emphasis on contrast; but here it is specially stressed—the tiny seed and the mature bush. In favourable situations in the Holy Land mustard *Sinapis niger* reaches a height of eight or ten feet, 'as tall as a horse and its rider'.[25] The exaggeration in Matthew and Luke, which pictures the plant as a tree, is effective, not only in emphasizing the contrast in size between seed and bush but also in bringing the comparison into relationship with Old Testament allusions which, as we shall see presently, are important for the interpretation of the parable.[26]

There is similar characteristically Oriental exaggeration in the parable of The Leaven which we may regard as its twin, though we cannot assume that they were originally associated.

In common with The Sower and The Leaven the parable of The Mustard Seed has a Palestinian atmosphere and the language has traces of Semitic constructions. When it is translated back into Aramaic alliterations and play on words are disclosed.[27] Luke's version, however, introduces modifications which suggest a non-Palestinian background to his thought. For example, his remark that the mustard seed was sown by a man 'in his garden' indicates that he was not acquainted with local customs which forbade the cultivation of mustard in garden beds.[28]

Birds figure in this little tale as in The Sower, but not as marauders. They profit by the shade which the plant offers and 'lodge' in the branches—the earlier meaning of the word being 'to pitch one's tent'. The goldfinches and linnets which frequent the plants perch there but do not nest; for the frail fronds would not provide suitable nesting sites. Mark, by stating that it 'grows taller than any other herb' shows he is aware that mustard does not reach the normal dimensions of a tree; yet he alludes to the branches growing so large that the birds 'settle in its shade' or 'roost in its shadow'. Thomas embroiders the expression—'It sends forth a great branch and becomes a covering for the birds of heaven.' The enlarging of the mustard plant to the proportions of a tree suggests associations with Old Testament prophecy. In the book of Daniel (iv. 11–12) we are told of Nebuchadnezzar's dream in which he watched the growth of a mighty tree which reached unto heaven 'and the fowls of the air dwelt in the boughs thereof'. The vision is of a great empire offering shelter and support to vassal states. Ezekiel (xvii. 2–6) relates the divine allegory of an eagle carrying away seed and twigs to plant 'in a land of traffick'. Later (xvii. 22) the Lord declares that He will pluck twigs from a tall cedar, and continues: 'In the mountain of the height of Israel will I plant it: and it shall bring forth boughs, and bear fruit, and be a goodly cedar: and under it shall dwell all the fowl of every wing; in the shadow of the branches thereof shall they dwell.'[29] Moreover, in rabbinic teaching, birds in such contexts represent the Gentiles. In the third century A.D. Rabbi Johanan, commenting on Jeremiah xxx. 18, predicted that 'the land of Israel which is narrow below will in the future extend and rise on all sides like the fig tree, and the exiles shall return and rest in its shade'.[30] Accordingly the parable suggests the exuberant growth and wide extension of the Kingdom.[31] Furthermore, it teaches that the Kingdom offers shelter, refreshment, and salvation to all attracted to it, including the Gentiles.[32]

This comparison of the Kingdom to a sanctuary of repose is not easily reconciled with the conception of the Kingdom as imminent Judgement. It is close to the thought found in the Assumption of Moses, written apparently between A.D. 7 and 30, where God's Kingdom is spoken of in terms of the future splendour and prosperity of Israel. Such imagery appears to be implicit in this parable.

Mustard grows quickly as compared with trees properly so called, especially in the warm conditions of the Middle East. 'Look at this! A seed. And now, a few weeks later—a tree!' Jeremias, in line with his views on our Lord's declaration of the imminence of Judgement minimizes the reference to growth and places all the emphasis on the contrast between the small band of Jesus' disciples and the great multitude of the people of God in the time of salvation. In common with Dodd he interprets these parables of growth as a confirmation of the eschatological nature of the Kingdom proclaimed by Jesus. This is a scholar's interpretation rather than that of a Palestinian peasant.[33] Contrast, indeed, there is; but what countryman, hearing this parable, could fail to be impressed most of all by the rapidity and extent of the plant's growth?

Leaving aside the unlikely suggestion that the birds are introduced into the parable merely to emphasize the magnitude of the mustard bush, we may assume that our Lord, or at all events His early followers, thought of the birds as representing those from afar, including the Gentiles, who would participate in the Kingdom. This is the more probable as the word translated 'lodge' is elsewhere used eschatologically of the incorporation of the Gentiles into the people of God.[34] However we interpret the parable the picture it suggests is of a rapid accession of people into the Kingdom to share its blessedness. It was a call to the disciples to faith and hope.

Given some extension of its meaning the relevance of the parable to conditions today is clear. The Church offers a spiritual home to multitudes. Some may merely make use of it for their own ends, 'perching in the branches', but the leaves of this tree are 'for the healing of the nations' (Apoc. xxii. 1-2). Again, there are tremendous possibilities latent in little things, and seemingly insignificant events may have incalculable consequences. We must not despise the petty coin (Mk. xii. 42; Lk. xxi. 2) or the small child (Mt. xviii. 2, 5; Mk. x. 15; Lk. xviii. 17). Men and women who are considered of little consequence may one day be the salvation of many. The witness of a small Christian community may today seem of little avail; but who could have believed that our Lord's tiny band of disciples would achieve so much? The doctrine of the Righteous Remnant is basic to the understanding of the New Testament and it has always been a cordial for drooping spirits in the Church.

Moreover, the parable has its application to the whole realm of knowledge. The keys which unlock nature's secrets are often small. Harnessing the very minute gives man immense capacities for destruction or amelioration of life. Control of the atom may create mushroom clouds of destruction or may bring light and warmth to our homes. One molecule may make the difference between normality and mental deficiency in a child. An idea, springing up spontaneously in fertile soil, can change the outlook of humanity.

> One man with a dream at pleasure
>   May go forth and conquer a crown
> And three, with a new song's measure
>   May trample an empire down.[35]

THE LEAVEN

Mt. xiii. 33; Lk. xiii. 20 f.

ACTIVITY AND TRANSFORMATION

Two problems have been raised concerning the usual interpretation of The Leaven as portraying the Kingdom of God growing and extending throughout the world. Firstly, it is said that leaven was thought of in antiquity as an agent of putrefaction, corruption or infection (Mk. viii. 15; I Cor. v. 6; Gal. v. 9).[36] Secondly, some writers, as we have seen, hold that the Kingdom announced by Jesus comes rather than grows.

Those who take leaven to be symbolical of evil interpret the introductory phrase to mean that the parable depicts the Kingdom as infected by an evil influence which constantly threatens to overwhelm the good in it.[37] This would link its message with that of The Tares, and it would be a picture of the disciples and the early Church menaced by internal dissension and infidelity. Such an interpretation is not very plausible.

From early times the symbol of leaven as the agent of fermentation has been used in two opposed senses. The rabbis usually pictured leaven as a corrupting influence, but exceptions can be found. Rabbi Joshua b. Levi (first half of third century A.D.) said: 'Great is peace in that peace is to the earth as leaven to dough; for had not God set peace in the earth the sword and wild beast would have depopulated it.' Also it is to be remembered that leavened cakes were included in the sacred offerings at the Feast of Weeks (Lev. xxiii. 17, 20).[38]

Whatever the significance of leaven in rabbinical and other sophisticated circles may have been, it is unbelievable that women placing leaven in dough, or their husbands seeing them doing so, thought of it as a putrefying agent. In Syria today leaven is held 'in high and reverential esteem'. It represents fertility, and therefore a lump of leavened dough is pasted on the lintel of the door by which a bride enters her new home. As she does so her friends say: 'May you be as blessed and fruitful as the *khamera*!' A woman says, 'God bless', as she takes the leaven, which has been preserved in flour to keep it 'from corruption', and 'hides' it in the meal.[39] Even if it was rather unusual to make leaven an illustration of a beneficent process, it is characteristic of our Lord's parables to contain surprising features (pp. 20, 165). Moreover, to many people any mention of leaven would, by association, suggest bread, which, in the Gospels, is symbolic of God's generosity and blessing.

The prodigality of its distribution in the Feeding of the Multitude (Mt. xiv. 13–21, xvi. 9; Mk. vi. 30–44; cf. Lk. vi. 1–5) may be regarded as a foreshadowing of the glories of the Heavenly Feast.

Jeremias (p. 148) denies that either The Mustard Seed or The Leaven is concerned 'merely to describe a process'; but to anyone who has watched yeast at work, the dough heaving, swelling, bubbling and erupting, the aspect which forces itself on his attention is the spectacular activity and growth. Indeed, it seems probable that the association with putrefaction sprang from an instinctive reaction. An occult power seemed to be at work; and among unsophisticated people such mysterious activity may well have suggested a potency for evil as well as for good. But once the art of baking leavened bread was discovered it became clear that what was harmful in some circumstances could, with God's blessing, be helpful in others. Our Lord thus used leaven as an illustration of the mysterious power of God in the world. His own ministry and message created a ferment which has pervaded the world. Indeed, The Leaven might be described as a parable about parables. Whatever their primary application and first audience— the small band of people in whom they were first 'hidden'—they have continued their creative work through the power of generating associations, activating energy, arousing imagination and inspiring discipleship.

To our Lord's hearers the idea of growth apart from divine power was quite alien; to them the parable suggested the spectacular coming of the Kingdom through divine creative power. For us, too, it is full of encouragement. As a tiny nucleus of leaven can activate an immense mass of meal (cf. Gen. xviii. 6)—enough to provide food for many people—so the Word has given life to mankind and the Church has grown from a few adherents 'hidden' in the recesses of some Middle Eastern towns to a Society of such magnitude that a few years ago it could be stated there were organized communities of Christians in every nation save three—Tibet, Saudi Arabia and Afghanistan. This is the doing of the Holy Spirit. The parable of The Leaven tells us that the Church is an organism rather than an organization and that the power 'hidden' in it is the power of God unto salvation.

In these three parables, The Patient Husbandman, The Mustard Seed and The Leaven, each contrasting with the others, we are given pictures of growth at different tempi—the stage by stage gradual growth of the seed growing secretly, the speedy, obvious development of the mustard bush from seed to 'tree', and the spectacular growth before our eyes of the leavened dough through the injection of inward, mysterious dynamic. The wheat grows gradually, the mustard rapidly, the dough sensationally.[40] The wheat thrives in the soil which vitalizes it, the mustard bush soon spreads its fronds to give shade beneath, the morsel of leaven in the vast quantity of dough injects life into it, creates an initially concealed ferment, permeates, enlarges and transforms it. As salt can change the flavour of a bowl of soup so can Christians transform society (pp. 133–135), but leaven symbolizes the transforming power of God in the hearts of individuals and in society. It would, indeed, be strange if the intention inspiring these parables were merely to point the contrast between small and great, initiation and consummation, and not to call attention to the different kinds of growth. Together the three parables portray the varied nature of the transformations which God effects as He ushers in the Kingdom. They are even more complementary to one another than the three Parables of the Lost and Found (pp. 169 ff.). The Kingdom of God is like the creative power revealed in the spontaneity of growth from the life-giving soil; it resembles the growth in size and unfolding of verdure of the mustard bush; it is comparable to the working of leaven, at first hardly perceptible, then seen as spectacular inward vigour. In all three parables the emphasis is on God's power, not on what man can do. Look around, compare the past with the present, note where God has been, and is, at work, and take heart.

THE BUDDING FIG TREE

Mt. xxiv. 32 f.; Mk. xiii. 28 f.; Lk. xxi. 29–31

JOY AND PROMISE

The Budding Fig Tree is another parable counselling expectation, hope and faith. Unlike the cedar, ilex, locust, olive and palm trees the fig loses its relatively large leaves during the winter, and stands holding its gaunt branches to the sky. Thus the sprouting buds herald the coming of more favourable weather as the daffodils signify to us the return of spring. Tristram (p. 351) noted the buds 'rapidly pushing at the end of February', though he suggests that this was rather early.[41] The old saying, 'Cast not a clout until the may (hawthorn) is out', now often corrupted into 'till May is out', reminds us that our forefathers, living close to the good earth like the dwellers in Palestine in the first century, paid much attention to their country calendar of seasonal signs. In the Song of Songs (ii. 12 f.) the lover dwells on the budding greenery, the springing flowers and singing birds—assurances that winter is past. To us, living in a more rigorous climate, the suggestion of the parable is that spring, rather than summer, is nigh. There is an Arab proverb much quoted in Palestine: 'February scarifies, kicks and strikes, but it has the smell of summer.'[42]

The fig tree is not only a harbinger of pleasant weather; its leaves provide shade from the sun and its fruit, fresh or dried, is tasty and nourishing. Only those who have plucked ripe figs from trees on hot eastern hillsides can appreciate how luscious and refreshing they are. Moreover, in the ancient Middle East the fig had many associations with fertility. Joel (ii. 22) mentions its fruit-bearing as a sign of favour from the Lord; and to 'dwell under the fig tree' (I Kings iv. 25; Mic. iv. 4) was to enjoy peace and blessedness. Again, a rabbi of the first century commenting on Ezekiel's vision of a future Jerusalem 'broadened and widening upward' (Ezek. xli. 7) remarked: 'The land of Israel will in time to come extend and rise on all sides like the fig tree, which is narrow below, and the gates of Jerusalem will reach even unto Damascus.' [43] As the green canopy in summer constitutes the tree a vivid illustration of prosperous expansion, so the transformation of its gawky, withered-looking branches when it bursts into leaf in spring makes it an appropriate symbol of life from the dead.

Luke weakens the illustration for those acquainted with fig trees by adding 'and all the trees', evidently seeking to interpret it to non-Palestinian, town-dwelling readers. Mark, who is followed by Matthew and Luke, appends the parable to the passage concerning the woes which will precede the End, so suggesting that the budding fig tree is a warning of disaster. But, rightly interpreted, the parable foretells the joy of the Kingdom. It 'would seem to belong to the spring and the springtime of the ministry'.[44] In so far as the parable portrays the joy of new life and springing hope after the tribulations of winter it may be compared with The Pains of Childbirth (Jn. xvi. 21) describing joy after anxiety, suffering and sorrow —a parabolic saying carrying a veiled reference to Isaiah lxvi. 7–17 in which Jerusalem is compared with a mother in travail.[45]

Dodd (p. 102) thinks that the parable, like The Weather Signs, was meant 'to suggest that men ought to have the wit to see that the crisis is upon them' and Jeremias (p. 119) considers it 'another saying concerned with harvest-time'—an odd way of describing a reference to the leafing of a tree which buds in February. Vincent Taylor (p. 520) remarks despondently: 'The original meaning of the parable must remain a matter of conjecture.' The lesson drawn by the Evangelists is that the Kingdom is imminent—'at the doors' —and men should perceive the clear signs of this in the ministry of Jesus. But the parable itself, with its portrayal of the tree putting forth its leaves in spring suggests the events leading up to the ushering in of the Kingdom.[46]

When we apply this parable to our situation it invites us to take heart and renew our hopes; for God's blessings are as confidently to be expected as are leaves, blossoms and birds' songs in spring. Each year we see life springing from the dead and receive the assurance that God's hand is over all and that His love never fails. At times the vitality of the Church seems to be low, the chill wintry winds menace it; or, as individuals, we may feel ourselves spiritually dry; but after the winter, spring. Heed the lesson of the fig tree. Life from the dead!

THE BARREN FIG TREE

Lk. xiii. 6–9

TAKE HEED!

In contrast to a flourishing fig tree as a symbol of prosperity and deliverance, an unfruitful or decaying fig tree had the opposite meaning. Joel (i. 7, 12) refers to barked and languishing fig trees as signifying desolation, and Jeremiah (viii. 13) indicates the Lord's displeasure with His people by the words: 'There shall be no grapes on the vine, nor figs on the fig tree, and the leaf shall fade.' The result of man's wickedness is imaginatively linked with blighted trees and fruit gone bad. Evil men are like rotten figs (Jer. xxiv. 2–8) and people under condemnation, suffering war, pestilence and famine, are said to be 'like vile figs, that cannot be eaten, they are so bad' (Jer. xxix. 17). The failure of the fig tree to blossom is symbolic of calamity (Hab. iii. 17).[47] Thus the unfruitful fig tree symbolizes the outcome of the people's unresponsiveness. This is confirmed by a comparison with Ahikar's Parables (pre-fifth century B.C.) in which the father says: 'My son, you are like a tree which yields no fruit, although it stood by the water, and its owner was forced to cut it down. And it said to him, "Transplant me (or 'Let me alone this year'), and if even then I bear no fruit, cut me down." But its owner said to it, "When you stood by the water you bore no fruit, how then will you bear fruit if you stand in another place!"' Perhaps we have an echo of this story in The Servant entrusted with Authority (The Faithful and Unfaithful Servants) and there are

details in The Prodigal Son which recall the plea of the son Nadan
in the Syriac version of The Story of Ahikar. He cries: 'Forgive
me this my folly; and I will tend thy horses and feed thy pigs.' In
the Armenian version he says: 'Father, I have sinned against thee.
Forgive me and I will be a slave unto thee for ever.'[48] This tale
was widely current in the time of our Lord and apparently He made
use of its symbolism to construct a parable; but He altered the moral
from a final condemnation to a warning.[49]

Thus the parable pictures the patience of God, but it is at the
same time a reminder that men should not presume upon this.
Luke significantly places this parable after our Lord's declaration
concerning the need for penitence in all men since they do not know
what an hour may bring forth. There are some 'who bring forth
fruit with patience' (Lk. viii. 15); but we must not assume that
there is no hurry, and that choice and commitment can be in-
definitely deferred. A time comes when 'the axe is laid unto the
root of the trees' (Mt. iii. 10; Lk. iii. 9). We are once more reminded that the teaching of our Lord was not in terms of soothing
stories but as flames of fire, urgent exhortation, words white hot,
lest any should suppose the challenge was not for them.

The parables in general, and this parable in particular, confront
us with a paradox and dilemma inherent in the Christian faith. We
have to reconcile our sense of crisis with the need for patience and
perseverance. The Gospel must be presented as an urgent call to
commitment, as if the Final Judgement were just round the corner.
Confidence in God's loving-kindness must not lull us into putting
off decision. It is all too human to feel the need to reform, but, like
Augustine, to thwart these promptings by adding 'but not yet'.

Again, the parable reproves the common supposition that to do
nothing is to do no harm. This was the assumption made by those
condemned at The Great Assize (pp. 191–195). The five careless
wedding attendants were shut out because they left action until too
late. The tree 'cumbered the ground'; it occupied space and sucked
nourishment from the soil to no purpose. Christian living calls for
positive goodwill and creative effort; it must be outgoing. Our new

towns and housing estates are full of people who are kindly enough, but whose homes are their fortresses and whose leisure lives revolve around their TV and their car. Many think in terms of entitlement rather than self-giving. The tree continues to live, but if sympathy and sacrifice are lacking, what fruit does it bear?

Those attending to our Lord's words may have recalled Isaiah's sad parable of the vineyard—'the house of Israel'—fenced and planted with the choicest vine, which yet brought forth wild grapes and was consequently laid waste (Isa. v. 1–7) (pp. 146–149). The gardener's compassion for the tree, which represents unresponsive Israel, has its counterpart in our Lord's mourning over Jerusalem recorded by Luke in the same chapter (xiii. 34). But, while we are given grounds for cherishing hope for the tree, we know the fate which awaited the city whose children rejected the overshadowing of the Divine compassion.

Another aspect of the story is a source of inspiration and encouragement. The gardener did not give up hope. His sympathy led him to realize that the tree's unfruitfulness may have been due to neglect, poor soil, drought or other unfavourable environmental circumstances. His conscience may have reproached him with having failed to do his best by the tree. The significance of all this for us living in a post-Freudian age is evident. We are too ready to blame nature rather than perceive the deficiencies of nurture in a society which exalts freedom in conduct so highly that many are growing up unable to distinguish liberty from licence. Violence and sex are great money-spinners, and making money is widely held to be the criterion of success. We are apt to blame the young when we ought to be making every effort to reform and revitalize society, which, in spite of its flourishing appearance, is deprived of spiritual nourishment at its roots. This is a personal matter in which each of us is involved, for there are those around us who need, not condemnation, but patient understanding, sympathy and Christian support if they are to be productive of good.

There may come a time in our dealings with people when we are liable to despair of them. Then we should recall the teaching of this parable. The gardener was prepared to go on toiling in good hope of success. The lesson for us is clear; have a little more patience, give them another chance, and the longed-for fruit may yet appear. Often we have to be content not to see the fruits of our labours and pray: 'Show Thy servants Thy work and their children Thy glory' (Ps. xc. 16).

THE BIRDS OF HEAVEN
Mt. vi. 26; Lk. xii. 24
AND
THE FLOWERS OF THE FIELD
Mt. vi. 28–30; Lk. xii. 27 f.

TRUST

While the sayings about The Birds of Heaven and The Flowers of the Field are pictorial comparisons rather than parables, their affinity to parables is evident. Jesus warns His hearers against concentrating attention and energy on what to eat, drink and wear. As Jeremias points out (p. 214), the meaning is not simply that they ought not to worry about these matters, but that they should not waste unnecessary effort on them. Our Lord stressed in other contexts the need to conserve mental and physical energy for constructive ends. When the disciples were despatched on a preaching tour they were told to 'exchange no greetings on the road' (Lk. x. 4b; cf. II Kings iv. 29); they should not delay for those prolonged courtesies which were normally obligatory among eastern peoples— the 'oriental salutation, a copious flow of soul, whose intimacy and inquisitiveness are strange to the mentality of the West'.[50] The mission teaching was of such importance that no time or energy should be dissipated on subordinate matters.

If missionary urgency was such that even greetings, which were

observed with special punctiliousness by the Pharisees (Mt. xxiii. 7;
Lk. xi. 43, xx. 46), were to be regarded as a waste of time, the
disciples would have few opportunities to earn their keep. How
were they to live? By faith, was the answer. 'When did you ever
see a raven sowing or reaping, or notice one of these lovely purple
anemones spinning or weaving? They depend on God and so
should you.'[51] Jesus, as His disciples fully understood, realized that
God's gifts to men must be mediated by their fellowmen. But in
this gentle, humorous rebuke he called their attention to what is
more fundamental—the reliability of God. Even if they were called,
as He had been called, to renounce the ease which God had provided for the beasts and birds by endowing them with their instincts
(Mk. viii. 35; Lk. ix. 24) they should live putting their complete
trust in Him. Many who since then have left all for the Gospel's
sake (Mt. x. 29, xiii. 38) have found strength in the thought of this
identification with their Master.

> In such wise, He—
> Plucking His themes, as Syrian girls pull flowers,
> To spell dear names and speak the gentlest words,
> From common wayside things in Galilee—
> Taught us by Parable.[52]

In the Old Testament 'the grass of the field' signifies the transi-
tory nature of human life (II Kings xix. 26; Isa. xl. 6–8; Ps. xxxvii.
2, cii. 11, ciii. 15); Jesus characteristically gives the illustration an
unexpected twist so that men are called to appreciate the beauty of
what they neglect. Even if the suggestion that by 'the grass of the
field' He referred to gladioli and irises is somewhat strained
certainly these might be included in a reaping to be 'cast into the
oven' to bake bread.[53]

In The Flowers and Birds the emphasis is on trust in God—
faith which The Rich Fool lacked—and it is not accidental that we
are reminded of the Lord's Prayer for there are remarkable verbal
affinities between its phrases and these sayings—'Heavenly Father',
'Kingdom', 'will', 'this day' and 'tomorrow', which is probably the

true meaning of the word translated 'daily'—'our bread of to-morrow'. Both sayings and prayer suggest the thought of God's perennial loving care, the reliability of His gifts in nature and our duty to trust Him. The life of the completely dedicated Christian should manifest the tranquillity which is the fruit of trust in God as well as the purposefulness which issues from identification with God's will.

THE VULTURES AND THE CARCASS
Mt. xxiv. 28; Lk. xvii. 37

THE TREE AND ITS FRUITS
Mt. vii. 16; Lk. vi. 44

AND

THE WEATHER SIGNS
Lk. xii. 54–56; cf. Mt. xvi. 2 f.; Mk. viii. 11–13

God's Purpose Manifested in the Sequence of Cause and Effect

There were many during the time of our Lord's ministry who lived in expectation of strange, terrifying portents preceding the End but, as we have seen (p. 30) there is little evidence that Jesus endorsed such notions. 'The Pharisees came out and engaged Him in discussion. To test Him they asked for a sign from heaven. He sighed deeply to Himself and said, "Why does this generation seek for a sign? I tell you this: no sign shall be given to this generation" ' (Mk. viii. 11 f.).[54]

In contrast to such expectations of abnormal manifestations Jesus drew attention to the regular relationship of cause and effect to be seen in nature as a pointer to the kind of activity to be expected from God. In commenting on the carrion-devouring birds he may have been applying a proverb comparable with the current Palestinian saying: 'The flies know the house of the sour milk seller.' Eagles as well as vultures are attracted to carrion, but the allusion is more appropriate to vultures; for eagles prefer living prey. In Job (xxxix. 27–30) an enumeration of what popular writers of yesterday called 'the wonders of instinct' concludes with mention of a great bird of prey—evidently the griffon vulture: 'Where the slain are there is she'; and the writer says correctly, 'She seeketh the prey and her eyes behold afar off'; for vultures find dead bodies by sight and not by scent as Jeremias supposes (p. 162).[55] In the East African National Parks an assembly of vultures is such an infallible indication of a carcass that guides, wishing to show tourists lions and leopards, search around where they are to be seen.

Some commentators interpret this saying as a warning of the sudden coming of the Son of Man, but this can hardly be correct. It is the inevitability with which vultures flock to a carcass, not the abruptness of their coming, which is most impressive. This is the significance of the proverb. The prophets emphasized nature's regularities and the lessons to be drawn from them. Amos (iii. 4) enquired, confident that his hearers knew the answer as well as he: 'Will a lion roar when he hath no prey?'[56] Jeremiah reproved the nation: 'Yea, the stork in the heaven knoweth her appointed times; and the turtle and the crane and the swallow observe the time of their coming; but my people know not the judgement of the Lord.'[57] Nature does not contradict herself. Rejecting the visionary unrealities of Isaiah (xi. 6, lxv. 25) Sirach (xiii. 17) asks: 'What association can wolf have with the lamb?'

Jesus pointed out that inferences concerning God's judgements and the moral law could be drawn from vegetation as well as bird behaviour: 'Can grapes be picked from briars or figs from thistles?' (Mt. vii. 16; Lk. vi. 44). Moreover, weatherwise people could foretell imminent changes in the weather, arguing from the regularity of nature's laws. In referring to such forecasting Jesus reminded His hearers of a popular maxim as He did in mentioning the proverb, 'Physician, heal yourself' to the synagogue congregation at Nazareth

(Lk. iv. 23). When clouds were seen banking up in the west wise-acres knew that it was going to rain, and when the wind was in the south they could predict a heat wave.[58] Such people could be too obtuse to read the 'signs of the times' and too slow-witted to perceive the truth concerning the Kingdom of God proclaimed by Jesus. Thus they failed to heed the warning and to take the action called for from them, like a man who might miss the opportunity to settle the suit brought against him before being brought into court (The Defendant, Mt. v. 25 f.; Lk. xii. 58).

We should not let our assimilation of the separate lessons of the Nature Parables occupy our attention to the exclusion of the principles which underlie them. The parables proclaim implicitly that nature is a manifestation of the divine; in our contact with nature we touch the hem of the garment of God. We learn from them that the laws of nature must be respected and obeyed, and that reverence is required of us in all our commerce with the natural world. Science has acquired mastery by learning to respect and harness the forces of nature, but man's reverence lags far behind his capacity to destroy. His attitude, apart from the outlook in limited, enlightened circles, is comparable with that of the Rich Fool in its selfishness and shortsightedness. Only if man is gracious to nature can nature be gracious to him. The Christian sees the world in the light of the parables with appreciation and compassion. For him the bushes are afire with God. The Seed Growing Secretly depicts the happy relationship—man relying on the growth of the seed in the good earth—all 'under God'. He dare not assume that only he among living creatures has rights. He must learn personal self-control lest increase in his numbers make the earth inhospitable for innumerable other organisms and ultimately for himself. The fate of this lovely world depends on prudence, restraint and common sense, but, above all, on whether reverence succeeds in supplanting ruthlessness.

CHAPTER II

OPEN AND CLOSED DOORS

Warning and Assurance, Importunity and Opportunity

The Palestinian countryside with its trees and blossoms, birds and beasts, seasonal changes and regular sequences of activities in the fields and on the hillsides furnishes the homely background to the Nature Parables. Except when man maliciously interferes, as in The Tares, we see scenes revealing development and consummation, growth and harvest. The activities of nature being understood as manifestations of the divine these parables depict, in their presuppositions as well as their lessons, the paramount power of God. When we turn to the parables in which man's activities predominate we find ourselves in a different environment. In some, such as the three Parables of the Lost and Found (pp. 169–185) God's activity is adumbrated in man's; but many of the parables which we are about to discuss depict human predicaments. We do not find it difficult to think of ourselves as involved in them. We move from the orderliness and reliability of nature, governed by divine laws, to the disorderly complexity of the human scene, from the open air to the dwellings of men and what happens indoors. We may place these parables in an order which is, perhaps, somewhat arbitrary, so far as their lessons are concerned, by considering them in a sequence leading us from incidents taking place at the door to events and festivities inside (Chapter III). We will include with them certain related parables dealing with petition and prayer. The keynote of a number of them is the importance of watchfulness.

Our modes of thought are such that doors acquire symbolic significance. They figure in our memories, dreams and in the metaphors we use. To recognize this is to realize that the division between symbolism and allegory is more a matter of definition than a reality. The allegorizing procedure which led to such false interpretations of the parables involved attaching arbitrary meanings to items in them, but, as we shall see later, some parables include traditional symbols such as light, the vineyard and feasts. Only when we can be certain that in any apparently allegorical interpretation no traditional symbolism is involved are we entitled to consider the interpretation arbitrary.[1]

We speak of doors of opportunity opening or closing. Jacob, after his dream cries: 'This is the gate of heaven' (Gen. xxviii. 17) and St. John, in his vision, saw twelve gates of pearl (Apoc. iii. 8, 20). Matthew (xvi. 18) records the assurance to Peter concerning the Church that 'the gates of death shall never close upon it'. Perhaps the home ritual of the 'open door' on Passover Eve, still observed, influenced the imagery of the parables.[2] In our memories mingle pleasant recollections of lighted, welcoming, open doorways and sad recollections of closed doors representing disappointment, thwarted aspirations and lost opportunities. Painters have depicted the pathos of the closed door, as in Holman Hunt's 'Behold I stand at the door and knock' and Watts' 'Love locked out'; and other artists have symbolized faith, hope and joy in their pictures of the garden tomb with the stone—'the door of the sepulchre'—rolled away (Mk. xvi. 3). Hymn writers, from at least as early as the ninth century, have included doors in their imagery. Familiar to everyone is Bishop Walsham How's 'O Jesus Thou art standing outside the fast-closed door' and well-known lines in a Lenten hymn express the prayer:

> Lord on us Thy spirit pour
> Kneeling lowly at the door,
> Ere it close for evermore.[3]

Dante elaborated the 'gates of hell' metaphor in his description of the grim portal inscribed: 'Abandon hope all ye who enter here'.[4]

Christian passed throught the Wicket-gate at the beginning of his pilgrimage and the gate of the Heavenly City at the end. Thus in the natural activity of the imagination as well as in religious and literary tradition the door can symbolize appeal and opportunity taken or lost.

THE BURGLAR

Mt. xxiv. 43 f.; Lk. xii. 39 f.

BE PREPARED

The robber did not sneak in through the unlatched door. The house was 'broken into'. Economic distress, which was widespread and acute, drove men to desperate deeds. The parables with their references to murder (The Wicked Vinedressers), banditry (The Good Samaritan), extortion (The Unforgiving Official) and unemployment (The Labourers in the Vineyard) show us a state of society in which life and livelihood were insecure.

Evidence that this parable was widely known during the lifetime of first-generation Christians is provided by the use of the same illustration in I Thessalonians (v. 2 ff.), written about A.D. 51. This imagery is also found in II Peter (iii. 10) and the Apocalypse (iii. 3; xvi. 15). The picture of the Day of the Lord coming 'as a thief in the night' caught the imagination of Christians living in expectancy of the Final Judgement and Parousia—the sudden return in glory of the Son of Man. It is unlikely that our Lord intended The Burglar to be understood as depicting the Parousia. His immediate followers thought of it as a time of joy. Even less is it credible that the burglar represents God.

This illustration is one of a group of Crisis Parables in which our Lord stressed the importance of alertness and preparedness. It is a tocsin, a call in emphatic terms to heed His message. This challenge, as we shall see, was repeated in one vivid image after another. Men were to be as faithfully alert as a trusted doorkeeper or a servant given authority; they were to be as prepared as a bride's girl-friends awaiting the bridegroom; they were not to leave the final reckoning until too late.[5]

The early Church caught this spirit of urgency and bestirred itself to greater efforts and devotion. 'The hour of favour has now come,' wrote St. Paul, 'now, I say, has the day of deliverance dawned' (II Cor. vi. 2). God challenges each generation in un-expected ways and we urgently need this expectedness and fervour, the children's Christmas Eve anticipation, together with the warrior's girding himself for the battle. Past history reveals too many periods when the Church was somnolent or individuals sunk in lassitude and tolerance of evil. Like the householder, we realize our sins of omission too late. Suffering goes unrelieved and sin unrebuked. We drift into becoming spiritually moribund, dilettante Christians. We trifle with realities. An illustration used by C. S. Lewis might be considered an extension of this parable. He compares the com-placency of the relationship of many to God to the light-hearted feelings of children playing at burglars. But what if they become aware of a real burglar in the hall?[6]

THE STRONG MAN BOUND

Mt. xii. 29; Mk. iii. 27; Lk. xi. 21 f.

AND

THE DIVIDED REALM

Mk. iii. 24–26; Lk. xi. 17–20

THE POWER OF GOD AND THE IMPOTENCE OF SATAN

The parable of The Strong Man Bound is one of a group of sayings rebutting the charge that Jesus expelled evil spirits by grace of their prince. Matthew's version follows Mark, Luke has used source Q. In contrast to the surreptitious entry of the man described in The Burglar, this parable shows a householder confronting a would-be intruder at his doorway. Mark's account would seem to be the more authentic, for it bears traces of translation from the Aramaic, whereas Luke's version contains expressions typical of his style, Greek and Septuagint locutions. Moreover, he has heightened the drama of the situation by depicting a military figure, armoured and accoutred, defending his 'palace'. Further, Luke here, as elsewhere, shows special interest in the distribution of goods (Lk. xviii. 22; Acts iv. 35). In this parable, Jesus, by implicit allusions to Scripture, turns the edge of His critics' accusation that He was in league with the devil. Deutero-Isaiah (xlix. 24) had asked: 'Shall the spoil be taken by the mighty?' and he declared that the Suffering Servant 'shall divide the spoil with the strong' (liii. 12), but in the Septuagint translation of this passage the Suffering Servant is proclaimed as a victor overcoming the strong and distributing their goods. Thus it would seem that our Lord deliberately identified Himself with the Suffering Servant.[7] The concept of evil powers being 'bound' appears in Enoch (x. 4 f.; xxi. 1 ff.) and is echoed in the Apocalypse (xx. 2 f.).

Our Lord's critics (Pharisees in Matthew, scribes in Mark, the people in Luke) in trying to minimize and explain away His powers reveal that they are thinking in quasi-magical terms. They suspected Him of sorcery. According to Mark (iii. 21) even Jesus' family circle thought that He might be demented The magician can always account for any failure in his magic by blaming a more powerful magician. The realm of magic is a kingdom divided against itself where spirits war against spirits. Jesus repudiated the implied accusation that His cures were magical as He had earlier repudiated magic as of the devil during the Temptation. He declared that it was 'by the finger of God' that He exorcized evil spirits. He challenged His critics to face facts: 'If you see healing and happiness restored in surprising circumstances do not let your prejudices prevent you from perceiving that the Spirit of God is at work.' He countered the accusation by showing that, however interpreted, the kingdom of

Satan was doomed. It was either engaged in self-destruction or manifestly impotent against the powers of God. Indeed, it is of the nature of corruption to be self-destructive.

The Jews looked for the time when, in the words of The Assumption of Moses:

> His Kingdom shall appear throughout all His creation
> And Satan shall be no more,
> And sorrow shall depart with him.

Jesus declared again and again that Satan was being overcome. This claim appears not only in this parable and the narrative of The Temptation but also in the dialogue on exorcism (Mk. iii. 22–26; Mt. xii. 24–28; Lk. xi. 17–20), the saying, 'I watched how Satan fell, like lightning, out of the sky' (Lk. x. 18), the incident of the demoniac in the synagogue (Mk. i. 23–27) and the story of the Gadarene swine (Mk. v. 1–20).[8]

In our time the mentality of the believer in the divided realm appears in the bewilderment of the man in the street on finding that science, which can have such beneficent results, can also be so menacing. He naïvely fails to realize that unless morality overrules ingenuity and intellectualism is acknowledged to be no substitute for idealism the end is destruction. Reports of the experiments conducted in Nazi concentration camps have shown what happens when science, divorced from religion and morality, is divided against itself.

No doubt John Bunyan had the parable of The Strong Man Bound in mind when he described Christian's vision in the Interpreter's House of a 'man of a very stout countenance' who fought his way through the men in armour into the palace, and again, later, when Christian with this object-lesson in mind, put Apollyon to flight:

> He who would valiant be
> 'Gainst all disaster,
> Let him with constancy,
> Follow the Master.

The true armour of the Christian is spiritual (Eph. vi. 13–17). The man with morale vanquishes the materialist—who trusts in 'the arm of flesh'; he who goes forward in faith is endowed with power. But the parable has a deeper significance; it foreshadows the ultimate victory over evil and the triumph of truth and righteousness when 'every kind of domination, authority and power' (I Cor. xv. 24) will be overthrown and Christ will be 'all in all'.

THE UNOCCUPIED HOUSE

OR

THE DEMONS' INVASION

Mt. xii. 43–45; Lk. xi. 24–26

THE IMPORTANCE OF CONTINUED ENTHUSIASM

We are invited to picture an invasion in force. More than a posse of demons is involved; for 'seven' hints at a large contingent. Here there is no breaking in nor hand-to-hand encounter at the door. The demons, gathering from their desert ranges, 'prowl and prowl around' and slip in through the unguarded doorway, probably at night, the time when, traditionally, the hordes of evil are most active. The house has been set in order after the expulsion of the malicious spirit; but the naïve assumption that all would be well proves unjustified. So also is it true that this is not the kind of world in which the moral *status quo*, once established, will maintain itself. The forces of temptation and the forms of its assaults do not remain the same. Conversion is incomplete if it is only a negative attitude, a repudiation of, or regret for, the past, without vigorous resolve to seek positive righteousness in the future. True conversion means a new commitment. The carefully folded garment, stored away, is destroyed by moths, the unused tool is corrupted by rust (Mt. vi. 20); life without creativity deteriorates. Enthusiasm, which in its root meaning is the attribute of the God-possessed, is the only effective protection against invasion by sordid, evil, destructive agencies; and this, the Christian must maintain, is as valid of society as of the individual. The empty life is vulnerable. If the old maxim: 'Satan finds some mischief still for idle hands to do' is somewhat out of favour, we need not look far for evidence of its truth. Creativity is the true defence against corruption. The Christian must so equip himself for active service that he 'may be able to stand his ground when things are at their worst (Eph. vi. 13).

It was in an age when belief in the malignant activities of evil spirits was widespread that St. Patrick's Breastplate was composed, so it includes petitions for protection from 'the wizard's arts in-human' and 'each ambush of the devil', but its emphasis is on Christian affirmation:

> I arise on my way,
> With God's strength for my stay,
> God's Might to protect me,
> God's Wisdom to direct me,
> Christ be with me, Christ within me,
> Christ behind me, Christ before me,
> Christ beside me, Christ to win me,
> Christ to comfort and restore me.

The Christ-possessed life is fortified against invasion by evil.

THE CLOSED DOOR

Lk. xiii. 24–30

Opportunity Neglected

So strong is the similarity between Lk. xiii. 25 and the reply to the negligent wedding attendants in Mt. xxv. 12 that we may assume these passages to be derived from a common source. Dodd (p. 129) calls the Lucan passage the parable of The Closed Door; and

Jeremias (pp. 95 f., 175) also adopts this title and argues, plausibly enough, that the parable came into being from the fusion of some similes (Mt. vii. 13 f., 22 f.; viii. 11 f.) with the conclusion of The Bride's Attendants. There are affinities with Mt. viii. 22 f. (The Great Assize) in which sinners are pictured protesting their lack of negligence. Here the reply is: 'I never knew you: out of my sight, you and your wicked ways.'

The narrow door to the householder's dwelling is pictured standing open for a time, but those for whom he waits are dilatory and unenthusiastic. We may picture him as a kind teacher offering hospitality and instruction. He can wait no longer, but gets up and fastens the door. At length those to whom he has proffered realization approach and knock, imploring him to open; but he refuses, denying any acquaintance with them apart from the disclosure that they are evil-doers. The tardiness of their arrival may, indeed, be an indication of bad conscience or of a preoccupation with their own affairs nearly comparable with that of the guests who absented themselves from the Wedding Feast. They call through the closed door that they have feasted with him and that he has been in their neighbourhood teaching, but to no avail. They are typical of those people who, because they have accepted charity, advice or help of one kind or another from some person or organization believe that this entitles them to further help. They are like birds which perch in the branches of a mustard bush and feed on its seed. Charity accepted is regarded as entitlement earned. The problem is world-wide. The industrially undeveloped countries accept the largesse of powers competing for overseas influence, and when gifts come to them, inspired by generosity and Christian sympathy, they find it difficult to believe that the donors are not inspired by ulterior and selfish motives.

The opportunity symbolism of the door leads naturally to imagery in which a narrow entrance represents the acceptance of restriction on self-will and self-indulgence. After the parable of The Closed Door we are reminded that 'the gate that leads to life is small and the road narrow' (Mt. vii. 14). The humorous allusion to the camel trying to squeeze through the eye of a needle (Mt. xix. 24; Mk. x. 25; Lk. xviii. 25), a variation on another Jewish saying: 'Men are not shown (in a dream) either a golden palm or an elephant passing through the eye of a needle', reinforces our Lord's other exhortations to travel light and avoid setting one's heart on earthly treasure (Mt. x. 10; Mk. vi. 8; Lk. ix. 3; Mt. vi. 21; Lk. xii. 33 f.). Another natural association links the idea of a door, closed and locked, with the restrictive teaching of some religious leaders who shut the door of knowledge and take away the key (Lk. xi. 52).[9]

The commitment required by our Lord is not a matter of mere adherence. It calls for whole-hearted devotion involving the renunciation of evil and strenuous effort to 'buy up every opportunity'.

THE DOORKEEPER

Mk. xiii. 33–37; Cf. Mt. xxiv. 42

BE ALERT

In a country where acts of violence were not uncommon those who could afford to do so kept a watchman. The doorkeeper was, and still is, a familiar figure in Palestine. The last thing said to him when the householder goes out is, 'Turn your mind to the house.' He would be surprised if this farewell were omitted.[10]

In contrast to The Burglar and The Unoccupied House, but in common with The Strong Man Bound this parable tells of a guarded door. Its emphasis is on watchfulness. It has evidently become somewhat modified, absorbing some words (Mk. xiii. 34) from The Talents (Entrusted Wealth) (Mt. xxv. 14–30). The exhortation to stay awake all night is less appropriate in connexion with a return from a long journey (Lk. xii. 36) than in reference to a wedding feast. Possibly the transfer of authority to the servants is derived from the parable of The Servant entrusted with Authority (Mt. xxiv. 45; Lk. xii. 42–46). Matthew (xxiv. 42; cf. xxv. 13) simply records: 'Keep awake, then, for you do not know on what day the Lord is to come', and appends the parable of The Burglar.

We have a word-picture of a householder who, going out to a banquet, instructs his doorkeeper to be watchful for his return. Jeremias (p. 55) and others consider that the parable was originally directed against the scribes. But in endeavouring to identify the first audience of a parable it is all too easy to assume it to have been addressed to those to whom we ourselves think it most applicable. It may well have been addressed to a general audience, the Speaker relying on those whom the cap fitted to apply it to themselves.[11]

The allusions to 'day' and 'your lord' rather than 'night' and 'master of the house' indicate that in Mark's time the parable was interpreted in terms of Christ's return in glory to reward or reprove according to men's deserts (Mt. xxiv. 42; Lk. xii. 40). The Church, in its traditional observation of Advent, emphasizes the message of this parable. Be watchful!

> Call to each waking band,
>   'Watch, brethren, watch!'
> Clear is our Lord's command;
>   Watch, brethren, watch!
> Be ye as men that wait
> Always at the Master's gate,
> E'en though He tarry late;
>   Watch, brethren, watch![12]

THE IMPORTUNATE NEIGHBOUR

Lk. xi. 5–8

EARNESTNESS

The door is closed; but the visitor, unwelcome as his intrusion may be, is a friend. Amused glances may have been exchanged by those who first heard this story, if, as is not unlikely, it was inspired

F

by a recent incident involving the discomfiture of a neighbour. The shutting of the cottage door, left open throughout the day as in many village communities, was the signal that the family had retired for the night. A wooden bar thrust into sockets on either side of the door or through rings in its boards excluded intruders. Parents and children stretched themselves on a mattress or on sheepskins on the floor, father at one end of the row, mother at the other, 'to keep the children from rolling from under the cover'.[13] In such circumstances to pick one's way across the encumbered floor of an unlighted or dimly lighted room without disturbing the whole family would not be easy.

The weary householder has settled down for the night and it is not surprising that he should feel irritation and resentment as, half-awake, he realizes that someone is knocking with increasing violence on the door. He grumbles and calls out, 'Don't bother me. We are all in bed.' But the battering continues. At length he gets up and fetches three small loaves—a supply which was considered a meal for one person.[14]

The parable leaves to the imagination the prelude to the story. The belated traveller may be pictured arriving at the neighbour's house, arousing him, and, necessarily, his wife and family. They are covered with confusion on remembering that there is nothing to set before the visitor. So the good man goes, with compunction, but impelled by the duty of hospitality, to awaken his friend. We are not meant to dwell on the tardy response of the man whom the importunate neighbour arouses. His reluctance to get up was natural enough and would be appreciated by the audience. The point lies in the initiative and persistence of the neighbour which were inspired by his disinterested care for a benighted traveller.[15]

Some commentators have raised gratuitous difficulties by suggesting that the word translated 'importunity' really means 'shamelessness'. (The word occurs nowhere else in the New Testament and is rare in the papyri.) They suggest that the man was shameless in disturbing his neighbour for so trivial a reason. But this is to underestimate the imperious demands of hospitality in such a community, even though they would be less stringent than among the Beduin, of whom it was said that the host would slay his horse rather than have nothing to offer his guest.

It was to provide food for the visitor that the householder ventured to disturb his neighbour; he would never have done so merely to alleviate his own needs. We may see in this a reminder that we ought to pray for the satisfaction of the needs of others and *a fortiori* for their spiritual welfare. This is the most gracious out-pouring of prayer. When, in the Lord's Prayer, we say, 'Give us . . . bread and forgive us' . . . we pray for our neighbours and imply our willingness to share our bread and blessings with them.

The tradition of hospitality still persists in the Middle East, though it has been sadly menaced by the commercialism which accompanies the growth of the tourist industry. Those who have travelled there have grateful memories of refreshments provided at monasteries, roasted lamb in Arab tents, and of coffee served by hopkeepers in the bazaars.

The beginning of this parable and also of The Son's Request which follows, 'Which of you . . .? or 'Suppose one of you . . .' implies that the comment expected in reply is, 'We couldn't imagine such behaviour.' To act ungenerously in such a situation would be unthinkable even among those who are not normally models of good behaviour. How much more, then, we may be confident that God heeds our requests and helps us in our need. Realizing this we, too, should be ready to help a neighbour in distress. But the parable is not a moralizing comment on neighbourliness. It calls upon us to apply what we know of human kindliness to stir our imaginations to a realization of how much greater is God's care for us than the neighbourliness which society's conventions impose upon its members.

THE SON'S REQUEST
Mt. vii. 9–11; Lk. xi. 11–13

God's Love

If there could be a further degree of the unthinkable it would be that a father should offer his hungry child a snake, a scorpion or a stone, instead of bread, fish or an egg. (All three, mentioned in one or other of the accounts in the two Gospels were staple foods in Palestine.) 'How much more will the Heavenly Father give good things to His children!' 'Ask and it shall be given unto you' (Lk. xi. 9). In this, and the preceding parable, the theme is the approach to God in prayer and His outgoing response. In both we have assurances of God's love and grace. A man will help a friend when he is asked, a father will give the best available to his son, but God— how much more will He who is infinite love bestow His gifts on His children.[16]

This little parable leads us into the cottage where the family meal is being enjoyed, and although it is of general application its simplicity suggests a humble household, such as that depicted in The Importunate Neighbour and unlike the more wealthy households of The Doorkeeper and a number of other parables. It has the same intimacy as The Prodigal Son in which a feast is provided for the lad on his return to the farm. The symbolism suggested by the loaves and fishes links it with other Gospel contexts such as the Feeding of the Multitude (Mt. xiv. 13–21; Mk. vi. 30–44; Lk. ix. 10–17) and ultimately with the Lord's Supper, the Heavenly Banquet and the Life of the Age to Come (cf. Chapter III). The Son's Request may be regarded as the petition for bread in the Lord's Prayer set in parable form. The two are placed together by Luke. The culminating expression of the love, generosity and graciousness of God is the banquet prepared for the Prodigal Son. Meals in the Gospels and especially in the parables are expressions of love, joy, fellowship and blessedness. The richness of such associations being so great we should not let meticulous fears of succumbing to allegorizing interpretations prevent us from perceiving symbolism and radiating allusions here and elsewhere.

THE UNJUST JUDGE

OR

THE IMPORTUNATE WIDOW

Lk. xviii. 1–8

MAN'S URGENCY AND GOD'S RESPONSIVENESS

The parable already commented upon, The Son's Request, has in common with this parable and with The Importunate Neighbour that it is a request parable. We can think of these as making a triad of Request Parables, though if it were not clumsy to call them Parables of Granted Request we might thus more accurately indicate their content and significance. It is not out of a sense of justice or feeling of compassion that the judge hears the woman's suit and grants her plea. All three parables depict, in different ways, approach by prayer to the throne of God, but the judge in The Importunate Widow no more represents God than does the burglar in the parable of that name. He declares, 'I care nothing for God or man.' He is corrupt, 'a judge of unrighteousness' and the parable is based, not on the comparison between the judge and God but on a contrast.

As in The Dishonest Steward there is a surprising twist in the parable of The Importunate Widow. The moral is drawn from the behaviour of a person whose character is not to be admired or imitated. The judge capitulates because he is besieged to the limits of endurance. The widow batters down the door of his resistance.[17]

If such a callous rogue will grant a request because he cannot endure further pestering, how certain can we be that God, who is always ready to hear His children's pleas, will give heed to their petitions. He will 'vindicate His chosen who cry out to Him day and night'. Too often we think of prayer as polite request and forget how agonizingly urgent it can be and should be.

Throughout the Bible the widow is the type and representative of those in need of compassion and practical help (Exod. xxii. 22; Deut. x. 18; Ps. cxlvi. 9; Isa. i. 17, 23).[18] Widows might be quite young, and their status in society was very low. From the time when Jesus gathered His few disciples around Him there have been followers who might be compared with them, suffering insecurity and subject to contempt and injustice.

Canon Tristram witnessed legal proceedings at Nisibis in Mesopotamia which illustrate this parable. The Kadi or judge was seated on piled-up cushions while whispering underlings handed on bribes to him in order to influence the priority given to the cases and the judgement passed on them. A poor woman kept interrupting, crying out that she came there every day seeking justice. At length the judge asked what she wanted. Her son had been conscripted and she was being compelled to pay tax on land which she was unable to cultivate. After a few questions the judge said, 'Let her be exempt.'[19]

The reference to God 'avenging his chosen' has been explained as an allusion to the Jewish martyrs of the Maccabaean wars or an addition inserted during a period of persecution when Christians were liable to 'lose heart'. Jeremias (p. 156) suggests, not entirely convincingly, that the 'chosen' signified the poor or that the whole parable was an exhortation to the disciples to face persecution fearlessly. He thinks that Jesus added the interpretation to avoid shocking His hearers who might suppose the unjust judge represented God. They must learn to apply the 'how much more' principle in order to attain a more adequate conception of Him.

Neither this parable nor The Pharisee and the Publican was primarily intended to indicate how to pray. (The introductory verse may be due to Luke.) Commentators are not agreed as to whether the widow or the judge is the important character, and consequently as to whether the stress is to be laid on the petitioning or the granting of the plea. In all three Request Parables the thought is of individual rather than corporate prayer. As with a number of other parables it is difficult to devise any brief and satisfactory title for the parable we are discussing. The point of the story is the responsiveness of God to those who cry unto Him. It is such that they may be confident He hears their prayers.

In the Middle East importunity has not generally been regarded as reprehensible to the same extent as among us. In the industrialized West we consider it degrading to persist in petitioning and we tend to regard reiterated pleading addressed to us as an affront. But, where poverty is endemic, there is an accepted tradition that the poor are entitled to their keep and therefore that it is legitimate for them to solicit alms assiduously. A beggar's business is to beg; though those who have endured the insatiable pleading of mendicants in the Middle East have found scant comfort in this thought.

Our prayers should be as earnest as the widow's. 'Pray continually' (I Thess. v. 17). Prayer should be ardent and vigorous, 'like javelins hurled forth with might' as some of the early monks taught. We should have complete trust in God, but not presume on His goodness. These three Parables of Request are indeed Parables of Assurance. In the Old Testament and New Testament alike the faithful are assured, 'His ears are open unto their prayers' (Ps. xxxiv. 15; I Pet. iii. 12). 'Ask and you will receive; seek and you will find; knock and the door will be opened' (Lk. xi. 9).

THE PHARISEE AND THE PUBLICAN

Lk. xviii. 9–14

THE IMPORTANCE OF SINCERITY

There is more here than a comparison between the characters of two men. The parable deals with the relationship between God and man. It is framed in terms of reproof to legalistic piety and the self-righteousness which besets religious and irreligious alike, but is often a besetting sin of the former. It also provides teaching concerning the nature of prayer. But its primary message is that 'God is with him who is of a humble and contrite spirit' (Isa. lvii. 15). In being shown what is pleasing to God we have revealed to us His nature and His relationship to man.

As in The Good Samaritan the official representative of religion is depicted unfavourably, for thus the sins which all religious people are prone to fall into are shown most vividly. It is generally assumed that those mentioned in the introduction 'who trusted in themselves that they were righteous' were Pharisees, but we are not told so, and we should beware of shifting blame away from ourselves. If early tradition had identified them as Pharisees, Luke, with his anti-Pharisaic bias, would hardly have failed to be specific. The Pharisee congratulates himself on abstention from gross sins, mentioning adultery, avoidance of which is not considered an outstanding virtue in religious people; but in fairness to him we should note that he takes religion very seriously and does even more than his principles require. Not many of us are entitled to cast the first stone.

His prayer is not a caricature. It may be compared with a Pharisee's prayer dating from about A.D. 70 attributed to Rabbi Nehunja b. ha-Quara: 'I thank Thee, Jehovah, my God and my father's God, that Thou hast given me my portion with those who sit in the house of study and in the synagogues, and that Thou hast not given me my portion with those who sit in the theatre and circuses. I labour and they labour, I am zealous and they are zealous. I labour to inherit Paradise, and they labour to gain the Pit.[20] Each of these two prayers contains a comparison and expresses contempt. In the parable the publican concentrates on God and His absolute standards; the Pharisee thinks of how much more sinful other men are than he, and so fails to realize God's demands or to perceive his own shortcomings. He concentrates on his own efforts, the publican on faith in God's grace. The publican has his thoughts on Heaven, the Pharisee looks down on other men. One sees a vision of God, the other of himself. There is something of ourselves in both.

The impulse to claim merit as a way of commending oneself to God is a deep-seated impulse. It may be due to the survival of semi-magical ideas that the gods ought to do man's will and it should be possible to compel them to do so. We have already noted that ideas associated with sorcery persisted in the first century in religious circles (p. 73). How utterly different was our Lord's teaching is shown in the parable of The Great Assize (The Sheep and the Goats) in which the virtuous are shown to be those who unself-consciously, without thought of reward, perform acts of mercy— all in the day's work.

The Pharisee is commendable for the seriousness with which he takes his religious duties. He even goes the 'second mile' (Mt. v. 41), but 'every one who is arrogant is an abomination to the Lord' (Prov. xvi. 5) and his legalism conceals from his conscience the sinfulness of his self-congratulation and contempt for the other worshipper. Contempt is not merely a vice of the mean-minded; it springs from an assumption that one is entitled to occupy the seat of judgement and implies the querying of another's standing as a child of God.

Constantly, from the story of Moses at the burning bush (Exod. iii. 1 ff.) and the account of the call of Isaiah (Isa. vi. 1 ff.) to such expressions of devotion as the hymn, 'My God how wonderful Thou art',[21] religious literature has testified to the fact that true aspirations after sanctity and goodness start from a numinous realization of God's holiness. Yet it is still widely assumed that the criterion of goodness is to be no worse than one's neighbour. Legalism and an anthropocentric outlook go together; when they do, the true basis of morals in the knowledge of God and His righteousness is lost to sight.

Luke's conclusion that the humble will be rewarded by being exalted is a generalization which weakens the parable and cannot be original. The parable Master and Man teaches, that, when we have done all, we are still unworthy servants. Our so-called virtues give us no claim on God. Those who are more sure of themselves do not stand highest in His sight—a conclusion which seems obvious to the dispassionate observer. The Pharisee tried to 'justify' himself; but only God can justify. He justifies the selfless penitent and grants the prayer of the publican. Here is the doctrine of justification by faith in embryo. In his prayer the publican used the opening words of the 51st Psalm and we may infer that the subsequent verses were also in his thoughts: 'The sacrifices of God are a broken spirit: a broken and contrite heart, O God, shalt Thou not despise.' Moreover, we should note that this Psalm looks beyond sorrow for sin to the joy of the state of participating in forgiveness: 'Thou shalt make me hear of joy and gladness.'

The Authorized Version, which pictures the Pharisee praying 'with himself', gives an exaggerated impression of his self-centredness. All that is meant is that he stood in a prominent place and murmured his prayer or prayed inwardly. None the less his outlook betrays the same kind of self-satisfaction as corroded the lives of The Rich Fool and Dives. His prayer reminds us of the importance of thanksgiving in our devotions, but warns us of the thin line between thanksgiving and self-congratulation.

There are no grounds for believing that our Lord condemned all Pharisees or commended all tax-gatherers. The Gospels, in spite of the element of bias which we have seen to have been introduced by the Evangelists (p. 198 ff.), record friendly relations with Pharisees. Some of them were men of vision and integrity. Hillel (c. 20 B.C.), who was one of the most illustrious, advised: 'Keep not aloof from the congregations, and trust not in thyself until the day of thy death, and judge not thy fellow until thou art come to his place.'[22]

The directness with which our Lord challenged men is apparent in the stark contrasts characteristic of the parables. These appear in their literary structure, the 'antithetical parallelism' of some, in the 'twinning' of others, the featuring of two contrasted figures and in the extremes of character and of destiny depicted. The setting in opposition here of Pharisee and Publican illustrates this characteristic portrayal of people and events in black and white without intermediate tones. The Publican plays the same rôle as a contrast-character as the Samaritan does in the parable named after him. The Pharisee appears as a representative of the good who are not as good as they are thought to be or as they think themselves to be. This teaching device, coupled with oriental hyperbole, has constantly led to misunderstanding from the time of the oral tradition until now. Christian teachers have found it useful to be able to point to extreme examples of good and bad behaviour. Hence the Pharisee has become the 'image' of the reprehensible and hypocritical, and the Publican an illustration of the misunderstood righteous—although it is made perfectly clear that he was a sinner. Slanting of the record in favour of publicans must not pass unsuspected any more than the bias against the Pharisees. An aspect of our Lord's teaching has been exaggerated into contumely for one class of people and exaltation of another. The Publican is representative of those who were despised, and so this parable is among those, such as The Wedding Feast and the Parables of the Lost which constitute the Gospel of the Outcast.

As types we may regard the Publican as standing for those pre-occupied with finance or immersed in business, the Pharisee for those concerned with religious observances; yet the Publican is represented as the more devout of the two. Religious professionalism can drown the sense of the holy. Francis Bacon defined the true atheist as 'he who handles holy things without feeling'. On the other hand, close contact with the worldly may arouse a longing for the spiritual. The Publican, concerned with hard men and grim facts, realized the realities of sin and what he might so easily become. He sought the temple and saw a vision of God in His holiness. So, too, the Prodigal Son when he had experienced the hollow pleasures of materialism 'came to his senses' and returned to his father.

It might seem that we are involved in a vicious circle: Where sin is regarded as unreal there can be no clear vision of God. On the other hand, those without a vision of God fail to feel conscious of sin. But immersion in sin or materialism may generate self-disgust.

We are told that guilt is an outworn concept, and that conscience is a survival of obsessions from the past which hinder the enjoyment of promiscuous sex and the achievement of true happiness. The arguments of the hedonist and so-called humanist often tacitly assume that the satisfaction of animal appetites and the expression of the competitive drive ought to dominate the altruism, heroic virtues and spiritual illumination aspired after by men and women of noble character in all ages. But to set the vision of God and the consciousness of sin over against each other in terms of priority in experience is a falsification. As the lives of countless saints testify, growth in virtue and growth in the knowledge of God accompany each other. There is a virtuous circle of increasing joy, inspiration and conviction for those who strive to do the will of God. The Pharisee and the Publican are not to be set poles apart. Each of us needs some of the virtuous sense of the one and the consciousness of sin of the other if we are to experience spiritual growth.

The parable of The Pharisee and the Publican should be interpreted constructively and not as a scrutiny of the sins of different men under the microscope. It gives us positive teaching about God; for we are meant to infer His character from His way of 'justifying'. He looks with pity upon the heartbroken—and we remember that Jesus in the Nazareth synagogue declared that in Him God was acting to free the 'broken victims' (Lk. iv. 18–19). In its teaching about man's relationships the parable is concerned with matters more fundamental than the words uttered in prayer; it deals with the underlying character and soul-state of the petitioner. Simplicity, humility, integrity and sympathy lead to spiritual insight, but growth in these springs from the vision of God. 'How blest are those of a gentle spirit' (Mt. v. 5). Pascal, who divided men into Pharisees and publicans wrote: 'There are only two kinds of men, sinners who think they are righteous, and righteous who think they are sinners. The former are self-deceived, the latter are self-perceptive.' As we have noted, the matter is not quite so simple; there are times when the righteous are self-deceived and when sinners see themselves for what they are. 'Conscience may make cowards of us all.' If, and when, through the grace of God it enlightens sinners they may become saints.

The parables of opportunity and warning call upon us to recognize the strand of eternity giving significance to the web of life. For each of us the Kingdom of God is here, to be welcomed, responded to and rejoiced in. It is eternal life in the midst of time, opportunity, judgement, joy.

CHAPTER III

WEDDINGS AND FEASTS

The Opportunity of Joy

It might be expected that imagery drawn from marriage feasts and banquets would be prominent in the Gospels, for such symbolism was traditional. The banquet had come to be one of the most significant symbols of the Messianic Age. Isaiah (xxv. 6) had spoken of the time when death would be swallowed up in victory and the Lord would provide 'a feast of fat things, a feast of wines on the lees' (i.e. old full-flavoured wine). In II Baruch xxix. 4 ff. we are given a more detailed description of the fare to be provided on that great Day. The Gospels make little distinction between weddings and banquets, since a banquet usually signified a wedding feast. It was the community's most joyful social occasion, and so had become symbolic of heavenly joys. Christianity took over and elaborated this symbolism. In the account of the martyrdom of the heroic Blandina in A.D. 177 the chronicler, quoting Apoc. xix. 9, recorded that she went to her death like one 'bidden to a marriage supper'. In church we continue to express ourselves in the symbolism of the heavenly banquet when we sing the ancient hymn of St. Bernard of Marles:

> There is the throne of David;
> And there from cares released,
> The shout of them that triumph,
> The song of them that feast.[1]

Mention of feasts was particularly appropriate in parabolic teaching concerned with analogies between earthly and heavenly things, for recognition of the symbolism awakened associations in the minds of hearers and stimulated them to seek a meaning beneath the surface. Much of the power of mythology, great literature and inspiring teaching is due to the effective link of emotive memories with inspiring ideas. Moreover, as everybody is interested in weddings and feasts, Jesus knew that mention of such festivities would immediately engage the attention of those around, stirring pleasant memories and sympathetic responses in their hearts. At wedding feasts communal rejoicing reached a climax. According to a Jewish proverb: 'The six-year-old and the sixty-year-old will run after the sound of the marriage drum.' But, as in a number of other Gospel parables, an unexpected element is sometimes introduced into the wedding feast parables—a note of warning as well as a promise of joy.

THE SULKING CHILDREN

OR

THE CHILDREN IN THE MARKET PLACE

Mt. xi. 16–19; Lk. vii. 31–35

'Is It Nothing to You...?'

The parable of The Sulking Children must have been uttered during the later phase of our Lord's ministry. It is a moving portrayal of overtures rejected. The fleeting vexation of a few village children reflects the tears at the heart of things; the curtain is drawn aside for a moment that we may perceive, in the light of Christ's grief, how petty are our animosities and how distorted our values.

There is a devastating forlornness in the reactions of children to disappointment which, for all those who have not forgotten their childhood, gives the parable searching poignancy. The children complain, 'We wanted to play at weddings, but you wouldn't join

in; and when we said, "Let's play at funerals" it was just the same.'
According to Ecclesiastes (iii. 4) 'There is a time to weep and a time
to laugh' and a rabbinic proverb counsels: 'In the time of rejoicing,
rejoicing, in the time of mourning, mourning' (cf. Rom. xii. 15). But
this parable goes far beyond proverbial wisdom in depth of feeling.

We may picture boys and girls alike grumbling, for men danced
a round dance at weddings and women wailed dirges at funerals.
We need not go to the distant past for analogies. Until recently
women's keening was a feature of funeral rites in the remoter Celtic
areas of these islands. Luke gives the impression that the children
are quarrelling about the kind of game they would play; but
Matthew's wording suggests that the unavailing appeals are
voiced by the pipe players and singers.[2] They have been playing
preliminary melodies and singing snatches to induce their companions to join in, but nothing pleases them.

Often perversity may best be countered by a little wry humour;
for humour usually involves seeing two aspects of a matter, and
perversity implies the refusal to see any point of view but one's own.
Among the rabbinic sayings is a parallel to The Sulking Children:
'Jeremiah said to God: "Thou hast raised up unto the Israelites
Elijah, the man with long hair, and they mocked at him and laughed
at him—'See he curls his hair.' Thou has raised up Elisha unto
them, and they said to him, 'Go up, thou bald head, Go up, thou
bald head.' " ' Because John was unsociable people said he was
demented, and because Jesus was sociable they repudiated Him as
not respectable.

In this parable about children's play Jesus characterized His
message as having two aspects. It was a proclamation of joy, as He
had emphasized when He read the good tidings passage from Isaiah
in the synagogue at Nazareth (Lk. iv. 16 ff.); and, despite His having
to defend the Gospel against opposition, this theme of joy continues
to shine forth in His references to joyful functions and happily
shared meals. On the other hand, as the parables clearly illustrate,
the note of warning was often heard. The contrast with joy which
might have been heightens the tragedy in this lamentation of the

children in the story. We have a comparable contrast at the feast of welcome in The Prodigal Son when the whole-hearted jubilation which might have prevailed at the feast is clouded with grief and dismay when the elder son refuses to participate in the revelry. Here too, there was a perverse and ungracious refusal to join in music and dancing.

This parable awakens responsive echoes in the hearts of all those who have been rebuffed or disappointed in their efforts to influence others. There are times when, whatever our approach, there is apathy or even contempt. But what right have we to expect that more attention should be paid to us than was accorded to our Master? In God's sight we are all perverse and petulant children.

THE ARROGANT GUEST

Lk. xiv. 7–11

HUMILITY AND COURTESY

We should not attach much importance to the setting of this and a good many other parables; for, as we have noted (p. 14), in default of exact information the Evangelists had to fit the traditions which they handled into what they considered to be the most appropriate contexts. Here Luke has evidently gathered together a number of sayings, and given them 'a local habitation' as conversational topics at a feast. The picture of Jesus criticizing the guests and advising the Pharisee who was His host as to whom he ought to invite is incongruous and arouses the suspicion that teaching, actually given to a mixed group, has been directed against the Pharisees. Moreover, it would seem that Luke, in giving the saying a realistic setting has reduced it from being an illustration of humility in spiritual things merely to an attack on people whom he regarded as overbearing and malicious.[3]

Rules of etiquette at feasts are very ancient. In Proverbs (xxv. 6 f.)

the advice is given: 'Put not thyself forward in the presence of the king, and stand not in the place of great men: Far better it is that it be said unto thee, Come up hither; than that thou shouldest be put lower in the presence of the prince.' Similar advice is found in the rabbinic literature and, indeed, among the proverbs of many peoples.[4]

In Aramaic the saying forms a 'rhythmic couplet'—an indication that it was proverbial. It has affinities with the reply to the Sons of Zebedee (Mk. x. 35–45) and with the advice 'Whoever would be first must be the willing slave of all' (Mt. xx. 27; cf. pp. 118–122). The arrogant of heart and mind are 'put to rout'; and those who 'turn round and become like children' are greatest (Lk. i. 51b; Mt. xviii. 3 f.). These themes concerning the reversal of rôles and the transvaluation of values are found in several parables—the down-and-outs are entertained, Lazarus and the Prodigal Son are feasted, those rewarded at the Judgement are surprised.

The parable recalls our own proverb: 'Pride goes before a fall.' It reminds us that humility is the soul of politeness. The scientist realizes that nature yields truth to the humble and the philosopher knows that *hubris* blinds the soul. As pride estranges a man from his fellows so conceit in spiritual things alienates from God. 'God sets His face against the arrogant but favours the humble' (I Pet. v. 5; James iv. 6).

THE BRIDEGROOM'S FRIEND

Jn. iii. 28

THE JOY OF CHRIST'S PRESENCE

In St. John's Gospel the parable, The Bridegroom's Friend, is attributed to John the Baptist, though it has been suggested that a somewhat similar parable may have been included in earlier tradition as uttered by Jesus.[5]

Even though the Baptist's character was austere and his message stern he is spoken of as rejoicing in his rôle as the bridegroom's friend—the 'best man' next to the bridegroom. 'It is the bridegroom to whom the bride belongs. The bridegroom's friend, who stands by and listens to him is overjoyed at hearing the bridegroom's voice. This joy, this perfect joy, is now mine. As he grows greater I must grow less.'

The Gospel records make it clear that where Jesus came He brought joy. Once again we are reminded that joy is the keynote of the Gospel. 'Praising we plough and singing we sail.'

THE BRIDEGROOM'S ATTENDANTS

Mt. ix. 15a; Mk. ii. 18 f.; Lk. v. 34

THE JOY OF HIS PRESENCE

Again, as in The Sulking Children, we are made aware of the contrast between the teaching of John the Baptist and that of Jesus. When Jesus was asked why the disciples of John fasted and His disciples did not, He commented that wedding guests do not engage in austerities while the bridegroom is with them. He spoke of the joy created by His presence as being comparable with wedding celebrations. The experience of John's ministry was still recent and it was taken for granted, especially by those inclined to fault-finding, that all prophets should be like him, following the penitential tradition—'Sanctify a fast!' (Joel i. 14). But Jesus' presence was a justification for rejoicing. It could be compared with the week-long period during which attendants on those newly wed were exempt from rigorous religious observances. The Kingdom of Heaven was already manifesting itself. It was no time for mourning.

Whether the hearers understood Jesus to be making a Messianic claim or not, they may have recalled that in the Old Testament the relationship between God and His people is referred to in terms of a marriage contract (Hos. ii. 16–20; Isa. liv. 5 f., lxii. 4 f.). The rabbis used the metaphor of a wedding with reference to the coming of the Messiah. The interpretation of the parable has resulted in a more direct identification of Jesus with the Messiah than it had originally; for the reference in verse 35 to the departure of the bridegroom may have been inspired by hindsight. It is out of keeping with the main theme—the joy of the Kingdom.

The spirit of rejoicing by which the early Church was inspired is apparent in the gay representations to be seen in the Roman catacombs of Christ as the Good Shepherd walking in flower-decked meadows (p. 187). Later on, the crucifix became the Christian symbol. Powerful as its emotional appeal and emphasis on sacrifice and redemption have been, it has influenced the Western Church, and much of the world, to think of Christianity as less the religion of joy than it is.[6]

THE BRIDE'S ATTENDANTS
OR
THE TEN VIRGINS
Mt. xxv. 1–13

The Importance of Foresight

We are invited to picture a village at night astir with unusual activity. Lights shine from the open doors and clusters of people chatter in the street, pausing to look around expectantly from time to time. The bridegroom and his party may arrive at any moment. Over there the bride's girl-friends are waiting, all a-dither, to welcome him.[7]

The prolonged delay is too much for them and they become drowsy, each resting with her lamp beside her. At midnight when shouts are heard, 'Here comes the bridegroom' they put out their lamps to trim the wicks. The girls who were not sufficiently far-sighted to anticipate delay beg for oil from the others and, when these refuse, they scamper off, hoping that some store may still be open.[8] When they return the bridegroom has already been welcomed into the house. They plead with him to open the door, but he replies, 'I will have nothing to do with you', a formula used, e.g. by a teacher to intimate that he will not see his pupil for seven days. Their opportunity has come and gone. Lack of forethought and skimped preparations have robbed them of their chance to join in the festivities.[9] Sins of omission have tragic consequences (pp. 191–195).

The parable is one of several portraying a crisis and foreshadowing by it the crisis of the Kingdom. Several parables are concerned with the unanticipated or disconcerting; they employ, as we might expect, illustrations designed, firstly, to capture attention, and, secondly, to express the necessity to come to terms with the in-breaking of the Kingdom involved in our Lord's mission. They were meant to shake from their apathy those who took Jesus to be just another itinerant preacher. Some of these Parables of Warning have been discussed already and others are mentioned later. The Burglar breaks in when nobody is on the alert; the negligent or un-faithful Doorkeeper may be taken by surprise; the Builder of a house on insecure foundations may see it swept away; the Rich Fool dies just when he has feathered his nest. The Bride's Attendants fail in their trust. 'Can a bride forget her attire?' asks Jeremiah incredulously (ii. 32), and for bridesmaids to neglect appropriate preparations is inconceivable. Crisis and conduct are inseparably linked together. The great prophets of Israel not only warned of calamities to come but thundered against moral evils. Jesus fulfilled the prophets in proclaiming the imminence of crisis and Judgement. But there is no suggestion in the Crisis Parables of the acceptance of an 'interim ethic' of panic penitence. They teach consistently the importance of continuing virtue.

In ancient Middle Eastern wedding ceremonies the bridegroom was the main centre of interest; thus the non-appearance of the bride in the parable indicates that the story has not been distorted

by the concept, which arose at a very early date, of the Church as
the Bride of Christ (Apoc. xix. 7, xxi. 9; II Cor. xi. 2; Eph. v. 31 f.;
cf. Mk. ii. 20; Mt. xxii. 2; Jn. iii. 29). There is no suggestion in the
Old Testament that the Messiah could be pictured as a bridegroom.
Evidently the traditional interpretation of the story as symbolizing
the Parousia is due to the Church.

By adding to the story the moral, 'Keep awake then; for you
never know the day or the hour', Matthew tends to obscure its force
and approximate it unduly to other parables which inculcate watchfulness; for no blame is attached to the girls who, having laid in a
supply of oil fall asleep and in due course wake up to perform their
duties. The principal lesson is the importance of preparedness and
of single-mindedness in view of the challenge of the hour. The
improvident girls were not merely forgetful; they were culpably
careless and so they forfeited the opportunity to 'enter into the joy'
which might have been theirs.

A subsidiary point is that this is one of a number of parables in
which discourtesy, which is sometimes culpable thoughtlessness, is
implicitly rebuked; these include The Arrogant Guest, The Labourers in the Vineyard, The Prodigal Son and The Two Sons. This
deserves emphasis in view of misunderstandings which have arisen
concerning some sayings, particularly the advice to the disciples
to 'exchange no greetings on the way' (Lk. x. 4)—a warning not to
waste time in small talk with chance acquaintances or bands of
travellers (p. 64).

We may generalize the significance of the parable by interpreting
it as a warning that good intentions by themselves are not enough.
In contrast to the thoughtless girls the Good Samaritan saw what was
needed, knew how to do it and did it. Deep feeling and concern
which do not lead to adequate action are as uncreative as the rivers
which flow down the southern flanks of the Atlas mountains to lose
themselves in the sands of the Sahara.

If there are any people to whom the warning of this parable is
particularly applicable today it is to the young folk of a similar age
to the girls in the story. But we all need the admonition, 'Seize your

opportunities while you may.' Ibsen describes the kind of person who fails to do so in the name character of *Peer Gynt*. He is 'one who does nothing thoroughly'. When he walks over the heath he hears the leaves say, 'We are watchwords which you should have proclaimed' and the broken stones on the path cry out, 'We are deeds you left unperformed.'

THE TOWER BUILDER
AND
THE WARRING KING
Lk. xiv. 28–32

COUNT THE COST

Although these twin parables which appear together in St. Luke's Gospel do not refer to feasts their emphasis on prudence, forethought and responsibility links them with the teaching of The Bride's Attendants. In their context they are a challenge to face the consequences of the choice pressed upon men by Jesus, but their implications have not been given sufficient attention by those who stress the view that His message was dominated by the imminence of the End. The Tower Builder and The Warring King both imply long-term planning and careful assessment of future eventualities and resources. They were, and are, a call to that whole-hearted discipleship which has paused to count the cost, even to taking up the Cross, and is dedicated to persevering, long-continued effort. The would-be disciple must consider what is involved in putting his hand to the plough; he must be prepared to plod back and forth until the whole large field is furrowed (Lk. ix. 62). Concentration as well as pertinacity is required; for the ploughman, goad in one hand and plough handle in the other, must keep his eyes fixed on a landmark seen between the two oxen. The defaulting ploughman and the careless girls exemplify the tragic and humiliating consequences of failure to be thus single-minded. In The Tower Builder and The Warring King, as in The Bride's Attendants, we are, in addition, admonished of the need to think and plan ahead. Although the emphasis of The Two Builders is on building on a solid foundation it also teaches the importance of forethought. Those who would follow Christ must neither be unduly frightened by what is involved, nor rush into commitments which they will be unable to fulfil. Seeds which rapidly spring up, and then wither because the soil is shallow, bear no fruit (Mk. iv. 3–8; Mt. xiii. 3–8; Lk. viii, 5–8). Jesus called on those who would be His disciples to reconcile themselves to the abandonment of home comforts and face the vicissitudes of a vagabond and penurious life with Him (Mt. x. 10; Mk. vi. 8; Lk. ix. 3). Like Himself they might find themselves treated like the outcasts He came to save (Mt. viii. 20; Lk. ix. 58).

In any enterprise, and above all in the venture of being Christ's disciple, cool appraisal of the practical difficulties, the extent of future commitments and also, self-knowledge, are required. Failure and discomfiture are likely to ensue unless he who hears the challenge assesses his capabilities and resources in relation to the task and calls God to his aid. Prudence should partner enterprise. Despite our Lord's concern to awaken people to the urgency of decision He emphasized repeatedly that those who contemplated following Him must be in the fullest sense whole-hearted. Such is His claim on us and we quail at the thought of how much is required and how far we fall short. But if human frailty necessitates such admonitions divine compassion knows our limitations and grants grace to bring our intentions to good effect. We trust in God, the Supreme Planner.

These parables do not suggest renunciation of worldly ambitions as evil but call for integrity, forethought, cool decision and single-minded dedication. What is required of the disciple is described further in the parables of The Hidden Treasure and The Peerless Pearl, in which it is emphasized that lesser aims must be abandoned if the highest is to be achieved.

THE WEDDING FEAST

OR

THE UNWILLING GUESTS

Mt. xxii. 1–10; Lk. xiv. 16–24

GOD'S INVITATION

Careful reading of Matthew's version of The Wedding Feast reveals peculiarities. It is conceivable that insolent people might repudiate invitations to dinner at the last moment; but they would hardly murder the messengers sent by their would-be host. More-over, we cannot imagine a king sending an army to avenge such behaviour by burning up a city. These details go beyond oriental exaggeration. Clearly this version of the parable has been distorted. Matthew evidently associates it with The Wicked Vinedressers, which he records a little earlier, making the parable into an allegory emphasizing that the Gentiles will enjoy the blessings rejected by the Jews. It is possible to prune away accretions and penetrate to the earlier form of the story.

Some features which puzzle a reader today become intelligible when it is realized that the story is based on a folk-tale told in Egypt as early as 331 B.C. The Palestinian version recounted the unhappy fate of a poor scholar whose death passed unnoticed, whereas a wealthy tax-collector, Bar Ma'jan, had been buried with great pomp. It was thought shocking that God could allow such injustice, until the disclosure was made that Ma'jan, though not a man of un-blemished character, had died while he was performing a philan-thropic deed. He had provided a meal for the poor. The feast had been prepared and served for the city dignitaries; but, when they failed to appear, he invited beggars to fill the empty places rather than allow the food to be wasted. Evidently Jesus was acquainted with this tale; for He made use of it in the parable of The Rich Man and Lazarus (pp. 108–111).[10]

Since the story was widely known we may assume that those who gathered around Jesus would picture the 'certain man' of the parable as a publican anxious to curry favour with the influential. When these slight his hospitality he snubs them by inviting paupers to his banquet. (The practice of sending a servant to remind invited guests before the feast was customary in some areas of the Middle East.) 'Compel them' ('make them', NEB) as an instruction to the messenger slave need not mean more than that he should lay upon the invitees the constraint which an offer of hospitality implied and which the affluent had so churlishly rejected.

The Cinderella motif in which the downtrodden score over their oppressors or superiors has universal appeal. Listeners to such a tale as this, especially outcasts and the poverty-stricken, would identify themselves with the folk from the main thoroughfares, streets and alleys who secured a good meal in the place of the wealthy and at the expense of the affronted tax-collector. They would perceive with relish that Jesus was assuring them: 'The Kingdom of Heaven is open to you, despised, poor and oppressed as you may be. Yours may be the joys of the Kingdom.' Thus the story expresses the vital importance of seizing the opportunity of new life and joy open to those who recognize and welcome the Kingdom. Wherever the Gospel is proclaimed the theme is: 'Come to me, all whose work is hard, whose load is heavy; and I will give you relief' (Mt. xi. 28).

Luke, in accordance with his liking for literary smoothness, has a more detailed account of the excuses offered by the defaulting guests. The 'rule of three', involving the mention of three items in sequence, very common in folk-tales, is observed, and the preoccupations of those who had been invited mount in importance; first, land and crops, second, the draught animals and finally, a man's wife. As a whole they may be taken to mean every kind of excuse. The emphasis on the number of messengers is paralleled in The Wicked Vinedressers—another Refusal Parable. In the latter they are sent with orders, in the former with invitations; in both they are scorned.[11] The reference in Matthew to the destruction of the city is an allusion to the fall of Jerusalem in A.D. 70, and the second mission mentioned by Luke may correspond to the extension of the Gospel to the Gentiles after the Resurrection. This is the more probable as the first mission is in the streets of the town and the second farther afield, among 'the highways and hedgerows'. Moreover, there are verbal similarities with Mt. x. 13 ff., where the apostles, when being sent out on their mission, are told how to treat those who are 'not worthy'. Again, 'Go therefore . . .' corresponds to the command in Mt. xxviii. 19 f.—'Go forth therefore and make all nations my disciples . . .'[12]

Like a number of other parables The Wedding Feast was told as an invitation and an admonition. Probably by picturing the bringing in of outcasts and the rag-tag-and-bobtail to the feast Jesus was inviting 'publicans and sinners' to rally to his side after the scribes and Pharisees and other staid self-righteous folk had shown their opposition.

'I did not come to invite virtuous people, but sinners', He said (Mk. ii. 17; Lk. v. 32). Possibly also, as The Mustard Seed suggests, He was beginning to look beyond the bounds of Israel to those who 'will come from east and west' to feast with Abraham, Isaac and Jacob in the Kingdom of Heaven' (Mt. viii. 11). The threats with which the parable concludes in Matthew are typical of his style (Mt. xiii. 42, xxii. 13, xxiv. 51, xxv. 30; cf. Lk. xiii. 8), and represent the mind, not of Jesus but of the Early Christians.

To us this parable is another reminder that we are invited by the Gospel to join with others in rejoicing at the generosity and loving-kindness of God who offers both present and future blessings. The proffered feast is for us and all men an invitation to be active members of the Church, the family of God. But the story also contains a warning to sections and areas of prosperous Christendom. Men and women who respond to the invitation of evangelists working in regions where the Gospel comes as redemptive Good News are more ready to enter into its joy than those who live where Christianity has been long established and the blessings it has conferred are taken for granted. These latter may be tempted to reject the invitation to

'The Great King's Feast' because they are obsessed with worry about their own concerns or with striving to attain a higher standard of living or with desire to increase their domestic happiness. Certainly it is clean contrary to the mind of Christ to think that aspirations such as these are to be discouraged, but there are occasions when we are tempted to get our priorities wrong, or when we fail to face the challenge to personal sacrifice and the renunciation of the lesser for the higher good.

THE WEDDING GARMENT

Mt. xxii. 11–14

THE OFFER OF SALVATION

The episode of the guest without a wedding garment may be regarded either as a sub-parable or, preferably, as a separate parable. Some scholars consider it to be a parable which has lost its beginning. A guest, unexpectedly brought in from the street, could hardly be blamed for not being properly dressed for a festive occasion. Here, again, we have a modification of an ancient tale—a parable found in the Babylonian Talmud attributed to a rabbi who lived between A.D. 70 and 100 but which may be assumed to have originated earlier. It was said that when expounding Ecclesiastes ix. 8: 'Rabban Johanan b. Zakkai compared the matter to a king who invited his servants to a feast and did not appoint a time for the beginning of the meal. The wise adorned themselves and took their places at the door of the king's palace. They said, 'Is there anything lacking in a king's palace'? ('It will not be long now'), but the foolish among them went to their work. They said, 'Is there ever a feast without preparation?' Suddenly the king summoned his servants. The unwise among them went into his presence untidy as they were. The king rejoiced over the wise and was wroth with the foolish. He said, 'Let those who have adorned themselves for the feast sit and eat and drink; but as for those who have not adorned themselves for the feast, they shall stand and look on.'

There is a parallel story, ascribed to Rabbi Judah the Prince who lived about A.D. 200, which goes into greater detail, mentioning how 'the whitewasher went to his lime, and the potter to his clay, and the smith to his soot', so that when the time came to go in to the feast they were in no condition to do so. At the conclusion the host says: 'Let these (who are not fitly arrayed) stand upon their feet; let them suffer punishment by merely looking on and being angered' (cf. Isa. lxv. 13).[13]

The wedding garment of the parable would not be a special festal robe but a newly washed garment (Apoc. xix. 8). Its significance, in view of the rabbinic parable, may be preparedness and repentance. The wearer of such a garment would thereby signify his identification with the mind of his host. It could represent redemption and glory, just as the banquet symbolizes the happiness of the blessed in fellowship with God. In Isaiah lxi., a passage to which Jesus attached special importance, since from it He took His text in the synagogue at Nazareth (Lk. iv. 16), the prophet declared: 'He hath clothed me with the garments of salvation, He hath covered me with the robe of righteousness as a bridegroom decketh himself with a garland, and as a bride adorneth herself with jewels.'[14] In the Apocalyptic literature the Elect are said to be clothed with 'a garment of Life from the Lord of Spirits'; in Isaiah lxi. 3, a promise is given of 'a garment of praise for the spirit of heaviness' and in The Prodigal Son the robe and the ring which are given to the youth on his return signify restoration to his proper status. Thus in this parable, as in so many, there are notes of joy mingled with those of warning, the thought of opportunity being emphasized, as well as that of crisis. Moreover, there are similarities to The Bride's Attendants. The rejected guest, like the careless girls, had not taken the occasion seriously. Again, he is addressed as 'Friend', a term which occurs in three contexts in the New Testament (Mt. xx. 13, xxii. 12, xxvi. 50) and, as Jeremias points out (p. 137), maintains cordiality, but is also reproachful. But the deepest message of the parable is that God ever offers joy and salvation to those who accept the Gospel and seek Him in sincerity.

THE RICH MAN AND LAZARUS

Lk. xvi. 19–31

OPPORTUNITIES MAY NOT COME AGAIN

The parable of The Rich Man (Dives) and Lazarus includes the imagery of The Banquet and, in so far as the theme of exclusion is involved, The Closed Door. As has already been mentioned (p. 46) it is *par excellence* a parable of contrasts. Riches and poverty, heaven and Hades, compassion and indifference, inclusion and exclusion are set against each other in a narrative which, as in many folk-tales, depicts abrupt reversals of fortune. This resemblance to folk-tale is not fortuitous, for the parable is based to some extent, as we shall see, on a very ancient Egyptian story. Like The Generous Employer (The Labourers in the Vineyard) (Mt. xx. 1–16), The Prodigal Son (Lk. xv. 11–32) and The Wedding Feast, with its appendix The Wedding Garment (Mt. xxii. 11–14) it is double-edged or, more correctly, dual pointed. Its culmination is to be found in the second section. We are presented with successive scenes which lend themselves to vivid visualization. In interpreting the parables we must never forget the importance of picture-thinking among the people to whom they were told. Much Jewish thought was in dramatic scenes rather than abstract terms.

Some commentators assume that this parable was directed against the Sadducees who professed agnosticism concerning the after-life (Mk. xii. 18–27), but it is not stated that the Rich Man was a Sadducee. This seems to be an example of the propensity for critics, as for the Evangelists themselves, to find groups as the targets against which it is assumed the parables were directed, even when the teaching in them is applicable to all men. That some Sadducees were wealthy is no reason to believe they were the target of this story. Jesus was painting on a broad canvas, depicting types of character and perennial problems of conduct. We may assume that He refrained from giving a name to the Rich Man, although others have called him Dives, Niniveh or Phinees, and from mentioning his religious or social affiliations, in order to give the parable general application, just as in The Good Samaritan we are not given any details of the nationality, religion or race of the bandits' victim. Perhaps by calling him 'Dives' we subconsciously avoid that identification with him which we are intended to make. None of us, in the affluent society, can protest that we have little in common with him; nor, if we think, as we should, of our door opening on a world in which Africa and Asia are only a few steps away, can we plead that Lazarus is no concern of ours.

We need not regard the Rich Man as wealthy only in respect of house, food or clothing. He was rich also in privilege and in freedom from the gnawing anxieties which beset the poor; but these very privileges concealed from him his responsibilities.

Lazarus was 'laid' at the gates of the Rich Man's house. He was carried there, incapacitated by his ailments. It has been suggested that he was a leper, but a leper's presence would not have been tolerated. Readers today may think of the dogs which licked his sores as nuzzling him in a friendly way, offering him the companionship which his fellow-men withheld, but Middle Eastern dogs were, and in some places still are, notorious for their savagery. The rabbis classed them with wild animals. Dogs 'licked the blood of Naboth and Jezebel' (I Kings xxi. 19). In the latter half of last century Canon Stanley saw dogs snatching at offal and carrion on the ruins of Jezreel, Jezebel's city. Canon Tristram found 'every oriental city and village abounding with troops of hungry and half-savage dogs . . . devouring even the dead bodies of men when they can reach them'; and Doughty had to drive Arab dogs off with stones. In the Turkish countryside curs have given me some unpleasant moments.[15]

The mention of the dogs conjures up, in a phrase, the abject misery of the man. He may even have had to fight them off in order to obtain the morsels of bread. Except in one respect his condition is described in a rabbinic saying: 'There are three whose life is no life; he who depends on the table of another; he who is ruled by his wife, and he who is burdened by sufferings.'

Lazarus 'would have been glad to satisfy his hunger with the scraps from the rich man's table'. These were pieces of bread on which guests at a feast wiped their hands. We are reminded of the saying of the Gentile woman who came begging Jesus to exorcize the devil in her young daughter (Mk. vii. 28; Mt. xv. 27): 'Even the dogs under the table eat the children's scraps.'[16] Lazarus' plight was rather like that of the Prodigal Son who 'would have been glad to fill his belly with the pods that the pigs were eating' (Lk. xv. 16). Detested animals, scraps, misery, begging by people regarded with contempt, and a happy ending, link these three contexts.

One day Lazarus was found dead, and people who had done nothing for him had to carry away the skin and bones. The Rich Man had been unmoved by the sight of the beggar covered with ulcers, but he could not tolerate a stinking corpse by his door. No meal could be enjoyed in such conditions. The corpse had to be disposed of summarily. There is no mention of funeral or burial. The pack of pariah dogs was not far away. No greater indignity could befall a man than that his body should remain unburied, as is shown by the widespread folk-tale—The Grateful Dead. Uncovered blood cried for vengeance (Ezek. xxiv. 6 ff.) and unburied dead were believed to bring defilement and a curse upon the land. Later on, the Rich Man 'died and was buried'—a hint of the fine funeral he was given. No doubt the crowd of paid mourners rejoiced. So ends the first scene.

In telling this tale Jesus was apparently using ideas familiar to His audience. An Egyptian story, set about 1250 B.C. and preserved in a text of about A.D. 100, relates that a high priest saw two burials on the same day, one of a famous man, followed by mourners, the other of a poor man, with none. Later, in a glimpse of the other world, he saw souls being weighed and then rewarded or punished according to their deserts. The poor man was receiving honour by being garbed in the funeral robes of the rich man, while the rich man was undergoing punishment. The rabbinic story derived from this tale tells of a godly man whose funeral was unattended whereas a whole city followed the remains of a tax-collector to the grave. In a dream the pious man is seen in a paradise of trees and springs of water, while the tax-collector Bar Ma'jan leans over a stream with lolling tongue trying vainly to reach the water.

In the Egyptian version, which was translated into Greek in Memphis, the feasting with the gods is stressed while in the Greek Orphic version heaven, hell and the gulf between are mentioned. Evidently the Greek version was carried from the Jewish colony in Memphis to Palestine where it was translated into Aramaic with the addition of the allusion to 'Abraham's bosom'. As told by Jesus the story has been refined, the fantastic and metaphysical elements reduced and the ethical significance emphasized.[17]

Lazarus, having been transported by the angels, is seen 'in Abraham's bosom'. Significantly, what happens in the other world is sketched with greater detail than the earlier earthly scene. Lazarus reclines in the place of honour, as St. John reclined on Jesus' bosom at the Last Supper (Jn. xiii. 23). (In a rabbinic source the mother of seven martyred brothers encourages the youngest by asking whether he would be willing that all his brothers should lie in Abraham's bosom without him.) Thus Heaven, where Lazarus finds himself, is depicted in traditional terms as a banquet including the joys of feasting.[18] So Lazarus, faithful, as we are given to understand, to the religious and moral traditions of his forefathers, was gathered to them.

Thus in the otherworld there is a complete reversal of fortunes. The poor man is feasted, cherished and happy. We are thus assured that misfortune in life is no evidence of a man's wickedness, still less of the wickedness of his forefathers—a lesson which had only gradually been learnt (Jer. xxxi. 29 f.; Ezek. xviii. 1 ff.). Indeed, so tenacious was the belief that our Lord thought it necessary to contradict it (Lk. xiii. 4 f.; Jn. ix. 2 f.). It still lingers here and there among afflicted people who think of their sufferings as a direct punishment for their sins. The Rich Man's fate is also the reverse of his previous life. In the light of similar stories the audience might be left to imagine his sins of commission, whatever they might have been. His sins of omission were sufficiently glaring. His culpability lay, not simply in his lack of pity, but in his thoughtlessness and want of imagination. He was a materialist, caring for things more than people. Our world is a place of increasing numbers of people wanting more and more things. Seeds of contention are being sown which may grow and thrive unless selflessness triumphs over selfishness and compassion over cupidity. Few of us go out of our way to injure others; but we set a fence, often unwittingly, around our sympathies. It requires an effort to apply imagination. Moreover, to feel for others, and still more, to take trouble to help them is apt to hurt.

In the otherworld the Rich Man, like the Poor Man, found a complete contrast to his previous life. The flames encompassing him represent the annihilation of everything to which he had attached importance. Gone are his costly purple robes and linen undergarments, consumed by fire, and he is now one of the 'naked souls' such as Dante found lamenting miserably in the Fourteenth and Fifteenth Circles of Hell. Accustomed in the past to feasting daily, he now sees Lazarus reclining at the heavenly banquet, and in his utter deprivation longs for a drop of water. The 'might-have-beens' torment him, as, at times, they torment us all. But later, his concern for his brothers shows that he is ceasing to be dehumanised. The monster is becoming a man.

What is the strange scenery in which this drama is staged? As with all detailed pictures of the other world, including Dante's, there are inconsistencies in it—not surprisingly as it is a realm beyond reason. But the otherworld of this parable is what it is because of the refinements which had taken place in man's conceptions during the course of centuries. The Old Testament *Sheol*, often translated 'hell', is a dark underworld in which good and bad alike lead a pale and aimless existence and in which God's writ does not run. When the hope of a real life after death sprang up this conception changed. The dead went first to a place of waiting from which they eventually passed on, the wicked to Gehenna with its fires, the righteous to a place of reward. Even in *Sheol*, the place of waiting, different treatment was meted out to the righteous and to the wicked. Thus, according to Enoch (xxii. 10) *Sheol* has a place 'for sinners when they die and are buried in the earth and judgement has not been executed upon them in their lifetime. Here their spirits shall be set apart in great pain until the day of judgement.' On the other hand, the spirits of the righteous are where 'there is a bright spring of water' (xxii. 9). Thus Lazarus and the Rich Man were able to see one another and conversation across the dividing line was still possible.[19]

Hades, like the Realm of Bliss, is depicted materialistically according to contemporary ideas and because the human mind has to use mundane concepts in order to grasp the immaterial. So the scientist formulates conceptual or actual 'models' to give precision to his theories. The purpose of the parable is not to give us a picture of the underworld. The flames enveloping the Rich Man are traditional and symbolic and are not to be interpreted literally. His 'torments' include pangs of conscience and the thwarting of newly-aroused compassion. Although in the parable this is made clear, yet hell continued to be envisaged for centuries in terms of physical torture not very different from scenes one may see illustrated in Buddhist temples, as at Hangchow in China. But the Rich Man's agony includes the realization of the impossibility of reliving the past in the light of the insights he has gained. His condition is akin to that nightmare state in which, paralysed, we look on helpless as calamity bears down on those we love. Concern and affection for his brothers have awakened too late for him to help them.

All dignity set aside the Rich Man asks for aid from the man who had previously been beneath his notice. We had best give him the benefit of the doubt in this and not assume, like some critics, that in asking for Lazarus to be sent to his brothers he is treating him as a lackey.[20] Compassion, which he had not known before, has been aroused. Further, he can believe in it in others now that he is capable of feeling it himself. Suffering may increase or decrease compassion. It can arouse fellow-feeling; or it can turn the mind in upon itself and erode sympathy. For the Rich Man the flames have become a refining fire (Mal. iii. 2), but memory remains.

Dante, exalting much of this imagery to its highest symbolic significance, as well as giving it concrete portrayal, charged it with hope and beauty. Touched by his imagination the streams pictured in earlier descriptions of the otherworld, as in this parable and Enoch's vision, become more than thirst-quenching sources. Before he can ascend to Paradise the poet drinks of the waters of Lethe which banish from memory all taint of evil, and then the waters of Eunoë which requicken fainting virtue. 'I came back from those most holy waves,' he says, 'born again, even as new trees renewed with new foliage, pure and ready to mount to the stars.'[21]

The Rich Man begins, 'Father Abraham . . .' acknowledging the religious tradition to which he belongs, and Abraham, accepting him as belonging to it, replies, 'Son (or child) remember . . .' Unhappily, where he is there is no way in which he can make up for his neglect of that tradition. The past remains, with its sins of omission and commission. Regrets and good resolves cannot alter it.

In the parable all is vivid, pictorial, colourful. This parley could have been represented as a scene in an old Mystery Play enacted in an inn courtyard with Abraham and Lazarus reclining in one farm waggon and the Rich Man in another, conversing across 'a great chasm'. Again the style in which the parable is expressed shows it to be a cautionary tale and not a description of the afterlife.

The Rich Man makes a later than deathbed repentance, but to no avail. The 'great gulf fixed' is the recognition of the nature of things as ordained by God and experienced by man. No warning from the Rich Man can reach his brothers. No ghostly apparition would convert them. We are challenged to face what is in the nature of things and to act accordingly. 'Things and actions are what they are, and the consequences of them will be what they will be:

why then should we desire to be deceived?' wrote Bishop Butler. Those principles of cause and effect which science has so effectively investigated and exploited apply ineluctably in the sphere of morals, though, in the mercy of God, other and higher principles apply in the sphere of divine grace.

So, finally, we are brought back to earth—to the five brethren— a significant, inclusive number, based on the fingers of the hand. They represent ourselves. The reproof was to the Rich Man, the warning is to us. We have the Law and the Prophets, the Old Testament and the New Testament and two thousand years of Christian witness. They represent what God reveals and man discovers, all the channels by which knowledge accumulates, wisdom increases, insight matures and inspiration is achieved. Religion, science, philosophy and art enshrine what has been painfully learnt and conscientiously preserved. Each generation of men, inheritors of the past and recipients of divine grace, expresses in its own transient setting such love, compassion and adoration as it may. Each individual, debtor to all the past, stands before God, responsible for the manner in which he conducts his life. The time is now; the choice is ours.

The parable confronted and rebuked those who sought from Jesus a 'sign', the expected authoritative vindication of His mission. No sign was given them (Mk. viii. 11; Lk. xi. 16 ff.). If stark realities fail to convince, then spectacular portents, though they may astonish, will not convert. Would some spectral voice or apparition, such as appeared to Hamlet, convert a sinner? Men have long tried to persuade themselves that it would. Many people have had mystic experiences, ennobling their characters and making them vehicles of truth to their fellows; but every one of them, like St. Paul, owed much to 'the Law and the Prophets'. Revelation is never divorced from reason; and God seldom shatters men's stony hearts in order to enter and make His dwelling there. What we are told of the negative response certain to be evoked if Lazarus were to visit the Rich Man's brothers is also a reminder that spiritualist manifestations, being out of context, seldom carry conviction. So our

Lord's Resurrection must be understood in the whole setting of history, revelation and experience, 'the Law and the Prophets' which it fulfils and interprets and by which it must be interpreted.

Through these parables runs the promise of joy, pictured as fellowship with God and man, for the Messianic Banquet had associations with present experience and future consummation. St. John the Divine described the perfection of such fellowship in mystical terms—the angels, the souls of the righteous and every creature of earth and sea and sky joining in the exultant hymn, 'Worthy is the Lamb' (Apoc. v. 11–14). Our knowledge of earthly joy enables us to glimpse something of heavenly joy, and what we perceive of heavenly joy enriches our capacity for earthly joy. When Dante, nearing the end of his long pilgrimage heard all Paradise burst forth into praise of the Father, Son and Holy Spirit it seemed to him that he beheld 'a smile of the universe'.[22]

CHAPTER IV

WORK AND WAGES

Parables of Responsibility

Among country folk such as were most of the people of Galilee in the first century men's employment was inseparable from their dependence on nature. They looked to the land for their livelihood. There is, therefore, no rigid distinction to be drawn between what we have called the Parables of Nature and the parables which deal with work and wages, but in these latter the stress is on the relationship of men to one another rather than on the processes of nature. The number of these Parables of Responsibility is an indication of the extent to which Jesus accepted interest and involvement in affairs of this world as natural and proper. When He sought to lead His followers from earthly concerns to heavenly aspirations He recognized the importance of bread. As we have already noted (pp. 26–30) scholars who make central in the teaching of Jesus expectation of the imminent End have given inadequate recognition to the extent to which He dwelt on the tranquil, regular processes of nature; nor have they taken sufficiently into account that the background of the parables is a workaday world in which people have to order their lives according to a regular pattern and make provision for the future by their foresight, industry and perseverance. No shadow of cosmic catastrophe hangs over the husbandman, the shepherd, the merchant or the slave in the parables as he goes about his business. His problems are moral and social, and fundamentally religious—the ordering of his life in a world which is God's world, but is also a world in which there are dishonest and discontented people, extortioners and men of violence.

MASTER AND MAN

Lk. xvii. 7–10

No Entitlement

Known by various names, such as From Field to Kitchen and The Farmer and his Slave, this parable reminds us that Jesus' teaching was adapted to appeal to the relatively well-to-do as well as the outcast. Men of substance figure in a number of His stories. This parable implies an audience of such people: 'Suppose one of you has a servant ploughing or minding sheep . . .' Would they treat such a man as an equal or a superior? When he came in from the fields would they invite him to take it easy? Not at all. Certainly he would not expect such treatment nor would he understand his master acting out of character to this extent. So with men in their relationship with God. They should not preen themselves on their merits like the Pharisee in The Pharisee and the Publican but realize that when they have served God faithfully they have done no more than their duty.

It is difficult for twentieth-century man to accept this teaching, for his thoughts tend to run on what he is entitled to and what his wits have achieved. There are people whose hackles rise at the very thought of a master and man relationship. With all its social blessings the welfare state has had the side effect of nurturing this presumptuous attitude. The influence of assumptions of desert and entitlement is apparent in the irreligion and spurious religion of our time. Why should we offer thanks or worship or the service of our lives? It is commonly not accepted that to do so is ennobling, quite apart from the claims of gratitude or duty. The flippant and facetious references to God and religion by novelists and dramatists betray, not only arrogance but also a lack of sensitivity which demeans man.

Of course the parable is not an approval of the institution of slavery any more than The Dishonest Steward is about commendable morals or the finder of the hidden treasure to be admired because he bought the field without disclosing his reasons. It tells us that we should be whole-hearted in God's service. In field and kitchen alike there is work to be done. When we have done our best we still should not consider it good enough. The faithful servant is one whose life is a joyful offering of work and worship, whole-time dedication such as Paul showed and expressed in a phrase which illuminates what the Christian life should be: 'For to me life is Christ' (Phil. i. 21).

The context in which this parable is placed clarifies its meaning. The servant should labour, as expressed in St. Francis Xavier's well-known prayer, asking for no reward save only that of knowing that he is doing the Master's will; the disciple should set no limits to his readiness to give and forgive. Faith and fealty should be unbounded. Pharisaism laid emphasis on the contractual, so influencing people to think, sometimes subconsciously, of limitations on fervour and insight. The problem involved in setting a precise 'target' whether spiritual, moral or financial, is that if we come near achievement we too readily relax, regarding ourselves as 'worthy servants'.[1]

Christian service entails toil throughout the day indoors or out, bearing the yoke (Mt. xi. 29 f.) and carrying the Cross. Garibaldi, calling on the Italian people to fight for freedom, promised them blood and tears, and Churchill echoed his words when freedom was menaced in our own time. There is a Cross in every Christian's life if he is living creatively. My 'reasonable service' to Him 'who loved me and gave Himself for me' (Gal. ii. 20) must be sacrificial commitment. His service is perfect freedom, but, *si crucem portas, portabit te*: Carry the Cross and it will carry you. What Christian devotion requires and offers is indicated in a passage from a letter which St. Francis Xavier sent from India to his Society at home: 'I have nothing more to tell you except that so great is the intensity and abundance of the joy which God is accustomed to bestow upon those workmen in His vineyard who labour diligently in cultivating this barbarous part of the same, that, for my part, I do really believe that if there is in this life any true and solid happiness it is here.'

THE SERVANT ENTRUSTED WITH AUTHORITY
OR
THE FAITHFUL AND UNFAITHFUL SERVANTS
Mt. xxiv. 45–51; Lk. xii. 42–46

FAITHFULNESS

It is generally assumed that this parable was originally addressed to the scribes, set over God's 'household', who had failed to honour their responsibilities—but would listeners identify them with the bullying sots of this story? Like The Doorkeeper it was later interpreted as referring to Christ's return. The emphasis is on vigilance, as in The Doorkeeper, but it goes beyond this to stress the importance of acting responsibly and conscientiously. It would prick the conscience of any bearer of responsibility who was not hardened against self-examination.

The fate of the unfaithful servant in Matthew—to be 'cut in pieces'—is so surprisingly drastic, and the transition to punishment in hell so abrupt that we look for an explanation. It is generally agreed that the Aramaic has been incorrectly translated, though there is doubt as to the correct rendering. 'Give him blows' and 'divide him his portion with the unfaithful' have been suggested. It is possible that the parable has been coloured by what happened to Nadan in the Story of Ahikar, preserved in many languages and introduced into the *One Thousand and One Nights*. The Aramaic version dates from the fifth century B.C. Believing his uncle, the King of Assyria, to be dead, Nadan gathers 'vain and lewd folk' to a feast and strips and whips the menservants and handmaidens. He is found out and flogged; whereupon he swells up and bursts asunder (cf. Acts i. 18).[2]

In both Gospels this parable is linked with teaching concerning imminent crisis, but the Evangelists view the crisis each in his own way. In Luke the story follows a crisis parable, The Burglar, and is uttered in response to Peter's enquiry: 'Do you intend this parable specially for us or is it for everyone?' but this question seems not to have been derived from the earlier source Q, for it is omitted by Matthew. This suggests that Luke was in some doubt as to the interpretation of this teaching. Matthew, on the other hand, regarded it as referring to the Second Coming. Thus we are given a glimpse of the process by which the words of Jesus, counselling vigilance as the crisis of His ministry approached, were variously reinterpreted after the fall of Jerusalem when the Crucifixion was a memory. The emphasis shifted from watchfulness to faithfulness—in terms of imagery, from the vigilance of the doorkeeper to the faithfulness of servants. It moved, too, from concern about 'times and seasons' (Acts i. 7 f.) to the moral sphere. 'No servant can be the slave of two masters' (Mt. vi. 24; Lk. xvi. 13) (The parable of Divided Service); he must have his mind on his duty and be faithful to his trust (The parable of The Talents). Matthew shows us the Church realizing that, more important than the date of the Parousia, was that the followers of Jesus should be loyal; they must be 'found faithful' when called to give an account of their stewardship. The Christian must be at all times a 'trusty and sensible man' (Lk. xii. 42), 'a faithful and wise steward' (Mt. xxiv. 45). (We are reminded of the 'wise' virgins.) In our age when vast vistas of time have opened out we may easily fail to hear and proclaim the note of urgency in the Gospel; but urgency and faithfulness are inseparable. God has all time and eternity to work in, but we have not.

The changes in understanding through which this parable has passed are instructive. We see that from the earliest period of oral transmission parables have been subject to reinterpretation. They have lived within the Church, the constructions put upon them and the inspiration derived from them evolving with it. The nature of parables, as vehicles of eternal truth, is to speak to individuals and the Church in varying accents as insights and needs alter. As has already been emphasized (pp. 19–21) it is proper to let the mind brood over them and the imagination savour and enjoy them, bringing out from their treasure what is new and old (Mt. xiii. 52). To confine them to their original application is to fail to recognize the leading of the Holy Spirit.

THE INSTRUCTED AND UNINSTRUCTED SERVANTS

Lk. xii. 47–48a

RESPONSIBILITY RELATED TO KNOWLEDGE

The verses which follow The Servant entrusted with Authority constitute teaching in 'antithetic parallelism' comparable in form and teaching with The Two Sons (pp. 177 f.).[3] Perhaps they may have been part of another parable which we may consider under the title of The Instructed and Uninstructed Servants. It stresses that culpability is related to knowledge. A servant who knows what is expected of him and fails to do it is more blameworthy than a man who does not know his master's wishes and so does not carry them out. This was appreciated by the rabbis, who discussed whether study was more important than practice and argued that it was the more important as practice followed from knowledge. A second-century rabbi said: 'He who has learnt the words of the Law, but kept them not, his punishment is more severe than that of him who has not learnt them.' He added a parable teaching that a man who planted trees and cut them down is more blameworthy than a man who neither planted trees nor cut them down. Verse 48b may be a separate saying: 'Where a man has been given much, much will be expected of him; and the more a man has had entrusted to him the more he will be required to repay'; if so, it illustrates the inherent capacity of a parable to elicit generalizations and specific applications beyond its primary reference. The saying would be appropriate as a comment on The Talents.

Ignorance may be pleaded before the throne of God, but hardly lack of feeling, moral obtuseness and spiritual blindness, as we are reminded in The Great Assize. Failure on the part of the enlightened is culpable. In any society special moral responsibility lies with the educated. To 'fail one's class' in this respect is more than tragic; it is the *trahison des clercs* and betrayal of the truth— the special temptation of the liberal-minded and those who pride themselves on being advanced thinkers. This teaching is linked with the preceding parable and also with our Lord's comments on those who betray or lead astray little children (Mt. xviii. 6; Mk. ix. 42; Lk. xvii. 2). Much is expected of those to whom much is given. Today not only Christian leaders should ponder on this little parable but also broadcasters, journalists, and not least, scientists, since their pronouncements, even on subjects on which they have no expert knowledge, are regarded by many as having special authority.

THE WAITING SERVANTS

Lk. xii. 35–38; cf. Mk. xiii. 33–37

FAITHFULNESS REWARDED

The beginning of this parable, 'Be ready for action, with belts fastened and lamps alight', is abrupt. It seems as if the lighted lamps may be a reminiscence of the parable of The Bride's Attendants. Perhaps, also, there is an allusion to the virtuous woman of Proverbs (xxxi. 17 f.) who 'girdeth her loins' and 'whose lamp goeth not out by night'. The exhortation continues: 'Be like men who wait for their master's return from a wedding-party, ready to let him in the moment he arrives and knocks. Happy are those servants whom the master finds on the alert when he comes. . . . I tell you this: he will buckle on his belt, seat them at table and come and wait on them. Even if it is in the middle of the night or before dawn when he comes, happy they if he finds them alert.'[4]

If we compare this parable with The Doorkeeper (Mk. xiii. 33–37) it becomes evident that both are versions of one basic parable, and that Luke's source, or Luke himself, has interpreted it in terms of the return of Christ in glory and judgement, the Parousia. The Master awaited is Christ who will reward the faithful. Congregations proclaim this parable's teaching when they sing: 'Ye servants of the Lord.'[5] Similarly the Master of the House in Mark xiii. 33–37 is Christ, concerning whose return the early Church was in anxious expectation. The divisions of the night suggest the unknown length of the interval of waiting during which preparedness and patience are called for.[6]

The surprising reversal of rôles, the opposite of the situation described in Master and Man—the master setting to work to serve the slave—reads like a commentary on 'Yet here am I among you like a servant' (Lk. xxii. 27; Jn. xiii. 4 f.). Those who stand ready will be rewarded by receiving what they are prepared to offer. This is primarily a call to service, but its original point has been modified to give encouragement to the faint-hearted. As we have already noted, the notion of entitlement to reward by virtue of merit has little place in our Lord's teaching. When we have done all we are unprofitable servants (Lk. xvii. 10). Matthew characteristically introduces into his version promises of rewards and threats of punishment; but even so he recognizes that God's gifts exceed man's deserts or desires.[7] The parable of The Wedding Attendants is for our admonition, the parable of The Waiting Servants for our encouragement. The former is akin to those nightmare experiences in which we are too late or find ourselves ill-equipped, the latter has the texture of our day-dreams.

THE LABOURERS IN THE VINEYARD
OR
THE GENEROUS EMPLOYER
Mt. xx. 1-16

GOD'S GRACE

The significance of this parable is more clearly appreciated when it is noticed that this is one of a number of instances in which the Kingdom of God is likened to a reckoning (Mt. xxv. 14 ff.; Lk. xix. 12 ff.; Mt. vi. 2, 5; xxiv. 45 ff.; Lk. xii. 42 ff.; Mt. xviii. 23 ff.)—a concept stemming from very ancient ideas such as are symbolized in ancient Egyptian representations of the weighing of souls to assess their merit. In the background of much sacrificial ritual was the notion of a transaction by which a spirit or a god might be appeased or bought off. Sometimes there went with this belief the idea that a god should be punished, or at least shown the displeasure of his worshippers, when he failed to deliver the goods—as when, in China, the rain god, having been appealed to in vain, was dragged out into the burning sun.

This parable, in common with others, seems to have come to Matthew without details of its setting, but, once again, most commentators assume it to be a rebuke to the Pharisees. It has been interpreted as picturing them as discontented workers arguing, like the elder brother in The Prodigal Son, that they have not been treated according to their deserts. Perhaps significantly the parable is placed between Peter's self-congratulation on behalf of the apostles and the status-seeking by James and John which earns a rebuke from Jesus. But, in fact, the grumbles of the labourers are of secondary importance. It is the employer's behaviour which should engage our attention. We are invited to consider his magnanimity as mirroring God's relationship to men. The primary purpose of the parable is not to pillory anybody, though, pondering on it we may be led to realize the pettiness of our aspirations against the background of God's generosity. 'Why be jealous because I am kind?' asks the landowner when the labourers bluntly expostulate, omitting any courteous form of address. The comparison between the human and the divine and the contrast between jealousy and graciousness matter more than the details of the story. If Jesus, in his picture of the grumbling vinedressers was tilting at the Pharisees, they and others hearing it might naturally have assumed that the landowner was Jesus Himself and the generously treated labourers the 'publicans and sinners' whose friend they accused Him of being (Mt. xi. 19; Lk. vii. 34). But it is no more than an assumption that the parable has any reference to the controversy with the Pharisees.

The story is designed to startle us into an ashamed realization of how squalid are our valuations, tainted by envy. 'Why should these receive so much?' springs to our minds, inspired sometimes by the materialistic emulation characteristic of our society and sometimes by the self-righteousness which so often lies behind what we take to be our disinterested championing of justice. The unexpected twist in the parable should shock us into self-scrutiny; for thus we are betrayed into disclosing our egoism to ourselves. Our stinginess is never more forcibly brought home than when we perceive another's generosity.

Even though wider economic considerations may not have been in the mind of our Lord or His hearers, the parable can also teach us a lesson about man's relationship to his neighbour as well as about God's attitude to us. The standard payment for a day's labour at that time was a drachma or denarius and each received this amount. We should interpret the parable in terms of each man being paid, not according to the extent of his effort or duration of his labour, but according to his need. Payment on the basis of the number of hours worked would have meant that some of the men would have been without enough money to buy food for the family. The employer acted according to the dictates of mercy rather than of strict equity. He saw to it that each man was paid enough to prevent his family falling below the subsistence level—a principle accepted by the welfare state.

The assumption by Jeremias and others that the men were lazy-bones idling in the market-place is unwarranted. We are not told that it was the time of vintage when they might readily have found employment. Rather we should assume that the owner of the vine-yard, being a compassionate man, deliberately found jobs for those unfortunate enough not to have been offered a full day's work. God often finds work for those who are not considered much use by worldly employers.

Whatever the failings of mediaeval Christendom in regard to social justice—due in part to difficulties in relating distribution to production—the principle of the Just Price was recognized. 'The labourer is worthy of his hire' (Lk. x. 7; I Tim. v. 18) and his maintenance should be the first charge on the produce of his labour. Many subsequent economic problems have resulted from the non-recognition of this principle or have been due to social or economic complexities which have rendered it difficult to apply.

Although the primary teaching of the parable concerns the graciousness and generosity of God, yet Jesus, in picturing God's mercy in terms of human generosity was also championing the oppressed. The legally minded who cared more for their own prosperity than for the poor might wear the cap if it fitted them; but the parable rises above any such polemic to reveal a vision of God's compassion, comparable in some respects to that portrayed in The Prodigal Son. In both gracious outgoingness is manifested. The disillusioned youth thought in terms of being received back as a hired servant, but he was treated infinitely better. He was feasted and reinstated. (We should notice the contrast with the slave's treatment in Master and Man in which man's responsibility to God, rather than God's relationship to man, is stressed.) So the labourers taken on later in the day were treated with a generosity they did not expect—an out-of-this-world generosity.

The lofty teaching of this parable is thrown into relief when it is compared with a later rabbinic parable almost certainly based on it.

In it the master replies to the malcontents that a man who came last and worked only two hours had done more than the others during the whole day. The parable has been reduced to a commonplace.

THE TALENTS (THE POUNDS)

OR

MONEY IN TRUST

Mt. xxv. 14–30; Lk. xix. 12–27

BE FAITHFUL

There are three (or more) servants involved in this parable and we soon realize that we must identify ourselves with one or other.

We need not concern ourselves with additions and intrusions, such as Matthew's favourite comment assigning the defaulters to the place of 'wailing and grinding of teeth' (viii. 12; xiii. 42; xxii. 13; xxiv. 5) or Luke's reference, which may be part of another parable, to a nobleman who became a king and slew the rebels who scorned his rule (12b, 14, 15a, 19b and 27).[8]

The essence of the parable lies in the servants' conceptions of responsibility. They were all faithful up to a point. According to Matthew two doubled their money; Luke records that the success of at least two of them was even greater. At the end, one, with a virtuous air, handed back the exact sum entrusted to him. The others were rewarded by further responsibility, but this man was berated as a 'lazy fellow' and punished. According to Matthew the blameworthy servant had buried the money, but Luke makes him explain that he had wrapped it in a napkin. This was pointedly irresponsible, for in rabbinical law anyone burying money was regarded as having deposited it in a place of safety, but a person wrapping it in cloth was held legally responsible to the owner if it disappeared. According to a rabbinical saying, there was only one safe repository for money—the earth.

Even if Jesus had the scribes in mind, the message was, and is, of wider relevance. But it does not seem probable that His intention was to rebuke or pillory the scribes and Pharisees; for why should they, entrusted with the treasures of the Law, be likened to the servant responsible for the smallest sum? Jesus declared that He had come to call sinners to repentance, and among these were plenty for whom this parable would be a warning; for it is a commendation of responsible effort and a condemnation of close-fistedness and jealousy.

Money in Trust has affinities with The Barren Fig Tree and The Wicked Vinedressers. Jeremias includes it with The Burglar, The Bride's Attendants, The Doorkeeper and The Servant entrusted with Authority as among the parables interpreted as referring to the Parousia, but originally intended to bring men to a realization of the gravity of the situation disclosed in our Lord's ministry. In any case, its emphasis is on moral responsibility rather than on watchfulness. Despite the interpretations of some scholars this aspect is so prominent that it is difficult to believe it was not its primary intent. The suggestion that the treasure represents the religious heritage which the scribes and Pharisees believed should be kept intact, buried under a mass of regulations rather than invested wisely is somewhat laboured. It is a product of thinking which assumes that the original application of a parable can be determined by considering who were the people to whom it narrowly applied.[9]

The practical applications to modern conditions are clear. Too often we are not alert to seize the immense opportunities which life offers. Many of the ills of society result from lethargy or misdirection of energy, due to want of insight or lack of a sense of purpose. The malaise is fundamentally spiritual. To those able and ready to take opportunities further opportunities are presented. This is a law of life in the fullest sense for it underlies the processes of natural selection by which evolution proceeds. In the human sphere creativeness, not criticism, has the last word. Manifestly it brings its reward.

The parable is framed primarily to appeal to the individual. Each of us should make use of his particular talents. 'The gifts we possess differ as they are allotted to us by God's grace, and must be exercised accordingly' (Rom. xii. 6; cf. I Cor. xii. 4 ff.). The notion that faith is passive encourages inertia. Christian faith is active to the extent of moving mountains. We have to put our faith, both in God and other people, at risk. What use is buried money, a lamp where its light is invisible, salt which is insipid or an inert soul?

When we compare this parable with characteristic nature parables we see that what is commendable on one level of experience may not be so on another. Seeds, but not coins, become productive when placed in the ground: they obey natural laws. Coins, obeying economic laws, become productive in circulation. According to psychological and social laws thoughts and ideas laid out to interest bring profit, and according to spiritual law faithful work for the Master is crowned with blessedness. As Paul explains, there are different planes of being and living, each with its rules of cause and effect: 'Those who live on the level of our lower nature have their outlook formed by it, and that spells death; but those who live on the level of the spirit have the spiritual outlook and that is life and peace' (Rom. viii. 5–7). In a great peroration the apostle reviews all levels of reality, concluding with the triumphant declaration: 'I am convinced that there is nothing in death or life, in the realm of spirits or superhuman powers, in the world as it is or the world as it shall be, in the forces of the universe, in heights or depths—nothing in all creation that can separate us from the love of God which is in Christ Jesus our Lord' (Rom. viii. 38 f.).

THE LAMP

Mt. v. 14–16; Mk. iv. 21; Lk. viii. 16, xi. 33

AND

THE CITY SET ON A HILL

Mt. v. 14b

WITNESS BOLDLY

Matthew pictures a Palestinian one-roomed cottage with a lamp alight on its stand or in a wall niche throughout the night, serving to prevent any person moving about from stumbling over the sleeping forms on the floor (p. 80), whereas Luke describes the entrance to a Graeco-Roman house with a light in the vestibule (xi. 33). He refers also to the cellar, another indication that he was thinking in terms of Gentile dwellings, though, influenced by the notion of the importance of a light at the door of a house, he seems to have forgotten that lights are placed in cellars. In these respects the descriptions by Mark and Matthew are closer than Luke's to the parable as uttered by Jesus. To place an earthenware lamp with floating wick under a bed would, in Palestine, be to smother the flame under a rug, sheepskin or palliasse. It has been suggested that putting it under a meal-tub was a normal way of extinguishing it; but this is improbable. The NEB text omits this detail.

Being without information concerning its original context each of the Evangelists treated it in his own way. Matthew's version includes the comment, 'You are the light of the world', and then, surprisingly, he adds: 'A town that stands on a hill cannot be hidden.'[10] The latter saying is self-evident, but the illustration of the lamp owes its point to the fact that it can be hidden and so lose its function. In view of the parable of The Pharisee and the Publican, which is often interpreted as a criticism of ostentation in religion, the words which follow—'You, like the lamp must shed light'—are somewhat unexpected, though witnessing for Christ need not involve self-advertisement. Unless they are an insertion by the Evangelist they add force to the argument that the primary purpose of the parable of The Pharisee and the Publican was to stress God's relationship to man rather than to pillory the Pharisees. Yet, on any interpretation, the meaning of The Lamp is, 'Let the light shine.' So the Church later understood it. Israel, as recipient and upholder of the Law, had been spoken of in the past as the light or lamp of the world.[11]

The saying may have been originally addressed to the people, calling on them to be true to their high calling as the People of God to whom truth had been, and was being, revealed, but very soon Christians applied it to themselves. Paul wrote: 'For the same God who said, "Out of darkness let light shine" has caused His light to shine within us, to give the light of revelation—the revelation of the glory of God in the face of Jesus Christ' (II Cor. iv. 6), and, 'You . . . shine like stars in a dark world' (Phil. ii. 15). Mark, having a little earlier recorded the saying about 'the secret of the Kingdom of God' (iv. 11), apparently regarded the lamp as the revelation of the truth about the Kingdom. This, though it might be concealed for a time, was finally to be revealed. But we need not accept the notion that the nature of the Kingdom was to be kept an esoteric secret. Luke, on the other hand, as his context shows, interprets the lamp as truth shining by its own light. This does not fit well with the reference to the meal-tub extinguisher, as Dodd points out (p. 109), but the suggestion made by earlier writers and endorsed by him that The Lamp represents the Law smothered under tradition is rather too allegorical. All three Evangelists (and Thomas) speak of the absurdity of hiding a lighted lamp. They imply, not that anybody is doing this, but that it is unthinkable those entrusted with the lamp should do otherwise than display it. If the Evangelists had regarded the saying as aimed at legalists they would have reported it differently. Moreover, if the lamp symbolized the Law, then the 'bed' would stand for the smothering of it by accretions and interpretations. Such allegorizing is not plausible.

It is of the nature of light to give light, and of God's truth to be spread abroad; it is His will that everyone who has received the grace of His revelation become in his turn a light in the world.

THE BODY'S LAMP

Mt. vi. 22 f.; Lk. xi. 34–36

The Tragedy of the Blind Soul

Bad eyesight is used to suggest stupidity and spiritual blindness in several contexts (Mt. xv. 14, xxiii. 16 f.; Jn. ix. 39–41; Rom. ii. 19; II Pet. i. 9; Apoc. iii. 17). It is also used in the saying about The Mote and the Beam (Mt. vii. 3–5; Lk. vi. 41 f.) in reference to obtuseness, fault-finding and lack of self-examination. Thus The Body's Lamp, by its emphasis that physical blindness is a deprivation so terrible that it may lead to error, accident and uselessness, teaches the disastrous consequences of blindness of the soul.

THE DISCARDED SALT

Mt. v. 13; Mk. ix. 50; Lk. xiv. 34 f.

The Uselessness of the Functionless

The metaphor of salt was used to denote a quality of primary importance and that without which something essential is missing. A proverb expressed the vital connexion between soul and body thus: 'Shake the salt off, and give the meat to the dog.' Body without soul decomposes.[12]

Dodd (pp. 103 ff.) points out that since Matthew and Luke agree in differing significantly from Mark they must have obtained their version of the saying from a common source. He reconstructs the original as: 'If salt decays, with what will it be salted? It is good for nothing; they throw it away.' Black (p. 125) prefers: 'It is fit neither for the ground, nor yet for dung. But men throw it out and trample it down.' According to a soil scientist with experience in

Israel salt has been used very widely in the past as a fertilizer and therefore one can speak of 'salt for the earth'. In our own gardens salt is still sprinkled on asparagus beds to kill the weeds. Some gardeners believe that it fertilizes the asparagus. Certain kinds of Palestinian salt may lose their saltiness either 'due to the actual loss of sodium chloride or to the masking of its taste by gypsum'. Salt is strewn on the soil-covered flat roofs of houses, hardening the soil and so preventing leakage. As people use their roofs on which to walk about and take the air the salt is 'trodden under foot of men'.[13]

The general purport of the saying is sufficiently clear. What use is anything which has lost its *raison d'être*? Possibly the writer quoted above is justified in extending the interpretation: 'If we do not exert a saving influence on others, we are in greatest danger of not being able to save ourselves.' Its primary application may have been to Israel as a people. The nation's mission was to be like a City set on a Hill, a permanent and unconcealable witness. Shame on it if, having been entrusted with the Lamp of God's Word, it allowed the light to be smothered, or if, like salt which had become insipid, it ceased to count in the affairs of men. But the proverb is of such general applicability that Jesus very probably used it to inspire His followers to take their mission as heralds of the Kingdom with the utmost seriousness. Only the acceptance of the view that nearly all Jesus' recorded teaching had the iniquities of the scribes and Pharisees in mind could suggest that here, too, they are being specifically condemned. Once again speculation in regard to the original target of a parable viewed as a weapon has tended to deflect attention from its real significance.

Salt has had widespread symbolism in social intercourse. It was a symbol of fellowship and the common meal. In Oriental usage 'to betray the salt' was to betray the master, the host or other person to whom loyalty or devotion was owed. Leonardo da Vinci, in his fresco of the Last Supper, made Judas identifiable by the salt cellar overturned by his agitated movement.

If the parable's primary meaning is as a warning it also conveys

a message of encouragment to the individual Christian and to the
Church. It is just because salt is indispensable that it is disastrous
if it 'loses its savour'. So, too, it is because the disciple of Jesus has
been entrusted with a message so vital to the welfare of mankind
that failure to proclaim it as he should is so great a dereliction of
duty. Therefore let him never lose courage nor neglect his opportunities. His witness will be most effective if his faith is as pervasive
in his life as salt in a savoury dish.

THE PATCH AND THE WINESKINS
Mt. ix. 16 f.; Mk. ii. 21 f.; Lk. v. 36–39
AND
THE HOUSEHOLDER'S TREASURE
Mt. xiii. 52

THE RELATIONSHIP BETWEEN THE OLD AND THE NEW

Luke, in his version of the parable, refers to an absurdity; nobody
could be so silly as to cut up a new cloak to patch an old one. The
Sayings of Thomas state: 'An old patch is not put on a new garment,
since a rip will result.' This seems to be a clumsy interpretation of
an imperfectly understood proverb.[14] Mark and Matthew have the
original sense. To patch an old coat with unshrunk cloth would
only make the rent worse; to pour new wine into old wineskins
would burst them. In their setting the inference meant to be drawn
would seem to be that Judaism and Christianity are incompatible.
But the contexts themselves are patchworks, and apparently we
have to do with proverbial sayings which have been slanted to carry
this meaning by the early Church as a result of the disputes with
Judaizers mentioned by Paul in Romans and elsewhere in his
epistles. At what stage and to what extent, if at all, Jesus thought of

Himself and His followers as breaking with Judaism is a matter for speculation. But it is improbable that He ever taught this explicitly to His disciples in these terms; for He came to complete rather than to abolish (Mt. v. 17). That such was His attitude is confirmed by the obverse saying which tells of The Householder who brings out of his treasure what is new and old (Mt. xiii. 52). This combination of new and old is to be found in the Church—the household of God (Eph. ii. 19; cf. Gal. vi. 10) with the Old and the New Testament in her hands. In every generation the Christian's task is to combine old and new creatively and to make the tension between them constructive.

THE DISHONEST STEWARD

Lk. xvi. 1–9

PRESENCE OF MIND

The first reaction to this parable by a critical reader might well be to suspect that it has found its way into the Gospel by mistake; for it seems intolerable that sharp practice should be, not merely condoned but approved. On second thoughts he might change his mind; for the Evangelists are not likely to have included teaching which could supply ammunition to opponents of Christianity, ready to seize on anything in the tradition which, in their opinion, increased its vulnerability. Passages in the Gospels in which it might seem that questionable morals were commended, or in which our Lord admits ignorance (Mt. xxiv. 36; Mk. xiii. 32) are least likely to have been invented.

The difficulty of interpreting this parable was recognized by the Church of England when in the Revised Prayerbook of 1928 it provided the parable of The Prodigal Son as an alternative to the Gospel for Trinity IX. Again the moralizing additions by Luke

after verse 8 illustrate the uncertainty that was felt concerning its
meaning by him and the early Church, for three different morals
are drawn from it—the prudence of the 'sons of this age' compared
with 'the sons of light'; the advisability of making friends even by
the use of wealth which has been questionably acquired; and the
importance of not being dishonest if you wish to be entrusted with
true riches. As worldly wisdom the moral might be: 'If a bad man
will go to such lengths to procure friends good men should strive
harder for good ends.'

The interpretation which has been widely accepted for at least a
century is that it gives advice on these lines: 'In view of the ap-
proaching spiritual climax, be as prudent, resolute and foresighted
in regard to this crisis as was the dismissed steward in regard to
worldly affairs.' In favour of this interpretation it may be noted
that the word *phronimos*, used of the steward, means 'one who has
grasped a critical situation' (Mt. vii. 24; xxiv. 45). The appeal,
which may have been addressed to the unconverted, is to apply
such wisdom not only to their worldly affairs but also to their
spiritual decisions, and show themselves wise as serpents and as
harmless as doves (Mt. x. 16). In other parables, such as The
Burglar, lessons are drawn from the questionable activities of dishonest persons. If we exclude the possibility that the parable is
broad sarcasm or irony, an interpretation on these lines seems the
most plausible. But it has been shown that according to tortuous
Pharisaic principles in which the law of God and the law of man
were imperfectly reconciled and because of the ambivalent attitude
to usury the steward's action was legal.[15]

In some respects The Dishonest Steward is The Generous
Employer in reverse. In the latter parable some labourers grumble
against their employer because others of their number are paid too
much; in the former the master expresses gratification in a situation
in which he is paid too little. The two parables, each with a twist or
surprise element (as in The Good Samaritan, The Prodigal Son
and The Rich Man and Lazarus), complement each other. Although
in both the story is concerned with money, in neither is financial

profit the motive of the employer's action. Each parable is baited to catch the attention of those interested in money-making—and few are not; but each turns out to be concerned with something different. One shows compassion to be more important than profit; the other tells of a master who can admire human qualities, particularly resourcefulness, even though they have been used to his financial loss.

THE DEFENDANT

Mt. v. 25 f.; Lk. xii. 58 f.

FACE REALITIES

Taken at its face value this parable would appear to be a piece of worldly wisdom. It is better to come to an understanding outside the court than to risk the verdict going against you. Matthew, who differs from Luke in using a phrase amounting to 'be well disposed towards' rather than the stronger 'make an effort to settle with him' apparently thinks in terms of reconciliation with others—as a matter of expediency.[16] Interpreted thus the problem of finding edification in it is almost as great as with The Dishonest Steward, though it could be interpreted with only a slender degree of plausibility as simply advice to seek appeasement with an adversary rather than harbour resentment. It is unbelievable that the parable originally suggested coming to some sort of compromise in good time with God.

Luke has placed the parable with a number of warnings concerning the impending crisis, seeing it as an urgent call to be prepared for God's judgement. We may conclude that this was the original message. It is, therefore, one of the Parables of Crisis.

We have to translate these warnings into terms applicable to our Age of Crisis; for such it is, though many, as in first-century Palestine, do not perceive 'the signs of the times'. It is not pessimism which prompts reflective Christians to fear that the many stresses within society on a world-wide scale may reach explosive force. They see that class, national and racial rivalries in an age of unprecedently rapid increase in population when man sets attaining an ever higher standard of living as his primary aim may lead· to fierce competition and conflicting ambitions. So long as there is the underlying incompatibility of ideologies between those who accept the Marxian dogma of economic forces determining ethical standards and others who believe man is given spiritual guidance and grace to know, and act upon, what is right, there will be schism latent in society and man's soul. We live in a Day of Judgement.

Accepting the primary message of this parable need not mean that we should eschew developing its further lessons. We should seek reconciliation before any situation or relationship develops to the point at which events take charge and estrangement becomes final. Intransigence often sets in motion a chain of events which takes its inexorable, bitter course. As the victim is passed from his accuser to the judge, from judge to constable and then to jail so sins of omission or commission, which might have been avoided in time, initiate a series of grim consequences. Foresight must be allied with prudence in confronting the problems of our age, whether individual or international.

THE UNFORGIVING OFFICIAL

OR

THE UNMERCIFUL SERVANT

Mt. xviii. 23–35

MERCY AND FORGIVENESS

The parable of The Unforgiving Official, less appropriately called The Unmerciful Servant, is another dealing with reckoning and judgement. It is placed by Matthew at the end of a section dealing with relations between Christians and the need for discipline within the Church (cf. Rom. xii; I Cor. iii). Like the Lord's Prayer it teaches that forgiveness and forgivingness must go together. It may be compared with The Sheep and the Goats, which pictures the Last Judgement in terms which emphasize the lesson that compassion is required of each and all in their dealings with others. 'How blest are those who show mercy; mercy shall be shown to them' (Mt. v. 7).

The Unforgiving Official, like The Sheep and the Goats, makes clear that the essential virtue, so far as concerns man's relationship to his fellows, is compassion. As elsewhere in the parables an aspect of the character of God is represented in such a way as to make clear our duty to reflect that aspect in our conduct. Where the Final Judgement is adumbrated or depicted we are shown the absolute standards which should govern our daily life.

We must picture the man who is over head and ears in debt as an important official, perhaps in somewhat the same relationship to the king as Joseph is represented to have been to Pharaoh. Unlike realistic parables, such as The Good Samaritan and The Hidden Treasure, this parable reflects ordinary life only up to a point. Like The Rich Man and Lazarus it has a folk-tale flavour. Everything is larger than life. Our imagination is stretched. The sum owed by the official 'runs into millions'. The threat to sell, not only the man's wife, but also his children—an impossibility under Jewish law—meant the disposal of everything he possessed to the extreme limit.[17] Even if the man's family had been sold into slavery the sum accruing would have been a drop in the ocean compared with the vastness of the debt. The reference to torture, also forbidden under Jewish law, adds another melodramatic touch. The tiny debt— some five pounds—must be settled there and then in the open street. Violent hands are laid on the debtor. (We are reminded of the man in The Defendant in danger of being dragged—not called— before the judge (Lk. xii. 58).) Every detail is painted in lurid colours with the extravagance characteristic of many Eastern tales. As in The Rich Man and Lazarus the contrasts are extreme and hyperbole is used to heighten the effect. The pillorying of the powerful and the description of their downfall are characteristic folk-tale motifs.

How outrageous a monster was that official! Hardly believable that anyone could act like that! And then, realizing that we are seeing our squalid pettiness in comparison with God's boundless compassion we find conscience saying to us, as Nathan said to David, 'Thou art the man!' (II Sam. xii. 7).

Of more than incidental interest is the part played by the debtor's fellow servants. They are outraged at the savagery of the official's action and complain to the king on their comrade's behalf. Thus in the story we are shown, on the one hand, the magnanimity of the king, whose compassion is to be thought of as commensurate with the debt owing to him—infinitely great; and, on the other, the ingratitude and inhuman behaviour of the official. Intermediate between these extremes is the natural sense of justice felt by the fellow servants. Absolute malice is contrasted with infinite mercy against the foil of the innate revulsion against injustice which is natural to man. The behaviour of the official is contrary both to natural decency, as shown by the fellow servants, and divine grace, mirrored by the king's mercifulness.

The emphasis is on our dependence on God's grace. His compassion is of His very nature. It is His 'nature and property' to forgive, to 'shed abroad His love', to 'flood our inmost hearts' with love and grace (Rom. v. 2, 5); then, through Christ, we must respond by throwing ourselves on His mercy. The freedom of God is revealed in His unconditional compassion. So far from reducing our freedom it energizes it as we share in that compassion and reflect it in our behaviour to others. But 'We are not able of ourselves to help ourselves'. Our own humane feelings are not enough by themselves. In contrast to the arrogant self-sufficiency of so many today the Christian knows that he owes everything to God and that only through His grace and power can he live the good life.

This parable should be viewed in relation to prior and current Jewish teaching about mercy and forgiveness. In addition to exhortations, such as Micah vi. 8, we find statements such as Ben Sira's in Ecclesiasticus xxviii. 2–4:

> Forgive an injury done thee by thy neighbour,
> And when thou prayest, thy sins will be forgiven.
> One man cherisheth wrath against another,
> And doth he seek healing from the Lord?
> Upon a man like himself he hath no mercy
> And for his own sins doth he make supplication?

But these sentiments were not accepted into Jewish prayers for forgiveness. In the Testament of the Twelve Patriarchs, which is probably to be dated some time in the second century B.C. we read: 'Love ye one another from the heart; and if a man speak against thee, speak peaceably to him, and in thy soul hold no guile. And if he repent and confess, forgive him. . . . But if he be shameless, and persisteth in his wrongdoing, even so forgive him from the heart, and leave to God the avenging.' Another teacher said: 'Ever shall a man bestow loving-kindness, even on one who does evil unto him; he shall not be vengeful, nor bear a grudge. This is the way of Israel.' Nevertheless, our Lord's teaching concerning forgiveness as expressed in the Lord's Prayer is without parallel in the prayers of first-century Judaism. The expression 'as we ourselves forgive everyone who has sinned against us' is unique.[18]

In the first century the accepted belief was that God rules the world by mercy and judgement, but the latter belonged to eternity: 'The Most High shall be revealed upon the throne of judgement and then cometh the End, and compassion shall pass away and pity be far off and longsuffering withdrawn; but judgement alone shall remain' (IV Ezra vii. 33 f; cf. vii. 74, 105).[19]

Jesus not only taught but embodied compassion. It shone forth in His care for the anxious, suffering and bereaved, for widows and children. He touched the untouchables (Mk. i. 41). 'His heart went out' to people (Mk. vi. 34). He forgave those who crucified Him (Lk. xxiii. 34). In His acts of compassion He illustrated the lesson He taught His disciples: 'Be compassionate as your Father in

Heaven is compassionate' (Lk. vi. 36). Justice there must be, but God is a God of mercy; and men, who find it difficult to be just, should ever have before them the divine quality of mercy.

Shakespeare expressed this parable's teaching in *Measure for Measure*, II. ii. 75 ff. and in Portia's well-known speech extolling mercy:

> 'Tis mightiest in the mightiest: it becomes
> The throned monarch better than his crown;
> His sceptre shows the force of temporal power,
> The attribute to awe and majesty,
> Wherein doth sit the dread and fear of kings;
> But mercy is above this sceptred sway,—
> It is enthroned in the heart of kings,
> It is an attribute of God Himself;
> And earthly power doth then show likest God's
> When mercy seasons justice.
>
> (M. of V. IV. i. 187–196)[20]

THE RICH FOOL

Lk. xii. 16–21

THE FOLLY OF WORLDLINESS

Folk-tales and moralizing stories among many peoples illustrate the folly of attaching undue importance to material possessions. In the Apocrypha there is this comment on the affluent man:

> What time he saith: I have found rest,
> And now I will enjoy my goods—
> He knoweth not what lot shall befall;
> He shall leave them to others and die.
>
> Sirach xi. 18 f.

In the *One Thousand and One Nights* we hear of a king who built himself a palace reaching to the sky—the Tower of Babel motif

(Gen. xi. 9)—indicating overweening arrogance. As he congratulated himself on having treasures to enjoy throughout a future long and happy life the angel of death summoned him. There is no reason to believe this story to be influenced by the parable, but possibly both owe something to Sirach.

The teaching is not specifically Christian but constitutes a foundation essential to Christian conduct. 'Man proposes, God disposes.' Unfortunately the idea that 'the love of money is the root of all evil' (I Tim. vi. 10) led to an exaltation of poverty as such which in later ages hindered the resolute grappling with economic problems, but the parable emphasizes the folly of evaluating life according to materialistic standards. There is an inherent tension in which the individual Christian and the Church are alike involved, requiring the reconciliation of legitimate aspirations after a higher standard of living with the renunciation of cupidity. Secular thought has always tended to dwell on pleasure-seeking as man's primary goal and the most effective defiance of the flight of time. Ecclesiastes (viii. 15) expressed the sensualist's view of life: 'Then I commended mirth, because a man has no better thing under the sun than to eat and to drink, and to be merry' and the writer of the Book of Wisdom (ii. 7–11) said cynically: 'Let us fill ourselves with wine . . . and let no flower of the spring pass by us, let us crown ourselves with rosebuds before they are withered. Let our strength be the law of justice.' A verse attributed to Rufinus in the Greek Anthology runs:

> Come let us bathe and let us crown
> Our heads with roses. Let us drown
> In wine our troubles, while we call
> For bigger tankards. Soon to all
> Old age and death an end will bring,
> And youth and joy are on the wing.[21]

On a Roman grave memorial is inscribed: 'Friends who read this do my bidding. Mix the wine, drink deep, wreathed with flowers, and do not refuse to pretty girls the sweets of love.'[22] In the forum

of Timgad, in North Africa, may still be read the inscription:
Venari, lavare, ludere, ridere, hoc est vivere. 'To hunt, to bathe, to
play, to laugh, this is to live.' St. Paul was not caricaturing a widespread philosophy when he wrote: 'If the dead are never raised to
life, "let us eat and drink, for tomorrow we die" ' (I Cor. xv. 32).
The attractions of the life of pleasure were elegantly set forth
in Edward Fitzgerald's translation of the Persian poet:

> O come with old Khayyam, and leave the Wise
> To talk; one thing is certain, that Life flies;
> One thing is certain, and the Rest is Lies;
> The Flower that once has blown forever dies.

The theme reappears in Robert Herrick's 'To Virgins, to make
Much of Time':

> Gather ye rosebuds while ye may,
> Old time is still a-flying:
> And the same flower that smiles to-day,
> To-morrow will be dying.

Thus hedonists throughout the centuries have drawn the inference from the transient nature of flowers that men should indulge
in luxury and sensuality during their brief time on earth—*carpe
diem*—but our Lord found in their ephemeral beauty a token of
God's prevailing, loving care.

The outstanding characteristic of the wealthy man in the parable
is depicted as something worse than cupidity. That vice was an
expression of his egoism. Like the affluent gourmet in The Rich
Man and Lazarus he had lost the capacity to be concerned for other
people. He was interested only in himself and his death was the
final stage in losing his soul. He had withdrawn from real life. His
soul had become enclosed within the hard shell of selfishness to
such an extent that it had been stifled. He was the centre of his
world. 'He debated with himself.' In the parable of The Pharisee
and the Publican we are shown the dangers to the spiritually

minded of becoming ingoing rather than outgoing; in The Rich Fool we see the fate of the introverted materialist.

In contrast to the hedonists who, in our time, are at least as vocal as those of any previous age, our Lord says: 'Set your mind upon His kingdom and all the rest will come to you as well' (Lk. xii. 31). Society today is menaced by an increasing acquisitiveness. It looks on 'what catches the eye' in St. Paul's phrase (II Cor. x. 7), but in a characteristically modern way we are liable to be duped or dazed; that is by the almost incessant flow of pictures, words and sensations undermining our capacity to reflect and to feel deeply. Those who have experience of people with a simpler culture, as in parts of Africa, notice that often persons who possess little have more poise and readier merriment than are characteristic of the members of industrialized communities. Industrialism itself is not to blame, but it fosters cupidity unless man's spirit asserts itself against pressures which may entail the loss of freedom and gaiety. Salvation lies, not, as some suppose, in increasing industrialization in the hope of more leisure time for everyone, important as that may be, but in cultivating the spiritual resources which God makes available for us; for true joy is inseparable from extending our spiritual reach increasingly both Godward and manward.

THE WICKED VINEDRESSERS

Mt. xxi. 33–41; Mk. xii. 1–9; Lk. xx. 9–16

REJECTION AND PERSECUTION

The parable as told in the Synoptic Gospels has been so much allegorized that its authenticity has been called in question. But scholarly scrutiny has revealed where modifications and additions have been introduced, so that scepticism in regard to the basic parable is unnecessary. Among such modifications may be noted:

Mark mentions a number of slaves and Matthew exaggerates the number even further, thus spoiling the symmetry of the story; Matthew elaborates by interpolating words from the Septuagint version of the Song of the Vineyard in Isaiah v. 1 ff.; Matthew and Luke alter Mark by making the killing of the son take place outside the vineyard, thus allegorizing it as a reference to Christ's Crucifixion 'outside the gate' (Jn. xix. 17; Heb. xiii. 12 f.).

When allowance is made for alterations and accretions the kernel of the parable is disclosed: A vineyard owner living abroad sends, in turn, two messengers requiring payment from his tenants. They refuse to pay and treat the messengers brutally. Finally he sends his son, but the tenants murder him, thinking thus to be able to secure possession of the vineyard. (This is rather like the version in Thomas, but is not evidence that his version is earlier. Almost certainly it is later.) The realism of such a narrative would be evident to its hearers. Much of the Galilean hill country was owned by absentee landlords, and in such a disturbed period tenants might assume that an owner could not interfere effectively from a distance with their malicious plan to appropriate his property. Foreign absentee landlords have never been popular. Moreover, in certain circumstances ownerless land could be seized by the first claimant.[23] Thus tenants, such as those in the parable, might reasonably hope that if they got away with murdering the only son they could eventually make good their claim to the property.

Since Israel was commonly thought of as a vineyard (Isa. v. 7; Jer. ii. 21) the parable would be interpreted by hearers as a description of God's dealing with His recalcitrant and rebellious people. It is generally assumed that Jesus told it in controversy with the Jewish authorities; but, according to Nineham (p. 309) 'the setting should not be pressed', though presumably He addressed the parable to the leaders of the people. He doubts whether, as told by Jesus, it carried a reference to Himself, though Dodd (pp. 97 f.) and Jeremias (pp. 55–60) think it did. Dodd considers the predictions 'a dramatization in terms of history of the moral realities of the situation'. Certainly the assertion that the vineyard would be given to others is a warning that evildoing would receive condemnation. Justice would prevail. No individual or nation could assume that God's arm was shortened.

The opinion of the reader must depend on whether he believes that Jesus used allegory in His parables to the extent required if He was indeed referring to the crisis overtaking Him. Dodd (p. 147) reviews the evidence that He foretold His own death. He points out that He said: 'This generation will have to answer for the blood of all the prophets, shed since the foundation of the world' (Lk. xi. 50) and sorrowed that Jerusalem had failed to recognize 'the way that leads to peace' (Lk. xix. 41-44). In His moving lament for the city He called Jerusalem 'the city that murders the prophets and stones the messengers sent unto her' (Mt. xxiii. 37). Whether or not Jesus had Himself in mind when mentioning the son in the parable—and it is difficult to believe that even when reduced to its simplest form, as set out above, He could have told it without some thought of His own treatment—the parable was prophetic. The absence of any reference to the Resurrection confirms that it was related by Jesus. Its later gradual elaboration shows how forcibly its fulfilment impressed the early Church.

This is one of the parables which may be most readily understood as referring to a definite historic situation. It has been argued that we are not entitled to generalize the meaning of this and some other parables (pp. 16 f.), but, as we have seen, there is disagreement as to the extent to which it was originally particularized. However, no teacher, using parables at a time when people were accustomed to memorize and ponder over such teaching could expect them never to find new meanings in them. So, too, in our meditation and teaching we are entitled to expand lessons implicit in the parables. The Wicked Vinedressers can make us realize afresh how carefully we should consider our opportunities, reflect on our decisions, and assess, so far as we may, their consequences. The parable illustrates the dangers of a sequence in which blunted conscience leads to increasingly serious depravity. It is a warning to all kinds of groups, communities and organizations that moral considerations can all too readily be disregarded where advantage is likely to accrue to the group. The temptation to gang up against others is strong. Indeed, in such circumstances it is fatally easy for individuals or groups to deceive themselves into thinking that they are acting morally and disinterestedly. The head of a family, when acting dishonestly, may salve his conscience by convincing himself that he owes it to his wife and family to acquire all he can for them; the members of a trade union may persuade themselves that a strike is justified, however much the public are inconvenienced; governments may excuse disingenuous policies on the grounds that it is their duty to protect the interests of their people. On such principles the Jewish authorities convinced themselves that it was expedient that one man should die for the nation. Not a few dictators have used such excuses to establish tyrannies and perpetrate atrocities.

The parable can today be interpreted in the light of the fulfilment of its warning and its predictions. History has confirmed its lessons and still the world refuses to learn the things which belong unto its peace.

THE TWO BUILDERS

Mt. vii. 24–27; Lk. vi. 47–49

ON WHAT FOUNDATION DO YOU BUILD?

The figure of a storm is frequently used in the Old Testament to signify tribulations due to the havoc caused by enemies or other agencies from without. There is a rabbinic parallel:

> Whosoever's wisdom is in excess of his works,
>   to what is he like?
> To a tree whose branches are abundant
> and its roots scanty;
> and the wind comes,

> and uproots it,
> and overturns it.
> And whosoever's works are in excess of his wisdom,
>   to what is he like?
> To a tree whose branches are scanty
> and its roots abundant;
> though all the winds come upon it,
> they stir it not from its place.

Another rabbinic parable of about A.D. 120, is rather closer to the Gospel stories:

> A man who does many good works and has learned much Torah, to what is he like? To a man who builds below with stones and then with (mud) bricks; and when much water comes and stands around the walls, it does not wash them from their place.
>
> But the man who does no good works and has learned Torah, to what is he like? To a man who builds first with bricks and afterwards with stones; and when little water comes it demolishes them at once.[24]

Both rabbinic parables emphasize that knowledge of the Law must be accompanied by fulfilment of its teaching. All such sayings are probably derived from ancient proverbial lore, such as:

> When the whirlwind passeth, the wicked is no more:
> But the righteous is an everlasting foundation.
>
> (Prov. x. 25)

Doubtless disasters from time to time renewed the aptness of such sayings for each generation. Rather more than forty years ago twenty-five houses at Nazareth collapsed in a downpour.[25]

It has been argued that Matthew's version is the more authentic because he expresses the parable in Hebraic parallelisms and envisages autumnal downpours, whereas Luke is thinking in terms of a river overflowing its banks. Jeremias (p. 194) comments that this is an unlikely eventuality in Palestine, but a torrent pouring down

TABLE OF THE PARABLES

CONSIDERED IN THIS WORK.

PARABLE-GERMS.

a *wadi* could undermine an unwisely sited house. Bishop (p. 86), fully acquainted with life in the Holy Land, remarks: 'There is no questioning the Palestinian description of Luke.' None the less, Luke weakens the point of the story, stressing the sound structure of the house instead of its firm foundation on rock. The cognate quotations from Proverbs and the rabbis, already quoted, all emphasize the importance of sound foundations.

Jeremias (pp. 169, 194) interprets this parable as a warning that the last hour is at hand, comparable with the warning to Noah before the Flood: 'Repent before the catastrophe occurs. The time is short.' But, as we have seen, the traditional message of this widely familiar theme was the importance of being rooted and grounded in sound teaching and, above all, righteous living. The contrast is between hearing and then acting according to what has been learnt, and hearing without doing.

This parable is placed by Matthew at the end of the first of his five collections of sayings of Jesus which he concludes with, 'And when Jesus finished these sayings . . .' (vii. 28; xi. 1; xiii. 53; xix. 1; xxvi. 1. Cf. Fenton, pp. 14 ff., 114). In both Gospels it forms the peroration to the Sermon on the Mount (Lk. 'the Plain'). It sums up our Lord's claim to be obeyed as a new Lawgiver and Teacher of righteousness. The ultimate criterion of allegiance to Him is action, building on the rock of His teaching. Even if the parable suggests a warning of the Final Judgement its primary intention is to stress the tremendous claims of Jesus, claims which incurred the deadly hostility of the Jewish authorities and finally brought Him to the Cross.

THE TWO DEBTORS

Lk. vii. 41–43

FORGIVENESS

The setting of this parable, so appealingly recorded by Luke, presents puzzling aspects. It is difficult to imagine how a prostitute could intrude upon a feast given by a Pharisee, although travellers in the Middle East a century ago have described dinners held where the court and guest-chamber were open and loungers could crowd in.[26] Taking into account how much of Luke's material is polemical and anti-Pharisaic it would seem that he has chosen a setting for the story which would make such a message most effective. This suspicion is reinforced when we note linguistic and stylistic peculiarities in his narrative which suggest that he may have remodelled its form.[27] It appears that there has been some interchange between the account of this episode and that of the anointing at Bethany (Mk. xiv. 8) for it would be too odd a coincidence that at both anointings the host should have been named Simon and that the ointment should be described in the same unusual terms and Jesus criticized for such a use of it. Possibly an episode in which Jesus was accused of impropriety for allowing a prostitute to approach Him has been interwoven with another incident when He was anointed by a woman (Mk. xiv. 3–9; Jn. xii. 3).

For Luke the incident illustrates the contrast between the self-righteous and the sincere, the Pharisee and the sinner, as in the parable of The Pharisee and the Publican. The Pharisee does not directly criticize the woman, but he is sceptical whether Jesus can be a prophet because He does not show knowledge of her past. It is implied that a genuine prophet would make it manifest that he was gifted with such insight. But it is the Pharisee who errs in underestimating our Lord's compassion, attributing His sympathetic attitude to obtuseness. Christian folk down the ages have sometimes been accused of being blinded by sentimentality or motivated by ignorance when, as events have later shown, sympathy enabled them to act helpfully.

The depth of our Lord's insight was manifested by His words: 'Her great love proves that her many sins are forgiven.' Here lies the point of the whole story—love covers a multitude of sins; for it is of God (I Jn. iv. 7). The common assumption was, and is, that a prostitute's profession of selling sex debars her from any experience of genuine human love and alienates her from the love of God. But our Lord did not regard sexual sin as worse than other sins; and, if sin excludes us from God's mercy, what hope have we? The woman's lavish expression of love was a clear proof that she had found favour with God; for if hatred indicates a sinful, unforgiving heart, love is the expression of a soul to that extent forgiven.

This parable may be compared with The Unforgiving Official in which the man who was forgiven much showed himself merciless and unforgiving. He was so utterly without any feeling of love that no manifestation of mercy, however great, could soften his heart, which had become completely callous. He could not believe in love, accept it or give it. He was a lost soul. Perhaps those most to be pitied in any society are not those who fail to receive love, tragic as is their plight, but those who are unable to give it.

Before considering the 'Lost and Found' parables in the next chapter we may end this chapter by considering two parables dealing with finders who discovered what they had not lost.

THE HIDDEN TREASURE
Mt. xiii. 44

AND

THE PEERLESS PEARL
Mt. xiii. 45 f.

JOYFUL SURPRISE FOR THE WHOLEHEARTED AND
SINGLEMINDED

In a peasant community there were difficulties in storing valuables. The poor man's safe was the earth (cf. The Talents, pp. 128–130). During turbulent times wealthy people, too, buried their treasures, and sometimes misadventures or the ravages of war prevented them from returning to retrieve what they had buried. Treasure trove was uncovered every now and then, and tales about fortunate finders were retailed by wishful thinkers throughout the countryside. In folk-tales the virtuous are sometimes rewarded by coming on hidden treasure, as in the rabbinic story of the good fortune which befell Abba Judan after he had philanthropically given all he possessed, except a cow and a field, to the needy. The cow fell into a hole in the field, breaking its leg, but in trying to rescue it Abba Judan found an immense treasure. In our sophisticated society only children can believe that a crock of gold is to be found at the foot of the rainbow, but a fortunate farmer may still unearth a treasure, while he is ploughing, as at Mildenhall, in Suffolk, when magnificently ornate Roman silver dishes were uncovered. In 1952 two heavily oxidized copper rolls were discovered at Qumran near the Dead Sea. The inscriptions recorded where treasures had been secreted, but diligent search revealed nothing.

Attention has been called to material differences between this parable and the version in Thomas and a rabbinic story. The latter, commenting on Cant. iv. 12, recounts the history of a man who inherited a place full of rubbish. 'The inheritor was lazy and sold it for a ridiculously small sum. The purchaser dug there industriously and found in it a treasure. He built therewith a great palace and passed through the bazaar with a train of slaves which he had bought with the treasure. When the seller saw it he could have choked himself (out of chagrin).'[28] Here the common folk-theme of the lazy or ignorant simpleton appears. In the Gospel of Thomas a son sells the land inherited from his father and the purchaser ploughs it, finds the treasure and becomes a money-lender. The contrast between these and the Gospel parable is immense.

The parable of The Peeless Pearl is twin to The Hidden Treasure, and the two may have been told together; for parallelism is a characteristic of Hebrew style, both in short clauses and in more elaborate compositions. Thus:

> If a kingdom be divided against itself,
>   that kingdom cannot stand.
> And if a house be divided against itself,
>   that house cannot stand.
>
> (Mt. xii. 25)

Other twin parables are The Mustard Seed and The Leaven, The Lost Sheep and The Lost Coin, The Tower Builder and The Warring King, The Patch and The Wineskins.

Pearls are not mentioned in the Old Testament, but from prehistoric times they were highly prized, in all probability at first for the magical properties attributed to them.[29] Pearl fishing was carried out in the Red Sea during the time of the Ptolomies and, according to Pliny, Cleopatra possessed a pearl worth £1½ million. In Palestine pearls came to represent the supremely valuable: 'Do not give dogs what is holy; do not feed your pearls to pigs' (Mt. vii. 6).

Thomas, who often abbreviates, expands or manipulates the sayings of the Synoptic Gospels records: 'Jesus said: The Kingdom of God is like a man who had a cargo (and) who found a pearl. He was a wise man. (Therefore) he sold his cargo and bought for himself the pearl alone. You seek for his treasure which does not perish, which abides where no moth enters to eat and worms do not destroy (anything).'[30] This version misses the point of the parable which is brought out by Matthew. The man was an expert, 'a merchant looking out for fine pearls'. He sold all to buy the pearl.

Jeremias (p. 200), assuming that 'the merchant was not an expert in pearls' prefers the version given by Thomas.[31] But this needs more justification than Jeremias provides. The man who had spent years seeking pearls and assessing their quality with a discriminating eye at last lighted on a supremely beautiful specimen. All else seemed unimportant compared with acquiring this superb pearl. Unlike the man, labouring in a field, who happened on treasure the merchant found what he had been looking for. His joy was that of a man who at long last achieves the culmination of his hopes. He might be thought of as a dealer risking all on an investment. If so, the emphasis would lie on the individual's commitment, but more probably the stress is on the delight of attainment. The risk and sacrifice necessary to secure the prize was as nothing compared with the rapture of success. This is the joy of the Kingdom, the reward of wholehearted devotion. 'Seek and you will find' (Mt. vii. 7; Lk. xi. 9). 'No one shall rob you of your joy' (Jn. xvi. 22). The keynote of both parables is the joy of attainment. The Hidden Treasure describes the delight of a find, hoped for, perhaps, but beyond all expectation; the Peerless Pearl the joy of lifelong aspirations consummated; together they encourage us to rely on the grace-gifts of God and to rejoice in the transformation of life through the inflowing of the Spirit.

The discoverer of the treasure trove was a comparatively poor man who chanced on the money, the pearl merchant was relatively wealthy; he came on the pearl in the course of business and sold his whole stock to acquire it. One man enters into the joy of the Kingdom unexpectedly, another gains it through the maturing of a lifetime's endeavour. Unlike the rich young ruler (Mt. xix. 21; Mk. x. 21; Lk. xviii. 22), when the supreme opportunity presented itself the pearl merchant was ready to invest everything. We are given to understand that his life had been devoted to acquiring ever more perfect pearls. Each, in turn, was a joyful attainment. So should the Christian's life be attuned to anticipating the insights and inspirations God gives as life goes on, confident that He has still finer things to reveal to us. We may not all have unexpected, glorious, mystical experiences, but we should aspire after clearer insights, some of which may have at least a little of the quality of that ecstasy enjoyed by Pascal. Sewn into his doublet, when he lay dead, was found this testimony:

> Certitude, Perception, Joy, Peace,
>
> .   .   .   .   .   .
>
> Joy, joy, joy, tears of joy.

CHAPTER V
LOST AND FOUND, FATHER AND SON

Compassion, Joy and Judgement; God's Care for the Individual

In this chapter it will be convenient to consider together some of the longer, narrative parables, those dealing with sonship and 'lostness' and the allegorical story of The Sheep and the Goats, which stands somewhat apart from the other parables, but is linked with some of them by the figure of the shepherd.

Among the aims of this whole discussion has been to probe below the parables themselves with the aid of the imagery in which they are expressed, utilizing it as a means whereby we may gain further insight into the mind and message of Jesus. Thus we may perceive more clearly those themes which constituted the essence of His teaching. In successive chapters we have noted how the imagery discloses our Lord's concentration on certain themes—nature as a means by which God's ways are revealed; appeal, warning and opportunity-seizing conveyed in picture-thinking concerning entering or being shut out; joy and salvation, represented by recurrent references to feasting; and the workaday world as the stage on which salvation may be gained. In this final chapter we trace the proclamation of the Gospel message set forth in terms of saving the lost and the relationship of love between father and son—the heart of the Gospel. These parables include the most appealing stories told by Jesus. They show how intensely He cared for people.

Although it is abundantly evident that the Fatherhood of God was supremely important in our Lord's teaching we have further confirmation in the imagery of the parables—the prominence of the sonship theme. In addition to The Loving Father there are five others dealing with sonship, if we include The Wicked Vinedressers, The Son's Request, The Two Sons and those in St. John's Gospel detected by Dodd (p. 39), The Slave and Son and The Apprentice Son. Just as the number and character of the Nature Parables indicates a basic premise of our Lord's thought—nature as an expression of the divine—so these references to fatherhood and sonship illustrate the relationship underlying all His life and teaching.

The parables of The Good Samaritan and The Prodigal Son, recorded only by Luke, diverge from most parables to such an extent that some writers place them, with one or two others, in a category of narrative 'example stories'. Outstanding in their simplicity and directness, breadth and depth of appeal, they are among the world's best-known tales. Children, captivated by their realism, re-enact them in their play and they provide teaching whereby Christian truth may be presented even to those brought up in traditions unsympathetic to it.[1] The two parables are complementary, to the extent that one illustrates the ideal Christian relationship between man and man, and the other the relationship between God and man. There are, too, parallels between features of the two stories. One tells of a lone wayfarer stricken down miles from his destination, his rescue and the loving care bestowed on him by the wayside and at the inn, the other of a youth's downfall in an alien countryside, his change of heart and welcome back home. In both there is a tragic figure who is 'lost' and then 'found', regarded as dead and then rejoiced over as restored to life; in both, also, help or welcome is withheld by those from whom it might have been expected.[2]

These two parables, especially The Good Samaritan, illustrate how mistaken is any generalization seeking to pin down the teaching of a parable to the particular situation in which it was uttered (pp. 14–16). Although the locality where the assault was made on the traveller is indicated with exactitude as a certain road from

Jerusalem to Jericho it is symbolical of the setting of all man's activities. The concept of life as a journey or pilgrimage, and the after-life as a continuation of it, may be traced into prehistory. Any person, hearing the parable, may picture himself as being on that road. Similarly, the Prodigal Son's departure for the far country awakens chains of subconscious sympathetic response in the minds of all those who know life as a perpetual going forth and return and the world as a place where the heart is both homeless and at home.

The parable of The Good Samaritan is represented by Luke as being told to a lawyer, but it has been commented: 'Luke's contrived contexts are so many that one suspects the parable must be independent of its context.'[3] The Prodigal Son is placed in a setting with 'tax-gatherers and other bad characters . . . crowding in to listen'. Discontented 'Pharisees and doctors of the law' are also present. It is difficult to picture a situation in which this motley crowd would associate together and possibly Luke, in view of the immense significance of the teaching collected into this chapter and its universal reference has emphasized all this by assembling into a congregation both those who welcomed Jesus' teaching and those who rejected it. Jeremias, assuming our Lord's teaching to have been usually directed against some particular group, concludes that these two parables were addressed by Him to His critics but, however this may be, they deal with universals and are applicable to every individual.[4]

THE GOOD SAMARITAN

Lk. x. 25–37

COMPASSION

The problem of neighbourliness becomes acute when the question arises: 'Where should limits be drawn?' All normal people, in addition to possessing self-regarding impulses have social inclinations of greater or lesser intensity. In this human beings are no different from most higher animals and some insects. We differ in being able to decide the bounds of our concern in the light of our personal advantage. Man's problem is, therefore, to muster sufficient disinterestedness, magnanimity and compassion to extend his sympathies commensurately with his widening social contacts. Within a group of people at the food-gathering stage of culture social solidarity is strong, and so naturally does each identify his interests with those of others in the small community that a starving man will share any morsel he obtains with his companions. But in a more complex society the conditions of life and accompanying psychological and social adaptations create tensions which can only be resolved on a much higher level. The extension of compassion ever further towards the ultimate ideal of Christian charity involves the overcoming of two obstacles, the practical difficulty of aiding all those we know to be in need and the emotional problem of self-giving beyond a limited circle. This problem presses upon all people of good will, and on how each of us resolves it depends the quality of his life. Gifts of grace are needed if we are to be able to give out lavishly to others, for beyond a certain point, self-giving, which normally should bring its own reward, may make excessive demands on a person's emotions and resources generally. The tensions which the Christian life involves have moral value, but they can only be constructive by God's grace.

This problem of achieving creative reconciliation between the personal and the social is analogous to the dilemma in which the Jews were so long, and are still, involved. Too great friendliness with others, individuals or nations, could lead to their assimilation, too little friendliness to resentment, isolation and conflict. The Jews became what they did because of these tensions. In the Bible, and especially the New Testament, we see their predicaments presented on a brightly illuminated stage. Exclusiveness became the refuge of a people constantly tempted to lower their standards. Thus, as a result of the immense strain of maintaining their identity and spiritual insights the Jews tended to add to the commandment,

'Thou shalt love thy neighbour as thyself' (Lev. xix. 18) the corollary 'and hate thine enemy' (Mt. v. 43). Intense loyalties within a group may foster coolness or worse towards those outside, and this may apply alike to families, trade unions, nations or other associations of people, especially when material interests are directly involved. Moreover, sympathies tend to become diluted the farther they extend.

For the Jew to love one's neighbour only made sense if 'neighbour' were understood as someone belonging to the Jewish community. Neighbourliness thus became being neighbourly to those within a defined circle of neighbourliness. Any such circle is liable to become a vicious circle of self-interest. Exclusiveness breeds exclusiveness. The Pharisees tended to add non-Pharisees to those who need not be loved, the Essenes were advised to 'hate all the sons of darkness', and a rabbinical saying stated that heretics, informers and renegades should be pushed (into the ditch) and not helped out.[5] The Dead Sea Scrolls have revealed further instances of sectarian exclusiveness during the first century.

Even now the precept to love a person while detesting his opinions is by no means easy to maintain in practice. To the Jews of the first century it was quite alien; indeed, the recognition of such an obligation is mainly due to Christian influence.[6] It is such a picture of neighbourliness that The Good Samaritan gives; for the characters set in contrast belonged, as we all know, to races which hated one another and regarded each other's views with abhorrence. Jewish–Samaritan antagonisms embodied most of the components involved in present-day animosities—racial, historical, religious, ideological and social. They illustrate the perverse streak in human nature which induces people to be particularly vehement in their dislike of those whose views have much in common with their own.[7]

The long-standing feud between Jews and Samaritans was perpetuated by this mentality though bitterness between them may not have been so continuously virulent as has commonly been represented. The people of mixed Assyrian–Jewish blood, who lived in the territory which was formerly the Northern Kingdom and practised a debased form of the Jewish religion, had quarrelled with the Jews who set about the rebuilding of Jerusalem on returning from exile, but at first the opposition was on political rather than religious grounds. The acrimony thus engendered between the two peoples was later accentuated by the establishment of a rival priesthood and temple on Mount Gerizim. However, it is not known when this temple was built and its construction need not have caused an irreparable breach between Jews and Samaritans. A temple was established at Elephantine in Egypt to serve the Jewish community there without arousing animosity. Apparently the feud developed gradually. By the middle of the third century B.C. and possibly earlier, the breach was complete.[8] Three incidents may be mentioned to illustrate this feud. About 128 B.C. the Jew, John Hyrcanus, overwhelmed Samaria and destroyed the Samaritan temple. In A.D. 6 Samaritans desecrated the Jerusalem temple by sneaking in at night and strewing human bones in the precincts. On another occasion Samaritans smuggled mice into the boxes in which doves were conveyed to the temple so that they scampered around when the boxes were opened. Such is the historical background to the parable.

For centuries the road from Jerusalem to Jericho, seventeen miles long, was notorious as the haunt of bandits. It is not necessary to assume that the assailants of the traveller in the parable were intruding Beduin as there were plenty of lawless men round about Jerusalem in the first century, driven to desperation by economic straits. Josephus calls the Jerusalem–Jericho road 'The Ascent of Blood', and Jerome refers to the rugged limestone valley through which it descends as the haunt of thieves. In 1118 the nucleus of the Order of Templars was formed to defend pilgrims on this track which winds steeply down some 3,000 feet to the Jordan valley. A century ago pilgrims descending it were given the protection of a force of Turkish soldiers.[9] Even in quite recent times there have been acts of violence on it. Vultures circle over the valley and at dusk a jackal may be glimpsed in the light of a car's head-lamps. But the assault described in the parable must be envisaged as taking place during daylight, unless we suppose the wounded man to have lain out all night; for it is unlikely that a number of people would have been travelling separately after dark along a road with such an evil reputation.

There was nothing exceptional in there being four persons on the road that day, for it was much used, Jericho being an important town with extensive date plantations close by. Sadducees owned land there and half of those on the officiating 'course' at the Temple were resident.

It is tempting to think of the story as having been first told at Bethany, which was situated about two miles from Jerusalem on the road to Jericho (Lk. xix. 29). The parable is followed immediately by an account of hospitality from Martha and Mary at their home in a village which John (xi. 1) identifies as Bethany.

The man lay by the roadside in the anonymity of nakedness. For all the priest and Levite could tell as they glanced at the body, or the Samaritan as he turned it over, the blood-smeared hulk might be Jew or Gentile. The victim might have been a Roman soldier robbed of everything which could indicate his profession. Members of the occupation forces were liable to be set upon by desperadoes.[10] However, the Jews who formed the first audience would probably picture him as a man of their own race. They were told only that he was a man. The temple officials manifested the extreme of un-neighbourliness in treating the victim as a thing rather than as a person—as Nazis were later to treat Jews. If instead of 'a man' we had 'a Jew' the rebuke to the priest and Levite would have been pointed and patently an attack on the temple authorities. Obligations accepted by Jews to members of their own community did not apply to others. In interpreting and expounding the parable the anonymity of the bandit's victim enables us to generalize its moral beyond the obligation to help those you hate to the responsibility to show love to all seen to be in need. We know less about the injured man than about the other figures in the parable. We may assume this to be intentional. Our sympathies should burst the bonds of all limiting categories, not only of race and religion but of prejudices and preconceptions, likes and dislikes. Christian neigh-bourliness has no place for restrictive thinking. In Mt. v. 44 ff. and Lk. vi. 27 ff. this teaching is carried to its ultimate point—'Love your enemies.' In our time we have seen this exemplified in the lives of men who suffered cruelly under the Japanese and after the war dedicated themselves to missionary work in Japan.[11]

The thought underlying the question addressed to Jesus was restrictive. 'Where should limits be drawn?' The enquirer, who, we are reminded, 'wanted to vindicate himself' and receive endorse-ment of his outlook was jerked into thinking in terms of opportunity rather than obligation, outgoingness rather than legalism. The story is framed to do this all the more effectively as it contains a characteristic twist. The question implied, 'What is the maximum neighbourliness which may reasonably be required of me?', but the reply is in terms of how practical neighbourliness should be expressed. The scribes and Pharisees thought in terms of legal definitions and ethical formulae. Our Lord taught that such modes of thought could stifle love. We have similar exhortations to think widely, lovingly and forgivingly in His reply to Peter (Mt. xviii. 21 f.), the parable of The Prodigal Son, and throughout the Gospels.

The parable might have been told in terms of a Jew who found an injured Samaritan by the wayside and befriended him. It would then have been a direct reproof to the Jews and their leaders, but not only would it have lost much of its artistry and imaginative impact but the universality of its teaching would have been obscured. As the tale unfolded listeners would catch their breath when, in-stead of the sequence, priest, Levite, Israelite, they heard 'Samari-tan'. To realize the startling and attention-compelling reaction evoked we need to imagine the effect created by a story of this kind being related to Jews under Hitler with a Nazi as the hero.

Rather naturally expositors, aware of how much of the priest and Levite there is in each of us, have emphasized their culpability, but the parable is not primarily designed as a condemnation of religious professionalism and legalism, but is positive teaching about un-bounded compassion.

In fairness to the priest and Levite we must take into account that a priest was forbidden by Sadducean ritual restrictions to touch a corpse (blood relations excepted), and was entitled to pass by a dead body. Also a Levite was required to maintain strict ritual purity during his duties (Lev. xxi. 1 ff.). But both men, when they saw the body 'went past on the other side', just as the Rich Man passed half-naked, ulcerated Lazarus on the roadside when he entered or left his house. They abandoned it to the scorching sun, the jackals and hyaenas as the Rich Man left Lazarus to be tormented by the dogs. They jumped to the convenient conclusion that what they saw was a dead body. The robbers might be lurking behind a nearby outcrop. It was obviously prudent to decamp rather than risk one's life meddling with a corpse. The priest and Levite were scared. Few of us would not have been. No doubt the Samaritan was frightened, too, but he examined the unconscious ('half-dead') man and found that he breathed. He knew that in halting to give first aid he was risking his life. Compassion conquered cowardice. Such was the splendid extent of his neighbourliness. He would give his life, if need be, for a stranger who, if a Jew, would have treated him as scum.

When the Samaritan appears on the scene there is a new fullness of detail. The stage becomes flood-lit. He was 'moved to pity' and 'bandaged his wounds', sacrificing his headcloth or undergarment. He bathed the man's injuries, which, it would seem, had been inflicted with sharp weapons as well as the bludgeons used to beat him up, employing emollient oil and antiseptic wine, the normal medicaments of the time.[12] Not only had he the courage and compassion to help but also the knowledge enabling him to do so. Good intentions are not enough. Implicit in these details is the reminder that once we have decided to be helpful we should set about obtaining the necessary knowledge and training. If we are to apply the story where it most directly belongs—to road traffic conditions—there are obvious lessons for all concerned.

We are not told whether the priest and Levite were mounted though it is improbable that they travelled on foot on a journey of this length. Mention of the injured man's being hoisted on to the Samaritan's 'own beast' suggests that he had another ass carrying merchandise. Such booty would have been an additional temptation to robbers. Apparently he was a commercial traveller on his rounds, for he was known to the innkeeper who would not otherwise have given him credit. The Samaritan nursed the injured man during the night and in the morning made reasonable provision for future expenses, giving the innkeeper 'two silver pieces'. The cost of a day's board was about one twenty-fourth of this.[13] His compassion was not a passing emotion but an acceptance of continuing responsibility—such as few of us shoulder with alacrity when strangers, or even friends, are concerned. He saw the matter through.

The innkeeper is a shadowy figure, but he deserves our attention. The Samaritan relied on his good will. No doubt he was a Jew, and Jews did not accept as valid any oath between Jews and Samaritans. If mine host had failed to fulfil his obligation the Samaritan had no hope of redress, while if the Samaritan defaulted the innkeeper would be at a loss. Both behaved according to an ideal relationship of trust between man and man so far as practical help was concerned (Lev. xxv. 35 f.; Deut. xv. 7 f.; Lk. vi. 35). The innkeeper was, indeed, paid in advance for some of the care to be bestowed on the invalid, but we must give the man his due; without his aid the Samaritan's efforts would almost certainly have been unavailing and if there had not been mutual trust the invalid would have been refused admission or turned out of doors. He is a representative of those auxiliaries without whose reliable background help much philanthropic work would fail. Heroic deeds and campaigns would seldom be possible without prosaic assistance. We are so accustomed to rely on those who fulfil the rôle of the innkeeper in the network of social organizations that there is some danger that we may too readily act like the priest and Levite, thinking, 'This is not my business', yet all who look below the surface of modern society know how much suffering there is—loneliness, anxiety, mental disturbance, spiritual dereliction—which goes unalleviated. A man in trouble needs a friend who, like the Samaritan, will 'come where he is'. The sympathetic relationship of person to person has healing power. Magnificent as is the work of our specialized social agencies St. Vincent de Paul's perceptive comment should not be forgotten: 'The poor will never forgive you for the good you do them unless you love them.'

The parable of The Good Samaritan, or, as we might call it, of The Man who was Found, in common with The Prodigal Son, emphasizes the importance of the individual as caring and cared for. Where the dignity of the individual is denied or taken little account of, as may happen in consequence of present-day political, economic, social and psychological pressures, callousness tends to displace compassion and the horrid vision appears of automated human beings and the ant-heap society. Arthur Koestler, one-time Communist, makes one of the magistrates in *Darkness at Noon* say: 'There are only two conceptions of ethics and they are at opposite poles. One of them is Christian and humane, declares the individual to be sacrosanct, and asserts that the rules of arithmetic are not to be applied to human units. The other starts from the basic principle that a collective aim justifies all means, and not only allows, but demands, that the individual may be subordinated and sacrificed to the community—which may dispose of it as an experimentation rabbit or a sacrificial lamb.'

It is the very life-blood of the Christian tradition to maintain the supreme value of persons as children of God. Man was made to mould society, not society to mould man. St. Paul's strongest argument against wronging another person is that for him Christ died (Rom. xiv. 15). This emphasis is prominent throughout the centuries. In the fifth century a Bishop, remonstrating with a governor in North Africa, declared: 'You are treating men as if they were cheap, but man is a thing of price, for Christ died for him.' The mediaeval scholar, Muretus, collapsed in a street in an Italian town and was laid on the operating table. He heard one doctor say to another, 'Try your experiment on this cheap life', and called out, 'Do you call a life cheap for which Christ did not disdain to die?' The change which Christianity wrought was in stressing, not that man is worth something to man, but that he is of inestimable value in the sight of God.

THE PRODIGAL SON
OR
THE LOVING FATHER

Lk. xv. 11–32

'WE LOVE BECAUSE HE LOVED US FIRST' (I Jn. iv. 19)

We have already noted points of similarity between the parable of The Prodigal Son and The Good Samaritan. Both stress the importance of the individual.[14] The Prodigal Son is the longest of the parables and some critics have maintained that it consisted originally only of verses 11–24a and ended with: 'For this son of mine was dead and has come back to life; he was lost and is found.' The second half is so integral to the story that this supposition, influenced by the assumption that a parable is designed to make only a single point, need not be taken seriously. Some superficial plausibility is given to the theory if we allow ourselves to be beguiled by the flowing artistry of the story; for the vicissitudes of the prodigal and the happy climax arrest our attention so fully that we are apt to forget temporarily that the parable begins: 'A certain man had two sons . . .' Moreover, the title by which the parable is known reveals a failure to appreciate that it deals, not with a young man's headstrong actions and dissolute behaviour, but with the character of a father and his relationship to his two sons. If it were not for the claims of brevity and tradition we might call it the parable of The Loving Father and his Two Sons. The contrast is not between an obedient and a disobedient son but between the reception given to the spendthrift by the father and that given by his elder brother—one representing God's love, the other the harsh reaction of the 'natural' man.

The farm is represented as of a fair size, large enough for 'hired servants', casual labour, to be employed, and small enough for there to be only one 'fatted calf' (cf. Mt. xxii. 4). When the younger son asked his father to divide his estate between himself and his brother in order that he might acquire cash to emigrate the elder brother became, with minor qualifications, the owner of the farm. The father continued to work the land with his son's help, for, legally, the usufruct remained the father's until his death.

It was by no means exceptional for a younger son to go abroad. Population pressure and economic stringencies were such that many young men had to emigrate if they were to make a living, even though they might prefer to stay in the land which was more than homeland to them, being where the faith was cherished that the Reign of God would be established. According to Jewish law the elder of two sons was entitled to two-thirds of his father's property on his death. Thus the meagre prospects of younger sons often compelled them to go overseas.[15] No doubt the story of Joseph inspired many youths with the hope that they would find a footing in foreign cities, even if their streets did not turn out to be paved with gold. Also, contemplation of the joyous outcome of Joseph's exile may have consoled grief-stricken parents. We should not suppose that the parable imputes blame to the lad for leaving home; nor does it suggest that the father tried to restrict his son's freedom. Those hearing it would recognize, as generations of Irish have done, that necessity is a hard taskmaster. Moreover, the parable of The Talents shows that Jesus commended enterprise. The tragedy lay, not in the penury to which the youth was reduced —though we are shown the connexion between imprudence, misery and moral deterioration—but in his unfaithfulness to the standards of conduct in which he had been brought up. Away from home and homeland the principles in which he had been reared were discarded. So it has been with many an expatriate since. As his confession on returning showed, he knew that he sinned against

God and man. That is, he came to acknowledge the principle which
is challenged today, and not only by the openly dissolute, that
morality is based on objective standards and their expression in
society.

In the far country he lived recklessly, not seeking a job while his
money lasted; but the accusation made later by his brother that he
had lavished his resources on prostitutes should not be accepted as
evidence of anything but his brother's malice, unless we assume, as
is possible, that rumours about his wanton conduct had filtered
through from where he had settled. The emphasis is on his wastefulness. Since 'no one gave him anything' he may have descended
to theft. As a swineherd his degradation was complete, for feeding
pigs, considered ritually unclean, put a Jew 'beyond the pale'. No
detail could indicate more completely how 'lost' he was—lost to
religious, racial and family loyalties. Starving, he envied the swine
their trough of carob bean pods. There was a rabbinic saying:
'When the Israelites have to eat of the carob tree, only then do they
repent.'[16]

All but alienated in mind the young man in the alien land 'came
to his senses'. Misery roused him from his almost animal condition.
Memory of happier times accentuated the contrast between his
present state and what might have been. But the thread of love
between father and son remained unbroken, though in that far land
it did not seem credible that the lad's father could be yearning for
him as he for his father. He realized that his father had given him
love which he had failed to return, now there would be retributive
justice in his suffering the pangs of unrequited love. He had learned
a lot about himself, but he had yet to learn the greatness of his
father's love. It was the hope of reconciliation, at least with himself,
not of restoration, which brought him home. He realized that on
leaving home he had abandoned freedom so lavish that he had not
recognized it in exchange for soul-destroying servitude—bondage
to strangers and to sin.

No parable calls more insistently for imaginative and emotional
identification with the principals. We must view it in terms of the

dramatic appeal with which it was originally presented and appreciated. Many days had passed since the lad's father had taken to
making excuses for going frequently to the door and looking out.
He could keep an eye on the land and the stock, he would say. But
his wife noticed that his eyes strayed in the direction of the path his
son had taken. So it was not altogether by chance that he happened
to be standing there when the dishevelled lad appeared over the
hill. 'While he was still a long way off' he saw him. Then, 'his
heart went out to him' regardless of the dignity on which such
elderly men set store 'he ran to meet him', flung his arms around
him and kissed him—as I have seen a sheikh in Jordan greet his
returning son. Haltingly the prodigal began his confession, but his
father could not contain himself. He broke in with orders to the
servants. There must not be a moment's delay in preparing the
household's welcome. No words of forgiveness to the son are
necessary; his actions have spoken for him. Some of those listening
as the story unfolded may have recalled the current saying: 'God
says, "My hands are stretched out toward the penitent; I thrust
no one back who gives me his heart in repentance." '[17]

As in The Good Samaritan, there is a fullness of detail at the
crucial point; in this case the welcome. The details may be
significant, for they embody symbolism harking back to very early
traditions. Parallels occur in status-giving ceremonial, including
royal enthronements, throughout the ages.[18] The son is vested
with a fine robe—as is customary in enthronement and coronation
ritual; a ring is placed on his finger—a symbol of status. He is
received as a son, not as a servant. (This procedure adds plausibility
to the assumption that the bestowal of the robe is more than a
substitution of an adequate garment for the youth's dirty rags.)
Shoes are placed on his feet, distinguishing him as a free man from
the poor, the enslaved and the oppressed. Musicians are sent for,
probably bagpipers, to provide an accompaniment for the men's
dance. All enjoy the feast which has been prepared—and we are
reminded of the symbolism of the heavenly banquet and the
constant association of feasting with the ceremonial recognition of

status. We should not fail to notice how significant is the setting of the parable. It was first related, according to the Evangelist, when 'tax gatherers and other bad characters' gathered around Jesus when they were sharing a meal (Lk. xv. 1 f.). Such table-fellowship reached its highest expression in the acted parable of the Last Supper. This section of the parable concludes, like the other Lost and Found parables, with community rejoicing.

There had not been much gaiety about the place for a long time; so the elder son is taken aback when, returning to the farm-house, he hears the sounds of revelry. Many puritanical Christians since have been shocked at the sound of music and dancing. His father, in transports of joy, hurries outside to bring him in—treating both sons alike in going out to them. To his amazement and grief he finds the young man in no mood to share his delight. The self-righteous fellow heaps reproaches on his father, and such is his chagrin that he cannot bring himself to mention his brother's name; as if, indeed, he wished him dead and forgotten. He is quick to impute sordid profligacy to him and assails his father with contemptuous spleen: 'I have slaved for you all these years'—as if he to whom the farm had been given had been treated as a serf. His brother's highest aspiration in the alien land had been to become his father's slave; the elder son felt himself to be a slave while all the delights and privileges of sonship were his for the enjoying. His father replies: 'My dear boy, you are always with me, and everything I have is yours. How could we help celebrating this happy day. Your brother here was dead and has come back to life, was lost and is found.' There is a tender rebuke in 'my boy' and 'Your brother here' in contrast to the young man's bitterly sarcastic, 'This son of yours.' The joyous transformation of the whole situation and the transposition from grief and sin to forgiveness, demand expression in terms of resurrection from the dead.

The father had been wronged, but his heart overflowed with forgiveness; the elder brother had not been wronged, but was unforgiving. We spontaneously condemn, and perhaps despise, him as we contrast him with the other two figures in the parable. We can see his unforgivingness turning into contempt and pride. His resentment kept him outside the house, outside reconciliation with his brother, outside the community rejoicing, outside peace with himself. It will be remembered that it was the Pharisee's pride which prevented him from 'going down to his house justified' (Lk. xviii. 14). A guilty conscience seeking self-justification readily passes over into pride, and pride into resentment; and rankling resentment is soul-destroying.

We should not fail to use The Loving Father and the Lord's Prayer to interpret one another as both emphasize the unique intimacy of the Father–child relationship (pp. 11 f.). The behaviour of the elder son illuminates by contrast our Lord's teaching on forgiveness in the prayer he gave His disciples—teaching without parallel in early Judaism, as has already been pointed out (p. 142)—'as we ourselves forgive those who have sinned against us' we trust in God's forgiveness. The elder son's behaviour is seen to be all the more reprehensible because he was unforgiving towards his father and brother even when their sins against him were products of his imagination.[19]

Yet we must be fair to the elder son. While his brother had been wilful and had kicked over the traces the elder brother had followed the rule of order and reason, showing both prudence and perseverance, two highly desirable qualities. Yet such staid behaviour can have its dangers. A young man or girl who remains aloof for fear of emotional entanglements may one day ruefully complain: 'Why is there so little music and dancing in life?' So, too, with religion. We may rely on reason when emotion needs free rein. Certainly faith needs to be firmly supported by reason, but it cannot be attained, nor can it be conveyed, by argument alone, however forceful. Emotion must be allowed to play its part. 'The heart has its reasons that the reason cannot know.'

So replete with meaning is this parable that the Christian faith may be expounded with it as starting-point, though, since it mentions no mediator between God and man, we cannot speak of it as containing all the essentials of Christian doctrine. It invites our thoughts into far countries of association and imagination. It compels comparison between the relationships portrayed and our own personal and social relationships. Above all, it presents us with a portrayal of the relationship of God to man which, if we fully accept it, must be life-transforming.

It is scarcely possible to stress too strongly the depth and intensity of the word 'Father' as used by Jesus. We cannot take to heart the parable of The Loving Father as we should unless we realize that when He spoke of God in terms of Fatherhood He did so with special restraint. If we take into account the frequency with which Matthew and John changed references to 'God' into 'Father', as critical comparison reveals that they did, we find that apparently Jesus seldom spoke of God in this intimate way except with His immediate disciples. In teaching them to use *Abba*, the child's colloquial address to his father (pp. 11 f), He opened to them the possibility of a deeper communion with God. Manson comments on the remarkable reticence in Jesus' references to the Father: 'The experience of God as Father dominates the whole ministry of Jesus from the Baptism to the Crucifixion . . . His experience of the Father is so profound and so moving that it will not bear to be spoken about, except to those who have fitted themselves to hear. At the same time it shines through His words and deeds in such wise that those who see Him see the Father. By what He is He makes the Father real to men. By being the Son He reveals the Father, so that men see the light of the knowledge of the glory of God in the face of Jesus Christ.'[19] The significance of this revelation of God's nature and relationship to man was at once grasped by Jesus' followers and before long this intimate form of address, '*Abba*, Father' was being used by the first congregations of Christians (Rom. viii. 15; Gal. iv. 6).

The parable depicts the tensions and strains within the individual, families and society, the folly alike of rashness and excessive prudence, the difficulty of reconciling conservative and radical temperaments and policies. We see disharmony and then the restoration of harmony with one son. It may be regarded as an allegory of man's freedom, comparable in some respects to the account in Genesis of man's fall. The father set no restrictions on his sons. They had their loyalties and responsibilities as members of the family, but they were expected to discipline their lives accordingly. Genesis tells of an angel with a flaming sword preventing any return to the Garden, thus representing how irrevocable are some decisions and how inexorable are causal laws, but The Prodigal Son assures us that higher laws prevail in the spiritual sphere. The prodigal is a very earthly son, but the father is an image of the heavenly. Often injuries cannot be compensated, nor insults withdrawn but forgiveness is a way of triumphing over events and altering their consequences, for it is a spiritual grace by which restoration is achieved and sin and error purged. Man could not return to the Garden of innocence, but the prodigal was welcomed and reinstated as a son.[20]

In the two sons we see portrayed much that is characteristic of our age. Some values, such as the recognition of scientific truth, are fully appreciated, but aspects of society betray the estrangement from reality and the waste of human effort depicted in the parable. A high proportion of the world's resources is squandered on the manufacture of armaments. In mass media of communication sexual intercourse as a physical experience is exalted to such an extent over other aspects of the relationship between man and woman that young people can grow up unaware how lovely is love and ignorant that marriage is the mature relationship in which bodily delights are integrated with joy in each other, loyalty, mutual respect, tenderness, devotion and self-giving. Affluence has led to wastefulness, the rapacious exploitation of the earth's resources, the devastation of natural beauty and the disregard of the needs of other forms of life. Lack of restraint threatens the maintenance of gracious living and even the survival of mankind. Strange forms of artistic expression reflect uncertainty, dissatisfaction, restlessness and deracination.

Like many other parables, The Prodigal Son conveys a warning as well as encouragement. In the unregenerate younger son we see selfishness, contempt for established standards, estrangement, loss of self-respect and depersonalization. In the elder son, lovelessness, resentment, joylessness and spiritual destitution. Both failed to appreciate the warmth of love surrounding them. One came to realize it, and we are to believe, responded wholeheartedly, but doubt remains as to the other. We are left in doubt, too, concerning the future of our Prodigal Society. But the parable is not an invitation to ruminate over or philosophize about the future of mankind. Its challenge is personal. It tells of the salvation of one son—for our encouragement, and leaves us in doubt concerning the other— for our admonition.

The supreme message is not a rebuke for man's sinfulness but an assurance of God's love. The parable, indeed, bids us consider where we are going and what sort of people we are, but it invites us, in this challenging age, to accept and use to His glory and the welfare of mankind the blessings which God in His love has so abundantly bestowed upon us.

THE TWO SONS, THE APPRENTICE SON AND THE SLAVE AND SON

Mt. xxi. 28–32; Jn. v. 19–20a; Jn. iii. 35

FATHER AND SON

The parable of The Two Sons proclaims that he who repents and does his duty is a truer son in God's sight than the person who fails to live up to his professions. It has affinities with The Pharisee and the Publican. Doing is more important than saying. Jesus declared that those who did the will of the Father belonged to the family: 'Whoever does the will of my heavenly Father is my brother, my sister, my mother' (Mt. xii. 50). It is not enough to say, 'Lord, Lord' (Mt. vii. 21). Excuses will not avail (Mt. xxv. 41–46), to falter at the plough is a betrayal (Lk. ix. 62), those who say and don't do, who preach without practising will be condemned (Mt. xxiii. 3).[21]

The well-intentioned who fail to carry out their promises or fall down on the job may hinder the carrying out of a project more than if they had given no promises. They are doubly defaulters, breaking their word and failing the cause. Moreover, as The Wedding Feast reminds us, such behaviour is discourteous, causes disappointment and upsets plans. On the other hand, what a joy it is when someone who has refused a request to help turns round and lends a hand. The greater the disappointment the deeper the joy. From our own experience we may get some inkling of the joy in the heart of God when a sinner repents (Lk. xv. 7).

Another brief sonship parable in which, as so often in the parables, two figures are contrasted, is The Apprentice Son. The father reveals to his son the details, known to himself as a master craftsman, of his creative activities. This may be compared with Mt. xi. 27 which, according to Jeremias, means 'only father and son truly know each other'.[22]

In The Slave and Son we are reminded of the honoured and permanent status of a son as compared with the menial and insecure status of a slave. The freedom of the children of God is compared with the slavery of those who are in the bondage of sin—a theme developed further by St. Paul and conspicuous in Church teaching ever since.[23] The contrast is implicit in The Prodigal Son, as we have seen. He exchanged the freedom of his father's household for bondage in an alien land. John reports Jesus as bringing this teaching and that of the parable of The Apprentice Son into relationship with His own Sonship and redemptive mission. It will be recalled that The Son's Request has some of the significance of The Prodigal Son, though lacking its artistic character and profound emotional appeal. If an earthly father can so care for his son, how much more will God care for His children!

THE LOST COIN

Lk. xv. 8–10

Things as Symbols of Supreme Values

The relationship between certain parables, due to similarities in structure, imagery, theme or teaching, is evident, but beyond a certain point the grouping of parables depends on matters of opinion, such as the point which, in any one of them, is held to receive most stress. Also, where preachers, teachers and writers are concerned, expository usefulness may determine the lesson emphasized. Large and rather loose categories have been indicated in our chapter titles and smaller groupings here and there during the discussion. Some writers regard the polemical parables as a large group, others distinguish numerous eschatological parables, yet others point out those which constitute the Gospel of the Outcast. Dodd regards some thirty as 'Parables of the Kingdom', while Hunter brings all into relationship with the Kingdom, its coming, its grace, its crisis and the people concerned in it. We have noted that some may be considered 'twins' (pp. 52, 155), but we must not allow recognition of groupings of this kind to obscure the extent to which the parables are linked together to form an organic unity. Thus, while The Lost Coin and The Lost Sheep may be regarded as twins, we may also consider them, together with The Prodigal Son, to form a triad. If we give due prominence to the stress these parables lay on the importance of the individual we must add the other 'Parables of Sonship' and The Good Samaritan to their number. Thus affinities link parable with parable and group with group. Moreover, we should not neglect the contrasts which bring parables into relationship with one another and stimulate our minds to look deeper into their truths. For instance, degrees of responsiveness are illustrated when we place some parables in series: The Samaritan gives aid without being asked, the father willingly grants his son's request, the neighbour responds to his friend's mportunity, the invited guests decline, the vinedressers respond with violence.

The interpretation of individual parables should not be permitted to obscure the effectiveness of related parables in complementing one another and illustrating different and, sometimes, contrasting aspects of truth. Parables of Growth contrast with Parables of Crisis, Parables of Joy with Parables of Warning, Parables of Importunity with Parables of Compassion. To treat the parables thus is to gain new insights and be reminded of the dangers inherent in the assumption that the meaning of a parable can be summed up in a phrase.

Some parables are designed to appeal primarily to men, others to women. Among such we have The Lost Sheep and The Lost Coin, The Mustard Seed and The Leaven, The Bridegroom's Attendants and The Bride's Attendants; also the saying concerning The Men in the Field and The Women at the Mill (Mt. xxiv. 40 f.). We might add The Patch and the Wineskins (Mt. ix. 16 f.; Mk. ii. 21 f.; Lk. v. 36–39 f.) and, perhaps, The Moth and the Rust (Mt. vi. 19 f.; Lk. xii. 33). The appeal of our Lord to the outcast is abundantly evident, but His concern for all conditions of men is manifested in the appearance in the parables of personalities ranging from king to slave—though, significantly, kings are much less in evidence than in the rabbinic parables.

The loss of a coin, equivalent to her husband's daily wage, was a disaster to the housewife. Taxation levied on the people of Palestine in those days amounted to 40 per cent, or even more, of their income. Little remained to buy necessities.[24] It has been suggested that the coin may have fallen from the woman's head-dress and constituted part of her dowry; but this is not very plausible. Even if it were true it would only add a sentimental touch to the parable and, possibly, a hint of great poverty.

The woman lights a lamp because the window in her home is small to keep out wind and rain and, therefore, admits little light. She sweeps the earthern floor with a palm frond besom, hoping to hear a tinkle or catch a gleam when the coin is disturbed. Her sympathetic neighbours, to whom she has confided her loss, congratulate her when she darts out to tell them that all is well. There will be no unpleasant news to break to her weary husband at the end of the day. The poor everywhere are very ready to share their joys and sorrows with one another.

The Lost Coin may be compared with a parable attributed to a rabbi of the second half of the second century A.D.: 'If thou seekest after the words of the Law as after treasures, God will not withhold from thee thy reward. It is like a man who lost a *sela*, or some other coin in his house, and he lighted a lamp until he found it. If, then, a man kindles many lights seeking that which affords but an hour's pleasure in this world, until he finds it, how much rather shouldest thou dig for the words of the Law which assure thee of life in this world and the next, than for treasures.'[25] This story falls short of The Lost Coin in brevity, clarity and compassion. One speaks of the importance of fulfilling the Law, the other of 'joy among the angels of God over one sinner who repents'. This emphasis on joy illustrates the difference between the teaching of Jesus and the legalistic rabbinic mentality. Again, The Lost Coin is concise and clear while the rabbinic parable is wordy and confusing; a lamp is used to search for something that has been lost and a mattock to dig for it.

To the scholarly and conventionally minded the story may have seemed to be about the comparatively trivial, a woman's lost coin. But it illustrates vividly God's fatherly love for individuals, however poor, or, from the worldly point of view, insignificant. There are no trivial people; nor are other persons' concerns trivial if they are to them anxieties. Only in so far as we are possessed by this outlook do our sympathies reflect, in however feeble a measure, the Divine compassion.

THE LOST SHEEP

Mt. xviii. 12–14; Lk. xv. 4–7

RESPONSIBILITY AS THE INSPIRATION OF CONCERN

We cannot be certain that the twin parables, The Lost Sheep and The Lost Coin, were uttered together. In Luke they are both expressed in an elaborate Semitic poetic form, differing in this respect from The Good Samaritan. Differences in vocabulary indicate that Matthew and Luke each obtained the parable from his own special source. In Matthew the stress is on the persistent search, while in Luke it is on the joy of the shepherd. Scholars disagree as to whether the original emphasis was on bringing encouragement to the needy, downtrodden and under-privileged or on reproof of the wealthy, well-educated and selfish for their disregard of them; but this problem arises from the acceptance of two assumptions, that parables are primarily polemical and that they are one-pointed. There is a measure of truth in both of these, as we have seen (pp. 38, 169); but relying too much on them may lead us astray. The individual hearer of a parable must interpret it as it 'speaks to his condition'. Because of its associative richness a parable, whatever the primary meaning, and however careful the attention to be given to this, may yet have other meanings which should not be neglected. Moreover, as a coin has two faces, both of which have significance, so a parable such as this has its obverse and its reverse. A message which gives encouragement to outcasts may also be a warning to those who neglect or oppress them. So it is with all three Parables of the Lost. To concentrate attention on their original settings, however important this may be in some respects, can distract attention from what is even more important, their spiritual and moral lessons. If we are to realize fully these spiritual lessons we need to consider the three parables together and so perceive how they complement one another.

No doubt Jesus told the three parables on different occasions and to different audiences, but He may well have intended to use them to emphasize different points in His teaching. For our purpose of comparing their teaching we may glance at some significant distinctions between them. We pass from the inanimate coin to the living animal, from the creaturely to the personal, from the predicament of a lost animal to the tragedy of a lost soul, from the searching shepherd, representing God's concern for the lost, to the welcoming father symbolizing His love. We have a sequence—object, animal, person; coin, creature, convert. The woman sought the coin because of its value, the shepherd the sheep because of his feeling of responsibility for it, the father welcomed the lad back because of his love for him. Each parable has its special point, but each lacks something contained in the others. The three parables take us increasingly far afield, from the home to the hillside, and then to the 'distant country'. The woman with her small hoard represents the poor, the shepherd with his flock the 'comfortably off', the father with his farm and 'paid servants' men of substance.

Compared with the parable of The Lost Coin the parable of The Lost Sheep shows accentuation of certain aspects, as in The Mustard Seed and The Leaven (pp. 52–58). The sheep is more valuable than the coin, the shepherd's area of search wider and his efforts more arduous than the housewife's. That he should go to more trouble to search for a much smaller proportion of his property emphasizes the depth of feeling impelling him. In all three parables the seeker is concerned for the lost, whether a coin which cannot feel itself lost or a living creature which can. Earlier commentators compared the coin to the ignorant sinner, the sheep to the stupid sinner and the son to the wilful sinner. Jesus saw tragedy even in the lostness of inanimate things; how much more in the forlornness of a sheep, and even more in the lostness of a man. Other sayings of His confirm how strongly he felt the tragic wastefulness of loss. 'Collect the pieces left over so that nothing be lost' (Jn. vi. 12); 'Salt is good but if salt hath lost his saltness wherewith shall it be salted?' (Mt. v. 13; Mk. ix. 50). The tragedy of the Prodigal Son lay in that for a time he became a wastrel.

The corollary of the tragedy of lostness is the supreme importance of seeking and saving the lost. Jesus stated His mission to be just this: 'I was sent to the lost sheep of the house of Israel' (Mt. xv. 24). 'Surely a man is worth far more than a sheep!' (Mt. xii. 12). He said: 'The Son of Man has come to seek and to save what is lost' (Lk. xix. 10), and 'I did not come to invite virtuous people, but sinners' (Mt. ix. 13; Mk. ii. 17; Lk. v. 32). This saying was significantly linked with a proverbial reference to a doctor's efforts to heal the sick, implying that sin is a sickness of the soul. How contrary to this teaching are the views of some self-styled humanists who regard, not sin, but the feeling of guilt and pangs of conscience, as unhealthy.

Matthew's version of the parable may be closer than Luke's to the original, at least so far as the phrase 'if he should find it' is concerned; for Luke's 'until he has found it' suggests that he was as likely to find it as the woman to discover the coin in her one-roomed cottage, though perhaps Luke's phrase is designed to call our attention to his resolute pertinacity. Luke gives more realistic detail, describing how the sheep was brought home on the shepherd's shoulders and the ensuing jubilation.[26]

Counting the flock in the evening was, and is, customary routine for a shepherd. Only when the flock has been rounded up can the number be ascertained. The first Dead Sea Scrolls were discovered by a shepherd lad who had counted his flock at 11 a.m. and noticed that a goat was missing. He had failed to make the routine check the previous evening. If the shepherd of the parable went off at once to look for the sheep, as his great concern for it would lead us to suppose, he would be taking risks by setting out at dusk, for after dark he might catch a foot in the fissured limestone or fall off a crag.[27] According to Matthew he leaves the flock 'on the hill-side', but in Luke he leaves the sheep 'in the open pasture', the 'wilderness', perhaps in an enclosure or in charge of one or more of his friends. When he returns he rejoices 'with friends and neighbours', a natural reaction if he had left companions at the sheepfold. Some scholars have suggested that these words were added by the

Evangelist to bring the parable into line with the others. But such repetition was a feature of oral teaching and might well have been used by our Lord in instructing His disciples. Here, as elsewhere, joy is pictured as shared, and rejoicing is shown as a community activity (Rom. xii. 15). The emphasis on joy after anxiety and sorrow unites the three parables and adds to their depth of meaning.

The lostness of the sheep lay particularly in the deprivation of the opportunity to express its essential nature. A sheep, in contrast to a cat, which walks alone, is a highly social animal. Removed from the flock it is not a real sheep at all. An isolated sheep becomes bewildered and even neurotic unless like Mary's lamb in the nursery rhyme, it can direct its social instincts towards a human being. It would be necessary for the shepherd to carry a sheep in this condition as it would not get to its feet and walk. Man's lostness is all the more devastating because he is the most social of all higher animals, and his search for community cannot be assuaged with less than fellowship with God and man. Naturally, therefore, these parables culminate in community jubilation: 'There is joy among the angels of God over one sinner who repents.'

B. T. D. Smith, commenting on these parables, says, 'What was certainly new in Christ's teaching was His belief that it was God's will that the sinner should be *sought* and not merely mourned for.' Moreover, a distinguished Jewish scholar has pointed out that God is here revealed as a 'seeking God'. 'What is new and startling in the teaching of Jesus is that this process of repentance takes an *active* turn. Man is bidden not merely to receive the penitent gladly but to *seek out* the sinner, to try to redeem him, and *make* him penitent.'[28] It is all too apparent that we are living today in an age of perplexity and muddled morals when lostness is widespread. Seekers of the lost were never more needed.

THE SHEPHERD, THE THIEF AND THE DOORKEEPER

Jn. x. 1–18

THE FAITHFUL SHEPHERD

It was natural that so familiar a figure as the shepherd should become prominent in Hebrew thought. The prophets used the image to suggest God's watchful care for His people. Handel's 'Messiah' has made Deutero-Isaiah's prophecy familiar to all: 'Behold, the Lord God shall come as a mighty one, and his arm shall rule for him; behold his reward is with him, and his recompense before him. He shall feed his flock like a shepherd, he shall gather the lambs in his arm, and carry them in his bosom, and shall gently lead those that are with young' (Isa. xl. 10 f.). Jeremiah (xxxi. 9 f.) depicted the joy which would follow the nation's tribulations: 'I will cause them to walk by rivers of waters in a straight way, wherein they shall not stumble: for I am a father to Israel and Ephraim is my firstborn. Hear the word of the Lord, O ye nations, and declare it in the isles afar off, and say, He that scattered Israel will gather him, and keep him, as a shepherd doth his flock.' Again, 'I will set up shepherds over them which shall feed them: and they shall fear no more, nor be dismayed, neither shall they be lacking, saith the Lord' (Jer. xxiii. 4). Ezekiel expanded the imagery of shepherd and sheep, speaking of faithless shepherds contrasted with God as shepherd of His people: 'Behold, I myself, even I, will search for my sheep, and will seek them out. . . . I will seek that which was lost and bring again that which was driven away, and will bind up that which was broken and will strengthen that which was sick. . . . And ye my sheep, the sheep of my pasture, are men, and I will be your God, saith the Lord God.' In the last verse of Psalm cxix. the Lord is depicted seeking for the lost sheep. Several of our best-known hymns are paraphrases of Psalm xxiii. or embody its imagery.

These familiar passages should not make us forgetful that the shepherd image is used with a different emphasis in some contexts of the Old Testament. Amos (iii. 12) pictures the plight to which

Israel has been reduced by its rebellion against God. All that will be left will be like the remains of a sheep after the lion had mauled it. In Isaiah xliv. 28, Cyrus is spoken of as the Lord's shepherd. Zechariah (x. 17) condemns the 'worthless shepherd that leaveth the flock'. Thus the Old Testament contrasts God as the Good Shepherd watchful over His flock with human rulers who act as faithless shepherds.

With such plentiful traditional associations the shepherd metaphor was used and further enriched by Jesus, both in His teaching about God's care for the lost, recorded in the Synoptic Gospels, and in teaching about His own mission, as recorded by John. Christians have continued to use this symbolism ever since. In the New Testament the writer to the Hebrews (xiii. 20) speaks of 'our Lord Jesus, the great Shepherd of the sheep' and in I Peter (ii. 25) He is 'the Shepherd and Guardian of your souls' and 'the Head Shepherd'. The leaders of the Church are exhorted to 'tend that flock of God whose shepherds you are' (v. 2 ff.).

It is almost impossible to exaggerate the influence of the shepherd symbol on the Christian imagination through the centuries. In the Roman catacombs Jesus was depicted as the Good Shepherd. Such representations were characteristic expressions of the early Church and have continued to the present day.[29] Many churches have been dedicated to the Good Shepherd and the bishop's pastoral staff is a reminder of the relationship between God and man, pastor and his flock. If we take into consideration the Good Shepherd symbol together with the symbolism of the Lamb of God in literature, visual art, ritual, hymns and musical settings we must assess their influence doctrinally and imaginatively as second only to that of the Cross.

In the parables, or series of parables, in John x., not only is there a reminiscence of the unfaithful shepherd of Ezekiel xxxiv, but the Synoptic imagery also reappears—the Shepherd, the Door and the Thief. It might seem that this recurrence of the Synoptic imagery is to be accounted for by the Evangelist's reflections on the records in the other Gospels. The attractiveness of such an explanation depends on the view adopted as to the nature of the Fourth Gospel —a vexed problem which cannot be discussed here. However, it may be mentioned that in recent years scholarly opinion has moved towards attaching greater value to it as an historical record. Dodd concludes 'that behind the Fourth Gospel lies an ancient tradition independent of the other gospels, and meriting serious consideration as a contribution to our knowledge of the historical facts concerning Jesus Christ'. This tradition can be shown to belong to the same reservoir of tradition as was drawn upon by the Synoptics. In regard to The Shepherd, the Thief, and the Doorkeeper he agrees with the Bishop of Woolwich (J. A. T. Robinson) who finds it to be two fragmented parables fused into one, the first ending with 'the doorkeeper admits him' (verse 3a), the second consisting of 3b–5, its opening possibly having been lost. In the latter the Shepherd and the Stranger are placed in contrast while in the former the contrast is between the Shepherd and the Thief. As we have seen, contrasted characters are typical of the Synoptic parables. Dodd also points out that the third character, setting off the contrast between the other two, approximates to the pattern of The Two Sons (Mt. xxi. 28–31) and The Prodigal Son (Lk. xv. 11–32).[30] Moreover, here, as elsewhere, the relationship between flock and shepherd reflects accurate knowledge of shepherding, the leadership and control of the flock, the appreciation by the shepherd of the individual characteristics of the sheep, the shepherd's concern for each animal and the plight of shepherdless sheep or a flock confronted by a stranger.

Again, as in the Nature Parables, the Shepherd Parables are redolent of the Palestinian countryside. We catch glimpses of scenes familiar to our Lord and the little crowds which gathered around Him. Even today, in the remoter parts of Europe and in North Africa and the Middle East one may see the shepherd with his flock, recalling the pictures of pastoral life in the Gospels, though trained dogs to aid the shepherd do not belong to the Biblical scene.[31]

According to what John tells us in verse 22 'it was winter'. At this season hungry wolves descend from their mountain and forest fastnesses to prowl around sheepfolds. In Italy, central Europe and elsewhere they sometimes enter villages in search of prey. There may be an association of thought between winter and the wolves mentioned in verses 12 and 13. If so, we have a particularly realistic reference to the shepherd's life. In II Ezra iv. 5–18 we hear of a faithless shepherd leaving his flock to the wolves.

Possibly the illustrative use of the figure of the shepherd by Jesus may have surprised or even shocked rabbinic circles. The shepherd's profession had long been regarded as menial and sheep were often tended by slaves. In patriarchal times responsibility for the flock was delegated to a younger son, or even, sometimes, to a daughter (I Sam. xvii. 13, 15; Gen. xxix. 9). The Pharisees included shepherds in their category of 'sinners' and in later Judaism shepherds were deprived of civil rights. Rabbis were puzzled that God could be called 'my shepherd' in the 23rd. Psalm. Moreover, the term acquired some military and political overtones.[32]

It is difficult to assess the extent to which such ideas were typical of, or confined to, certain sophisticated circles. Villagers, or even townsfolk, dependent on pastoral activities, can hardly have held shepherds in the contempt which some allusions might suggest, but in so far as derogatory opinions were current, additional significance might be perceived in the parable of The Lost Sheep and other references to sheep and shepherds by those who recognized in Jesus 'the friend of publicans and sinners' (Mt. xi. 19; Lk. vii. 34). Dodd and some other scholars detect in the sayings we are considering a challenge to the Jewish leaders. Certainly these authorities are viewed by the Evangelist as the successors of the unfaithful shepherds of the prophets. In the preceding chapter, they are represented as callous and spiritually blind—no better than 'hirelings'. In contrast, according to the explanation of the sayings, the Good Shepherd knows His sheep individually and is also the way, or entrance, into Life.[33]

THE DOCTOR AND THE SICK

Mt. ix. 12; Mk. ii. 17; Lk. v. 31 f.

HEALING OF BODY AND SOUL

This saying recalls Jesus' declaration in the synagogue at Nazareth that His ministry would be a ministry of healing (Lk. iv. 16 ff.). We must not think of healing in the terms customary today as a specialized medical matter, but rather picture the Good Physician in terms of the Good Samaritan who dealt with the whole predicament and not only with the man's wounds. In first-century Palestine there was no clear-cut division between bodily, mental, social and spiritual ills and any disability could affect a person's standing in society to such an extent that his miseries might extend to all four spheres. This is apparent when we reflect on the dreadful plight of the leper. Bodily suffering was generally thought to be punishment for sin (Lk. xiii. 1–5) and mental infirmity indicated demon possession so that even spiritual consolation was denied. The reading from Deutero-Isaiah was therefore our Lord's claim to be the Good Physician in terms of healing in the fullest sense as then understood—restoration to harmony within oneself and society, a promise of hope for the diseased, the misfits, the soul-sick, sin-oppressed and mentally disorientated, in a word, the 'heavy-laden' (Mt. xi. 28). Thus in His ministry forgiveness, bodily and mental healing, and restoration to active life within society were inseparable. His healing was essentially restoration to spiritual tranquillity, sanity of mind, soundness of body and social status—fellowship with God and man. Among the figures representing the saviours of the lost in the Gospels we must place the physician together with the shepherd and the fisherman (Mt. iv. 19; Mk. i. 17). If we seek in the parables for a glimpse of the good physician at work he is to be found tending a wounded man on the road to Jericho. Today, medical science has made it possible for magnificent healing work to be done to relieve man's various ills, but the ills of society are apparent, happy integration of the whole man in harmony with his fellows is elusive, the ideal of full restoration as exemplified in our Lord's ministry was never more needed.

THE GREAT ASSIZE

OR

THE SHEEP AND THE GOATS

Mt. xxv. 31–46

GRACIOUS GOODNESS CONTRASTED WITH SINS OF OMISSION

This drama or allegory of Judgement, which C. G. Montefiore (p. 152) regarded as 'one of the noblest passages in the entire Gospel' is, as we have it, an apocalyptic vision rather than a parable, but the description of the separation of the sheep from the goats brings it within the group of parabolic sayings in which the shepherd appears. The simile is true to life. Where grazing is sparse, as in arid areas of Palestine, North Africa and, in Europe, the Camargue in southern France, goats are run with sheep because, being more restless they feed more actively and thus keep the whole flock on the move so that grazing is more efficient. Although goats might appear to be more hardy than sheep they need shelter at night, and so they are divided from them in the evening.

In contrast to docile sheep which, as lambs, are often kept as pets, goats have long been suspected of affinities with the powers of evil. Just as the god of Ekron, Baalzebul or Beelzebub, became for the Jews the Prince of Demons (II Kings, i. 2; Mt. ix. 16; Mk. iii. 22) so it seems that the horned god of the ancient cultures of the Middle East was transformed in Hebrew thought into a devil. The ritual expulsion of the sin-bearing goat (Lev. xvi. 20–22) suggests this transition; and our use of 'scapegoat', the connexion of goats with witchcraft, and the horns and cloven hooves in traditional representations of the devil illustrate how tenacious are such associations. For quite different reasons ecologists regard the goat as an evil beast. It has reduced great areas of the world to quasi-desert conditions.

This narrative has characteristics distinguishing it from other parables and the material in it is generally agreed to have been subject to modification. But Jeremias endorses Manson's comment that it exhibits 'features of such startling originality that it is difficult to credit them to anyone but the Master Himself' and Preiss remarks that it is highly likely that these are 'the words of Jesus Himself'.[34] The pastoral simile is true to life and is in keeping with the shepherd imagery characteristic of our Lord's teaching. It includes technical terms used by shepherds. We have a vivid picture of the Judgement as like the separation of sheep and goats. The animals have been running together freely but in the evening they are parted, some to the right and some to the left. If we place The Tares, The Net, The Sheep and the Goats and The Bride's Attendants together we have four Parables of Selection in which plants, fish, mammals and people are respectively involved.

There is a vagueness concerning the rôles of the King and the Father which is not inappropriate to an apocalyptic scene but awakens the suspicion that we are dealing with a composite narrative or, at least, one which has been modified. The Bishop of Woolwich has pointed out that the story reflects three passages: Mk. ix. 37, Mt. x. 42, and Lk. xii. 8 f.: 'Whoever receives one of these children in my name,' He said, 'receives Me; and whoever receives Me receives not Me but the One who sent Me.' 'And if anyone gives so much as a cup of cold water to one of these little ones, because he is a disciple of mine, I tell you this; that man will assuredly not go unrewarded.' 'I tell you this: everyone who acknowledges Me before men, the Son of man will acknowledge before the angels of God; but he who disowns Me before men will be disowned before the angels of God.' The bishop believes that Matthew has skilfully woven these together with other features such as the figure of the shepherd, thus making the passage an allegory of the Last Judgement linked with the Parousia.[35]

This ingenious reconstruction attributes to Matthew greater ingenuity than some would concede, but it illustrates, together with other texts which could be cited, how effectively The Sheep and the Goats presents in dramatic form a great deal of our Lord's teaching. Perhaps Matthew may have depicted the Judgement as of 'all the nations' (verse 32), but the scene of Judgement is a spacious one and represents the fundamentals of God's relationship to man and of man's relationship to his fellows in the light of our Lord's doctrine, with, however, the qualification which appears below. The narrative embodies the teaching of a number of parables, those dealing with Warning and Opportunity and Parables of Compassion. We find in it a reminder that, however we may scrutinize the parables, we do not judge them. They judge us. In those rejected we see figures like the priest and Levite who failed to tend and clothe the naked, and the Rich Man who let Lazarus die on his doorstep but was doomed to crave for the drops of cold water he had not thought to give him. We see the self-satisfied who concentrate on building bigger barns and the unforgiving who recompense mercy with oppression. They are the people of any nation, especially the wilfully blind, who do not recognize their King in their needy fellow men.

The story contrasts with others having some affinities with it. In the Egyptian Book of the Dead and rabbinic tales souls at the Judgement proclaim their good works and argue that they merit reward. They declare: 'I have given satisfaction to God by doing that in which He delights; I have given bread to the hungry, water to the thirsty, clothed the naked . . .' In Jewish commentaries we find a similar point of view. But in The Great Assize the righteous are so far from self-righteousness that they are astonished at the verdict. Their lives have so naturally expressed compassion for others that their virtue has become unselfconscious. They have the purity of heart of those who see God. Such absolute, gracious, self-giving is God's ideal for man. It is of God's own nature, the expression of His love.

On a superficial reading it might seem that the consignment of the unrighteous to 'eternal punishment' in the allegory conflicts with Christ's revelation of God's love and St. John's moving proclamation of that love (I Jn. iv. 7–21), but more careful consideration shows that this is not so. We must have regard to Matthew's tendency to add a note of melodramatic threat to parables and also allow for the pervasive contrast-thinking of the parables. Artistic necessity demands that eternal punishment be opposed to eternal bliss, as in The Rich Man and Lazarus. Man's responsibility for others and the consequences of neglect must be depicted in the starkest terms—and man's lack of charity to man throughout the centuries indicates that even such warnings can be ineffective. But, having been shown in the parable that heaven judges compassion to be the supreme virtue possessed by souls on earth, we cannot regard the judgement on the sinners as absolute and final (pp. 141 f.). It is only so within its artistic and dramatic framework. If mercy should rank above judgement among men as we are shown it should, it must be paramount in heaven. If lack of compassion is an earthly sin it cannot be a heavenly virtue. In our Lord's teaching, notably the parable of The Prodigal Son, judgement is subordinate to mercy and forgiveness.

The Great Assize is concerned with more than judgement and mercy. It depicts the reciprocity between earth and heaven, the temporal and the eternal. What the souls were on earth is revealed in the light of heaven; what heaven is appears in the criterion of compassion by which the souls are judged. It is because heavenly light pierces earthly gloom and is reflected in human affairs that earthly stories can possess and express heavenly meanings. The earthly is enriched by the heavenly and is able to reflect its splendours. So earthly stories, like other earthly things, can reflect heavenly things; they can be sacramental, showing forth heavenly grace. 'In the words of the Lord are His works' (Ecclus. xlii. 15).

All life is the acting out of a parable, for life is an earthly story with a heavenly meaning. It is so because God is the Storyteller. His heavenly stories have an earthly meaning. God spoke in Creation, in the Word made Flesh and is ever speaking in and through men.

NOTES TO INTRODUCTION

1. Scholars agree in emphasizing the high importance of the parables, as indicated by the following representative quotations: 'There is no part of the Gospel tradition in which we can be surer of our contact with the mind of Jesus than the tradition of the parables' (J. Denney, *Expositor*, 1911, p. 136). 'Of all the Christian tradition it is perhaps the parables, with their kindly, intimate presentation of human character, their humour and their irony, which reveal to us most clearly Jesus of Nazareth' (B. T. D. Smith, *The Parables of the Synoptic Gospels*, Cambridge, 1937, p. 60). 'They have upon them, taken as a whole, the stamp of a highly individual mind. . . . Their appeal to the imagination fixed them in the memory and gave them a secure place in the tradition. Certainly there is no part of the Gospel record which has for the reader a clearer ring of authenticity' (C. H. Dodd, *The Parables of the Kingdom*, rev. edn, 1961, p. 13). The same writer comments: 'It is generally recognized that the parables as a whole have a strikingly individual style and character, which encourages the belief that they belong to the most original and authentic part of the tradition' (*History and the Gospel*, rev. edn 1964, p. 61). 'The student of the parables of Jesus, as they have been transmitted to us in the first three Gospels, may be confident that he stands upon a particularly firm foundation. The parables are a fragment of the original rock of tradition'. . . . 'In reading the parables we are dealing with a particularly trustworthy tradition, and are brought into immediate relation with Jesus' (J. Jeremias, *The Parables of Jesus*, rev. edn, 1963, pp. 11 f.).*

2. This attitude of mind can be more readily understood when we recall the supposed virtues and vices of animals, including fictitious

* The place of publication of books is London unless otherwise indicated. When only one work by an author is cited references after the first are indicated by name and page. When several of an author's works are quoted references subsequent to the first are by name and date. References by name and page to Dodd and Jeremias apply to their works on the parables. With a few exceptions New Testament quotations are from the New English Bible, by permission of the Cambridge and Oxford University Presses.

creatures, described in the Physiologus and mediaeval bestiaries which were long used as edifying embellishments in sermons and homiletic works.

It must also be remembered that Oriental thought, and to some extent mediaeval theology did not make the clear distinctions demanded by more recent Western thinkers between history and myth, fact and edifying story. This must be taken into account in interpreting accounts of Biblical miracles and prodigies attributed to the saints.

3. Augustine, *Quaestiones Evangeliorum*, ii. 19.

4. M. Adolfini, 'L'interpretazione delle parabole', in *Rivist. Bib.*, 9 (1961), pp. 97–111, has reviewed the various factors responsible for allegorization becoming popular and persisting so long.

5. C. E. van Koetsveld, *De Gelijkenissen van den Zaligmaker*, Schoonhoven, 1869; A. Jülicher, *Die Gleichnisreden Jesu*, Tübingen, 1890 (= 1910).

6. Cf. the works of P. Fiebig, *Rabbinische Gleichnisse*, Leipzig, 1934; *Die Gleichnisreden Jesu im Lichte der rabbinischen Gleichnisse des neutestamentlichen Zeitalters*, Tübingen, 1902; H. L. Strack and P. Billerbeck, *Kommentar zur Neuen Testament aus Talmud und Midrasch*, Munich, 1922–61 (in future cited as Bill.).

7. C. F. D. Moule, *The Birth of the New Testament*, 1962; R. Bultmann, *The History of the Synoptic Tradition*, Oxford, 1963.

8. S. O. Duilearga, 'Irish tales and story-tellers' in *Märchen, Mythos, Dichtung: Festschrift zum 90. Geburtstag Friedrich von Leyens*, Munich, 1963, pp. 63–82.

9. N. Morris, *The Jewish School*, 1937, p. 117. Cf. B. Gerhardsson, *Memory and Manuscript*, Uppsala, 1961; *Tradition and Transmission in Early Christianity*, Uppsala, 1964, pp. 197–199; M. Smith, 'The Dead Sea sect in relation to ancient Judaism', *New Test. Studies*, 7 (1961), pp. 347–360.

10. C. F. Burney, *The Poetry of our Lord*, Oxford, 1925; M. Black, *An Aramaic Approach to the Gospels and Acts*, Oxford, 1954; J. Jeremias, *The Sermon on the Mount*, 1961; H. Riesenfeld, *The Gospel Tradition and its Beginnings*, Uppsala, 1957; A. Finkel, *The Pharisees and the Teacher of Nazareth*, Leiden, 1964; *The Poems of Jesus*, edited by Dom Robert Petitpierre, 1965.

11. Eusebius, *H.E.*, iii. 39, cit. in J. Stevenson, *A New Eusebius*, 1957, p. 50; Irenaeus, *Adversus Haereses*, iv. 26.

12. C. W. F. Smith, *The Jesus of the Parables*, Philadelphia, 1948, p. 297; C. F. D. Moule, 'The parables of Jesus and the Lord of faith', *Religion in Education*, 28 (1961), pp. 60–64.

13. T. W. Manson, *The Teaching of Jesus*, 1935, pp. 105 ff., 207; F. Käsemann, *Essays on New Testament Themes*, 1964, pp. 37, 41.

14. J. Jeremias, 'The Lord's Prayer in modern research', *Expository Times*, 71 (1959–60), pp. 141–146; *The Central Message of the New Testament*, 1965, pp. 9–30; W. Marchel, ' "Abba, Pater." Oratio Christi et christianorum', *Verb. Dom.*, 39 (1961), pp. 240–247.

15. A. Nygren, *Agape and Eros*, 1953.

16. I. Abrahams, *Studies in Pharisaism and the Gospels*, I, Cambridge, 1917, p. 99.

17. B. T. D. Smith, p. 15. Cf. G. V. Jones, *The Art and Truth of the Parables*, 1964.

18. The following stories are included in a list of Old Testament parables compiled by Manson, 1935: The Ewe Lamb, II Sam. xii. 1–14; The Two Brethren and The Avengers of Blood, II Sam. xiv. 1–11; The Escaped Prisoner, I Kings xx. 35–40; The Vineyard and the Grapes, Isa. v. 1–7; The Eagles and the Vine, Ezek. xvii. 3–10; The Lion Whelps, Ezek. xix. 2–9; The Vine, Ezek. xix. 10–14; The Forest Fire, Ezek. xx. 45–49; The Seething Pot, Ezek. xxiv. 3–5. Cf. A. S. Herbert, 'The "Parable" (Māsāl) in the Old Testament', *Scot. Journ. Theol.*, 7 (1954), pp. 180–196. 'Many Oriental parables are expanded proverbs' (Abrahams, I, p. 98).

19. Josephus, *Antiquities*, xiii. 10. 6, xvii. i. 4. Cf. J. Z. Lauterbach, 'The Pharisees and their teachings', *Hebrew Union College Annual*, 6 (1929), pp. 69–139.

20. A. T. Cadoux, *The Parables of Jesus; their Art and Use*, 1931, New York, p. 13.

21. F. J. Foakes-Jackson and K. Lake, *The Beginnings of Christianity*, 1920–33, I, i., p. 32; Bill., II, pp. 182, 569.

22. In order to show that this position is widely accepted quotations from a number of authorities are appended. Although there is a consensus of opinion on this matter the implications for the interpretation of the parables are not always appreciated.

The NEB translators have relegated to a footnote the reading which ascribes to the Pharisees the accusation that Jesus cast out devils by the prince of devils (Mt. ix. 34) as it is missing from some important manuscripts.

B. T. D. Smith (p. 209), referring to Mt. xxi. 28–32, remarks that the setting involving high priests and elders has been supplied by Matthew. J. C. Fenton notes in *Saint Matthew* (*Penguin Gospel Commentary*, 1963, pp. 11, 364 ff.): 'Matthew's Gospel contains a strongly anti-Jewish note running through it'. . . . 'The scribes and Pharisees are used as lay-figures or representatives of practical atheism.' Manson (1935, p. 36), commenting on the material peculiar to Matthew, remarks that the violence of the abuse of the scribes and Pharisees 'raises the suspicion that there is more here than Jesus said'. W. E. Bundy (*Jesus and the First Three Gospels*, Cambridge, Mass., 1955, pp. 446 f.) remarks of Mt. xxiii: 'The extreme bitterness of these indictments may reflect the antipathies between the later Christian church and the Jewish synagogue rather than Jesus' own personal feelings toward the scribes and Pharisees.' B. H. Streeter (*The Four Gospels*, 1936, p. 253) stated that it read like 'an early Jewish–Christian polemical pamphlet'. D. E. Nineham (*Saint Mark*, Penguin Gospel Commentary, 1963, p. 334) referring to Mk. xii. 38–40, comments: 'In general the passage must be regarded as altogether too sweeping and unqualified in its attack on the scribes as a class.' He cites Bundy with approval: 'Scribes and Pharisees appear or disappear just as the compiler wants them. They are part of the stage property and scenery.' The bitter opposition of the Pharisees recorded in Mk. ii. and iii. can hardly have arisen so early in the ministry as the Evangelist suggests (D. H. Smith, 'Concerning the duration of the ministry of Jesus', *Expository Times*, 76 (1965), pp. 114–116). Others have pointed out how improbable is the appearance of the Pharisees in Mk. ii. 15–17. Commenting on the Woes in Lk. xi. 37–54, G. B. Caird writes in *Saint Luke* (*Penguin Gospel Commentary*, 1963, p. 158): 'It is unlikely that Jesus ever delivered a single great harangue such as this against the Pharisees, and still more unlikely that He did it while a guest in a Pharisee's house.' In reference to Lk. xvi. 14 C. G. Montefiore (*Synoptic Gospels*, 1927, II, p. 533) remarks: 'It is only one more of the attacks by which the Evangelists seek to blacken their Jewish opponents.' He regards Lk. xvi. 1 f. as merely an editorial *mise en scène* (p. 520). T. W. Manson (*Sayings of Jesus*, Cambridge, 1949, pp. 52 f.) agreed that the Evangelists show anti-Jewish bias. R. Bultmann (pp. 52 f.) states: 'There is an active tendency to represent the opponents of Jesus as scribes and Pharisees' and he supports this by citing a number of allusions which, in his opinion, cannot be original. Vincent Taylor (*Gospel according to Saint Mark*, 1952, p. 494), referring to the same passage, says that it reveals the strong anti-Jewish views of the Roman Church at that time. The bias in John is against 'the Jews' rather than the Pharisees. They are mentioned seventy times, the Pharisees twenty times (R. H. Lightfoot, *St. John's Gospel: A Commentary*, Oxford, 1956, p. 64). In the so-called Gospel of Thomas the Pharisees and scribes are blamed for hiding the keys of knowledge, but in the corresponding context in Lk. xi. 52 only the scribes are mentioned. The Dead Sea Scrolls are highly critical of the orthodox Jewish religious leaders.

There were two schools of Pharisees, the zealous, strict disciples of Shammai and the gentler adherents of the school of Hillel. Aspects of their doctrine were close to the teaching of Jesus. It must be assumed, therefore, that His criticisms were directed against the former. Cf. J. Z. Lauterbach, 1929; A. Finkel, *The Pharisees and the Teacher of Nazareth*, Leiden, 1964; L. Finkelstein, *The Pharisees: The Sociological Background to their Faith*[3], Philadelphia, 1962.

23. J. Jeremias, *The Sermon on the Mount*, 1961, pp. 22 f.

24. *Paradiso*, i. 100.

25. To believe that many parables inculcated general moral principles and truths concerning spiritual realities, as distinct from being condemnatory of those with views opposed to our Lord's teaching, does not imply that all the moralizing or homiletic comments at the close of parables as they have come down to us are from His lips. In a number of instances they almost certainly are not, but have been added by a Christian teacher or preacher. Jeremias (pp. 110–112) lists fifteen parables and similes with generalizing conclusions: The Lamp (Mk. iv. 22), The Measure (Mk. iv. 25), The Doorkeeper (Mk. xiii. 37), The Labourers in the Vineyard (Mt. xx. 16a, 16b), The Wicked Husbandmen (Mt. xxi. 44; Lk. xx. 18), The Wedding Feast (Mt. xxii. 14), The Ten Virgins (Mt. xxv. 13), The Talents and The Pounds (Mt. xxv. 29 par; Lk. xix. 26), The New Wine (Lk. v. 39), The Friend begging for Help (The Importunate Neighbour) (Lk. xi. 10), The Rich Fool (Lk. xii. 21), The Servant entrusted with Authority (Lk. xii. 48b), The Dishonest (Unjust) Steward (Lk. xvi. 10, xvi. 13), Pharisees and Publicans (Lk. xviii. 14b). A. M. Hunter (*Interpreting the Parables*, 1964, pp. 119 f.) adds The Tower Builder and The Warring King (Lk. xiv. 33).

26. Manson, 1949, p. 260; Jeremias, pp. 115, 202.

27. C. H. Dodd, *History and the Gospel*, rev. edn, 1964, pp. 63–72.

28. Jones, pp. 136 ff. Cf. pp. 107 f.

29. 'With one doubtful exception (The Two Debtors), the original setting of none of the parables and similitudes appears to have been preserved in the Christian tradition' (B. T. D. Smith, 1937, p. 49).

30. Jerome, *In Eccles*.

31. There are interesting and puzzling associations between some parables and passages of the Old Testament. Echoes of II Chron. xxviii. 15 occur in The Good Samaritan and in The Dishonest Steward and The Rich Man and Lazarus there are veiled allusions to Abraham's Steward Eliezer (p. 212). Perhaps such associations presuppose a greater imaginative and recollective liveliness on the part of our Lord's hearers than we are accustomed to attribute to them. It has been said:

'It is extremely likely that Jesus availed Himself of didactic methods which relied upon a copious memory of the sacred writings and their fanciful traditional embroideries The less literate His hearers the more likely they were to know the tales and utterly unhistorical associations of ideas in which the rabbis then and since have delighted. . . . Jesus may have been using existing habits of association at which none of His hearers would be astonished' (J. D. M. Derrett, 'Fresh light on St. Luke xvi; II. Dives and Lazarus and the preceding sayings.' *New Test. Studies*, vii., 7, 1961, pp. 364–380).

32. E. Sitwell, *The Sleeping Beauty*, 1924, p. 66.

33. *Collected Poems*, Dublin, 1964, p. 110.

34. M. Black, *An Aramaic Approach to the Gospels and Acts*, 1954, pp. 123, 157.

35. These and other suggestions are discussed by T. A. Burkill, 'The cryptology of parables in St. Mark's Gospel', *Novum. Test.*, I (1956), pp. 246–262. Cf. L. Cerfaux, 'La connaissance des secrets du royaume d'après Matt. xiii. 11 et parallèles', *Novum. Test.*, I (1956), pp. 238–246. Nineham (pp. 136 ff.) conjectures that if the saying is not due to the early Church it may have arisen from a comment by Jesus that only His disciples understood Him and His mission—as the prophets had foretold. Later, through a mistranslation, the saying may have been regarded as applying to the parables. The admonition, 'If you have ears to hear, then hear' inserted after this and another parable and also after two similes may indicate uncertainty on the part of the Evangelists as to their application. It appears after five parables in Thomas, the compiler of which wished to give them, or supposed them to have, a gnostic interpretation.

36. Manson, 1935, p. 65.

37. Estimates of the number of parables vary according to different concepts of what constitutes a parable. Trench discusses thirty, Jeremias forty-one, Jülicher lists fifty-three, Hunter sixty, B. T. D. Smith sixty-two and Manson sixty-five. I. H. Marshall, in *Eschatology and the Parables*, 1963, finds that there are just over forty parables and twenty parabolic statements in the Synoptic Gospels, the parables being distributed as follows: Mark 6; Q 7; Matthew 11; Luke 18.

38. C. G. Montefiore wrote in 1927 (I, p. 106): 'The actual bringing of the Kingdom is not the work of man; . . . it is God's work; he (Jesus) has to proclaim that God will rule, and that man must prepare himself for that rule and make himself worthy of it. This is quite good Pharisaic, Rabbinic doctrine, as opposed to the violent policy of the Zealots.'

39. *The Interpretation of the Fourth Gospel*, Cambridge, 1953, p. 447 n.

40. C. H. Dodd, *Historical Tradition in the Fourth Gospel*, Cambridge, 1963, p. 401; cf. C. H. Roberts, 'The Kingdom of Heaven (Lk. xviii. 21), *Harvard Theological Review*, 41 (1948), pp. 1–8. N. Perrin, *The Kingdom of God in the Teaching of Jesus*, 1963, pp. 58–63, 67 f., 159, points out Dodd's modification of his earlier view that the Kingdom was wholly present. Cf. pp. 65 f. and 201 ff. for comments on interpretations by Dodd and Jeremias of the ethical teaching of Jesus.

41. Perrin, 1963; cf. Manson, 1935.

42. H. B. Swete, *The Parables of the Kingdom*, 1920.

43. Rules concerning the treatment of draught animals and restraint in exploiting nesting birds (Deut. xxii. 6, 10, xxv. 4) may have been motivated more by conceptions of good husbandry and conservation than by compassion. St. Paul's query in I Cor. ix. 9 has been misunderstood because of the AV translation: 'Does God take care for oxen?' The NEB makes it clear that no disregard for the animals' welfare is intended. If an animal's welfare is to be considered much more should there be consideration for the human labourer. Cf. I Tim. v. 18.

44. Fiebig, *Altjüdische Gleichnisse*, 1904, p. 25.

45. Abrahams, I, p. 99; A. Feldman, *Parables and Similes of the Rabbis: Agricultural and Pastoral*, Cambridge, 1927.

46. Cf. *Church and School Hymnal*, 182.

47. The word may mean 'fox' or 'jackal'.

48. *Concerning the Ministry*, 1936, pp. 37, 62.

49. Sir Edwin Arnold, *The Light of the World*, 1896.

50. *Paradiso*, xxvi. 64–66. Tr. D. Sayers.

51. Nineham, pp. 339–362; Fenton, pp. 378–403. Even when 'redeeming the time' is stressed, as in the sending forth of the disciples, Jesus avoids mention of catastrophes, such as flood and earthquake, which might have been cited as illustrations of the vital urgency of decision and action. The prophecies of terrible portents in Lk. xxi.—great earthquakes, famines, pestilences, terrors and 'great signs from heaven' are a composition based on Old Testament passages concerning the Day of the Lord (Deut. xxxii. 35 f.; Isa. xxxiv. 8, xxxv. 4, lxi. 2, lxiii. 4). Luke, writing after the fall of Jerusalem, regards the crisis predicted by Jesus as having occurred and looks forward to a period of uncertain length before the End and the consummation of the Kingdom (Caird, pp. 227–233). It has been suggested that the solar eclipse on 29 November A.D. 29 inspired the reference to a 'sign' by the scribes and Pharisees. (Cf. E. F. F. Bishop, *Jesus of Palestine*, 1955, p. 118.) Other writers of about this period stress the apocalyptic portents (II Esdras v. 4; I Enoch lxxx. 4–7; Assumption of Moses x. 5; Sib. Orac. v. 504 ff.), but in the

teaching of Jesus such allusions are few and it is not certain that all of these are correctly reported (cf. Lk. xvii. 29—Sodom and Gomorrah; Mt. xxiv. 37–39; Lk. xvii. 26—Deluge; Lk. xii. 49—Fire).

52. C. J. Cadoux, *The Life of Jesus*, 1948, pp. 134–137.

53. Cf. Seneca, *Ep. Mor.* xxxviii. 2, referring to words which unfold into larger growth.

NOTES TO CHAPTERS

CHAPTER I

1. D. K. White, 'The parable of the sower', *Journ. Theol. Studies*, 15 (1964), pp. 300–330.

2. *De re rustica*, I. xliv. 2.

3. C. F. D. Moule, *The Birth of the New Testament*, 1962, pp. 149–152. He comments (p. 150): 'Here is a parable about the reception of Jesus' own parabolic teaching—a parable so circumstantial that it appears to be a ready-made allegory'. N. A. Dahl, 'The parables of growth'. *Studia Theologica*, 5 (1951), pp. 132–136; C. E. B. Cranfield, 'St. Mark iv. 1–34', *Scot. Journ. Theol.*, 4 (1951–52), pp. 398–414; 5, 49–66.

W. Neil ('Expounding the parables II. The Sower', *Expository Times*, 77 (1965), pp. 74–77) argues that when Mark compiled his gospel the parable had been transformed from 'A ringing call for faith in God's power to bring his purposes to their triumphant fulfilment, into a searching challenge to self-examination. In the parable the spotlight is on the harvest, in the explanation the spotlight is on the soil.'

4. C. W. F. Smith, *The Jesus of the Parables*, Philadelphia, 1946, pp. 58 f.

5. Manson, 1949, pp. 304–305. For another point of view, see Bultmann, pp. 200, 418. Cf. W. O. E. Oesterley, *The Gospel Parables in the Light of their Jewish Background*, 1936, p. 80.

6. Typical of Dodd's 'realized eschatology' is the following: 'In the few explicitly (non-parabolic) statements which Jesus made about the coming of the Kingdom, it is neither an evolutionary process nor yet a catastrophic event in the future, but a present crisis. It is not that the Kingdom of

God will shortly come, but that it is a present fact' (p. 133). He stresses the thought of harvest rather than of growth. Dahl (p. 157) states that in a certain sense 'we may say that Jesus taught two stages in the coming of the Kingdom, one corresponding to the time of sowing and growth, the other corresponding to the harvest'. In any consideration of these matters it must not be forgotten that some authorities maintain that according to Semitic modes of thought time was considered to be made up of separate points rather than as a flowing process.

7. C. H. Dodd, 1963, pp. 366–387.

8. Although space is not available to discuss our Lord's symbolic actions, such as those at The Last Supper, The Washing of the Disciples' Feet (Jn. xiii. 1–17) and The Writing on the Ground (Jn. viii. 3–11) their relevance in throwing light on the word symbolism in the parables should not be overlooked. In St. John's Gospel the symbolism of events is often emphasized.

9. Dahl, p. 155.

10. H. Schmidt and P. Kahle, *Volkserzählungen aus Palästina*, Göttingen, 1918, pp. 31 f.; Bill., I, p. 672.

11. G. Dalman, *Arbeit und Sitte in Palästina*, Gütersloh, 1932, II, pp. 308 f. Some of the writer's assumptions that ancient agricultural methods were similar to those which he observed should be treated with caution. M. Rihbany in *The Syrian Christ*, 1920, p. 106, speaking of the fairly recent past, states that attempts to weed out tares were often in vain. Women sorted out the grey darnel seeds after threshing.

12. Fenton (pp. 16, 225) points out that the sentence, 'He then dismissed the people, and went into the house where His disciples came to Him . . .' (Mt. xiii. 36) which is set between the parable of The Tares and its explanation, is slightly less than half-way through the Gospel and marks a turning-point in the ministry of Jesus, anticipating His turning from the Jews to the Gentiles. Mark, it is important to note, assigns the first teaching by parables to the time when He turned from the synagogue to His ministry in the Galilean countryside.

13. Manson, 1949, pp. 197 f.; cf. F. W. Beare, *The Earliest Records of Jesus*, 1962, pp. 118 f.

14. J. Manek, 'Fishers of Men', *Novum. Test.*, 2 (1958), pp. 138–141, comments on the association between water and the underworld, rising from or drawing water, and salvation.

15. The Lake of Galilee is rich in species of fish, some definitely unpalatable. H. B. Tristram, in *The Natural History of the Bible*[5], 1877, p. 291 wrote: 'The greater number of the species on the lake are rejected by the fishermen and I have sat with them on the gunwale *while they went*

through their net, and threw out into the sea those that were too small for the market, or were considered unclean.' At Capernaum and in East Africa the cichlid fish served in hotels are good eating. In this group of 'mouth-breeders' the females shelter the eggs and young in their mouths. The story of The Coin in the Fish's Mouth (Mt. xvii. 24–27) evidently relates to a fish of this kind.

16. The parable of The Great Fish in Thomas appears to be a composition based on this parable and The Pearl: 'Man is like a wise fisherman, who cast his net into the sea and drew it out of the sea when it was full of little fishes. Among them the wise fisherman found a large fish. He cast all the little fishes into the sea. He selected the large fish without difficulty. He who has ears to hear, let him hear.' This cannot be authentic. The comparison pictured in this parable is not with the Kingdom of God but with man enlightened by esoteric Gnostic knowledge. Cf. R. M. Grant and D. N. Freedman, *The Secret Sayings of Jesus,* 1963, pp. 120 f.

17. J. Weiss, *Die Predigt Jesu vom Reiche Gottes*[2], Göttingen, 1900.

18. A. Schweitzer, *The Quest of the Historical Jesus*[3], 1954.

19. Beare, pp. 113 f.

20. Dodd, 1963, pp. 369 ff., refers to Jn. xvi. 21 as the parable of The Pains of Childbirth. The metaphor of labour preceding the delivery of a child appears in the Old Testament to indicate the woes expected to precede the joys of the Messianic Age (Isa. xxvi. 16–19, lxvi. 7–14). F. A. Schelling, in 'What means the saying about receiving the Kingdom of God as a little child', *Expository Times,* 77 (1965), pp. 56–58, argues that Mk. x. 15 and Lk. xviii. 17 may be interpreted: 'Whoever does not receive the Kingdom of God as though it were a child will not enter into it.' If this were correct it might favour the interpretation of the Kingdom as growing.

21. Dahl, pp. 132–136. A Syrian writer comments that to the people among whom he was brought up reproduction is 'the most sublime manifestation of God's life' (Rihbany, p. 19). He recalls his father fondling the swelling buds of the vines and murmuring: 'Blessed be the Creator. He is the Supreme Giver. May He protect the blessed increase.'

22. Vincent Taylor, pp. 252, 266.

23. The symbolism was given further currency in The Battle Hymn of the Republic:

> Mine eyes have seen the glory of the coming of the Lord.
> He is trampling out the vintage where the grapes of wrath are stored,
> He hath loosed the fateful lightning of His terrible swift sword.
> His truth is marching on.

24. Cf. Oesterley, p. 76, for examples from rabbinic literature.

25. W. M. Thomson, *Central Palestine and Phoenicia*, 1883, p. 163.

26. In English usage we may occasionally use 'tree' to denote a large herbaceous plant. The Tree Mallow *Lavatera arborea* which grows around our coasts to a height of eight or nine feet is thus named to distinguish it from smaller, related species. The Tree Lupin *Lupinus arborea* of our gardens is a more shrubby plant than the commoner herbaceous species.

27. Black, p. 123. Jeremias, p. 147, believes that the datival introduction indicates that 'the purpose of the parable is to compare the Kingdom of God with the final stage of the process', but he admits, p. 102, that in some parables it may be a later insertion.

28. Bill., I, p. 669. In a number of contexts Luke shows his familiarity with a Gentile rather than a Semitic environment (p. 131).

29. The eagle and the Tree of Life with birds perched on it had great significance in the iconography and literatures of the Ancient East. The motif is found as far east as Mongolia and was incorporated into Christian art in Armenia and elsewhere. Cf. W. Willetts, *Foundations of Chinese Art*, 1965; T. Talbot-Rice, *Ancient Arts of Central Asia*, 1965; M. Eliade, *Shamanism*, 1965; E. O. James, *The Tree of Life*, Leyden, 1967.

Shelter afforded by the fronds carries the associations of God's care (Isa. xxxii. 1 f., xlix. 2).

30. Feldman, p. 151. Cf. Cadoux, pp. 94, 164; Dodd, p. 142. In the Sibylline Oracles 3,767 ff. there is a reference to a world-wide pilgrimage to Zion.

31. Bishop, p. 128, thinks that implied in the parable is the self-seeding and rapid spread of the mustard plant, but this is an extension of its significance rather than implied in it.

32. Manson, 1935, p. 133.

33. Arguments against interpretations which minimize the stress on development in this and other parables have been set forth by Dahl, Cranfield and others. Bultmann, pp. 200, 418, denied Dahl's interpretation and is doubtful of that of Jeremias. He holds that the Kingdom of God was not thought of either by Jesus or the early Church as a human community and that therefore there can be no talk of its growth; consequently it is not surprising that he finds the original point of The Sower and The Leaven irrecoverable. For his views and those of his followers see Perrin, pp. 112–129. The latter argues that the coming of the Kingdom of God is not actually an event in the course of time. In the crisis of decision in which man stands, every hour is his last.

34. Ed. P. Batiffol, 'Le livre de la prière d'Asenèth', *Studia patristica*, I, Paris, 1889, pp. 61.9 ff. Cit. in Jeremias, p. 147. C. G. Montefiore, I,

p. 108, and others have expressed the view that the parable reflects a situation in which Christianity had already achieved wide extension among the heathen, but this is not a necessary inference.

35. A. O'Shaughnessy, *The Music Makers*. For discussion of the germination of ideas in the minds of geniuses and others, cf. R. Harding, *An Anatomy of Inspiration*, Cambridge, 1940; E. A. Armstrong, *Shakespeare's Imagination*, rev. edn, Nebraska University Press, 1963; A. Koestler, *The Act of Creation*, 1964.

36. Plutarch, *Quaest. Rom.* 109, uses it in this sense, but for Philo and Persius it symbolizes vanity—being 'puffed up' with conceit.

37. P. P. Levertoff and H. L. Goudge, *A New Commentary on Holy Scripture*, ad. loc.; Beare, p. 115.

38. Abrahams, I, pp. 51 f.; Bill., I, pp. 728 f.

39. Rihbany, pp. 106–108. The term *khamera* in Syrian dialect = dough. The root in Semitic languages = ferment. Leaven in Biblical times consisted of a piece of fermented dough from a previous baking.

40. Bultmann's opinion (p. 172) that the parable of The Leaven grew by accretion from The Mustard Seed is not convincing, but suggests his recognition of the former as an illustration of speedier growth than in The Mustard Seed.

41. Tristram, 1877, p. 351.

42. Bishop, p. 235. The Beduin also say 'Here is March, an hour of sun, an hour of rain and an hour of the partridge calling. Cf. V. Howells, *A Naturalist in Palestine*, 1956, pp. 95, 114 f.

43. Feldman, p. 151.

44. B. T. D. Smith, p. 91.

45. Dodd, 1963, pp. 369–373.

46. Dahl, p. 145; R. H. Fuller, *The Mission and Achievement of Jesus*, 1954.

47. Similarly in *Macbeth* and *King Lear* unnatural events in nature are associated with man's wickedness and perversity. Cf. Armstrong, 1963.

48. A. S. Lewis in R. H. Charles, *The Apocrypha and Pseudepigrapha of the Old Testament*, II, Cambridge, 1913, pp. 715 ff.; F. C. Conybeare, R. Harris and A. S. Lewis, *The Story of Ahikar*[2], op. cit.

49. The cursing of the barren fig tree (Mk. xi. 12–14) is omitted by Luke. It may have been another parable similar to this or it could have originated from some legend attached to a withered fig tree on the way to Jerusalem. Another suggestion is that Jesus quoted Micah vii. 1: 'My soul desireth the first ripe fig', expecting His disciples to recollect the remainder of the passage and understand that He was commenting on the state of the nation. Instead they supposed He was hungry. Cf.

J. N. Birdsall, 'The withering of the fig tree', *Expository Times*, 73 (1962), p. 191; A. de Q. Robin, 'The cursing of the fig tree in Mark xi: A hypothesis. *New Test. Studies*, 8 (1962), pp. 276–281.

50. Rihbany, p. 181.

51. The raven (Lk. xii. 24), a species whose range extends from the arctic to the tropics, provides an appropriate illustration as it has long been noted as a bird adapted to live alike in flooded areas (Gen. viii. 7) and arid habitats (I Kings xvii. 4–6). It is prominent in mythology and folklore in Europe, Asia and America. Cf. E. A. Armstrong, *The Folklore of Birds*[2], Dover Publications, New York, 1967.

52. Sir Edwin Arnold, 1896.

53. Bishop, p. 80.

54. Nineham, p. 211. A scribe who gave a ruling on the Law not in accordance with majority opinion could be called upon to authenticate his opinion with a 'sign'.

55. The turkey vulture of the New World hunts by scent to some extent, but it is not a true vulture. Two species of vulture and six species of eagle occur in Israel. Cf. P. Arnold, *Birds of Israel*, Haifa, 1962; F. S. Bodenheimer, 'Birds of the Bible' in *A New Dictionary of Birds*, ed. Sir A. L. Thomson, 1964.

56. V. de Watteville in *Speak to the Earth*, 1935, p. 124, noted: 'Lions in the wild state roar only after they have fed.' She was thoroughly familiar with the behaviour of lions, but this is too sweeping a generalization.

57. Authorities differ on the identification of these birds. The 'crane' of the AV may be the swift, and the 'swallow' the crane.

58. According to Bishop, p. 133, The Weather Signs in Mt. xvi. 2 f. are European, not Palestinian. But most authorities believe these verses to be additions to the text. Tristram (p. 33) noted that in forty-three days on which rain fell the wind was invariably west or south-west.

CHAPTER II

1. Jones, pp. 108, 128, 212, points out that 'symbols may be allegorical, but a symbolical tale is not necessarily an allegory. . . . The Pearl is a symbol of the Kingdom; the parable is not an allegory.' The distinction between the symbolical and the allegorical depends mainly on the extent to which an identification, association or comparison is readily made or is artificial. Recognition of symbolism springs from natural association and the acceptance of tradition.

2. Abrahams, II, p. 196.

3. *Hymns A. and M.*, 198 and 94.

4. *Inferno*, iii. 9.

5. The Crisis Parables are usually understood to be The Bride's Attendants (Mt. xxv. 1–13), The Doorkeeper (Mk. xiii. 33–37; Lk. xii. 35–38; cf. Mt. xxiv. 42), The Servant entrusted with Authority (Mt. xxiv. 45–51; Lk. xii. 41–46) and The Talents (Mt. xxv. 14–30; Lk. xix. 12–27), but the atmosphere of crisis pervades other parables, such as The Defendant (Mt. v. 25 f.; Lk. xii. 58 f.).

6. C. S. Lewis, *Miracles: a preliminary study*, 1947, p. 114.

7. S. Legasse, 'L'homme fort' de Luc. xi. 21–22', *Novum. Test.*, 5 (1962), pp. 5–9; W. Zimmerli and J. Jeremias, *The Servant of God*, 1957, pp. 98–104; Taylor, p. 241.

8. C. H. Dodd, 1964, pp. 67 f.

9. Thomas (40) (88. 7–13) includes the Pharisees among those addressed and appends the saying concerning Serpents and Doves (Mt. x. 16 f.): 'Jesus said: The Pharisees and the scribes received the keys of knowledge; they hid them and did not enter in, and did not permit those who wanted to come in. But you be wise as serpents and sincere as doves.' The contrast between serpents and doves was proverbial. Cf. G. Dalman, *Jesus-Jeshua*, 1927, p. 227.

10. Bishop, p. 234.

11. The admonition to 'all' may have been a later addition giving practical application to the parable; but it cannot be assumed that the original audience was a mixed crowd. Moralizing comments giving a general application, which we find appended to a number of parables (Mt. xx. 16, xxii. 14, xxv. 13, xxv. 29; Lk. xii. 21, 48b, xiv. 23, xvi. 10, xviii. 14b) may have been added. A greater or lesser degree of generalization is inevitable in the course of the tradition of parabolic teaching (cf. pp. 17 ff.).

12. *Hymns A. and M.*, 681.

13. Rihbany, pp. 153 f.; J. M. Crum, *The Original Jerusalem Gospel*, 1927, p. 54. Cf. Lk. xvii. 34.

14. Lack of bread does not necessarily indicate poverty; it could be the result of the length of the intervals between bakings. Authorities are not agreed as to how long the interval would normally be. A baking would provide bread for more than one family so that as families could not anticipate calls on supplies occasioned by unexpected visitors they had to rely on the helpfulness of neighbours in such emergencies.

15. Dodd, 1964, pp. 373–379, as noted earlier (p. 39), detects a parable, The Benighted Traveller, in Jn. xi. 9 f.

16. Jeremias, p. 144, following Cadoux, accepts this parable as being a polemical utterance. He regards it as countering opponents who objected to Jesus' mission to outcasts. However this may be, it states plainly the divine compassion. The assertion of a conviction not generally accepted can always be represented as polemical.

17. The NEB translation which represents the widow as 'demanding justice' is more correct than the AV 'avenge me of my adversary' as comparison of the language used in the papyri has shown. 'Adversary' is the usual word for the opponent in a lawsuit. Cf. J. H. Moulton and G. Milligan, *The Vocabulary of the New Testament*, 1906–63, s.v. *enkakeo*.

18. Abrahams, I, pp. 79–81, commenting on Mk. xi. 38–40, claims that the Pharisees defended the cause of widows.

19. H. B. Tristram, *Eastern Customs in Bible Lands*, 1894, p. 128.

20. Bill., II, p. 240; B. T. D. Smith, pp. 178 f.; Manson, 1949, p. 311.

21. *Hymns A. and M.*, 169.

22. Manson, 1949, p. 309.

CHAPTER III

1. *Hymns A. and M.*, 228.

2. Bishop, p. 104.

3. In Mk. xii. 39 the scribes are said to choose the places of honour at feasts. Vincent Taylor, p. 494, comments: 'Mark, or a predecessor, desired to show how completely Jesus had broken with the Rabbis. The selection of the sayings reveals the strong anti-Jewish temper of the Church at Rome, for Mark himself indicates that the relationships of Jesus with the scribes were not always hostile.' Cf. xii. 28–34.

4. Theophrastus and Lucian ridiculed those who gate-crashed important seats at feasts. R. Simeon ben Azzai (*c.* A.D. 110) said: 'Stay two or three seats below thy place and sit until they say to thee, "Go farther up."'

5. Dodd, 1964, pp. 283, 385 f.

6. In the Greek Orthodox Church the emphasis is rather different. Thus the wooden crosses carved on Mount Athos show the Baptism on one side and the Crucifixion on the other.

7. The details of procedure are uncertain. There may have been local variations as there are today. The girls may have prepared to welcome the bridegroom at the entrance to the village. In most modern ceremonies the climax is the bridegroom's nocturnal entry to the paternal home. At weddings of Palestinian Arabs the bridegroom is received with lights,

and delays in his arrival may occur owing to the convention that discussions about the bride's dowry should take place to emphasize her importance. J. A. Findlay, in *Jesus and His Parables*, 1950, p. 111, describes seeing ten girls dancing along at the gate of a Galilean town, keeping the bride company until the bridegroom arrived. It has been argued that the girls in the parable were merely neighbours' children, on the grounds that otherwise some of them would not have been excluded, but the parable implies that they all had a definite rôle in the proceedings.

8. Jeremias, p. 174, refers to *lampades* as 'candles protected by a shade', but later speaks of them as lamps with wicks. Others refer to 'torches'. B. T. D. Smith, p. 101, mentions that the girls fell asleep 'leaving the torches burning', but it is difficult to picture how this could be done. Symbolically, anointing represented blessing and forgiveness (Ps. xxiii. 5; Heb. i. 9).

9. The shut door links this parable with others in the previous chapter. Its message resembles the teaching of the Closed Door and The Doorkeeper. Some critics have advanced the theory that it is an allegorized version of the former, but in view of the wealth and precision of the details this is improbable. It has sustained some modification in being adapted to become a warning to be on the watch for the Parousia.

10. W. Salm, *Beiträge zur Gleichnisforschung*, Göttingen, 1953, pp. 144–146; F. Ll. Griffith, *Stories of the High Priests of Memphis*, Oxford, 1900, pp. 41–66; H. Gressmann, 'Vom reichen Mann und armen Lazarus', *Abhandlungen d. preuss. Akad. d. Wissenschaft, Phil Hist.*, Berlin, 1918, No. 7, pp. 1–90; Bill., II, pp. 231 f.; IV, p. 1081; G. Maspero, *Les Contes populaires de l'Égypte ancienne*[4], Paris, 1911, pp. 154–181.

11. Oesterley, p. 126, suggested that Mt. xxii. 6 f. is a late addition approximating the parable to xxi. 35 f.—the killing of the slaves sent to receive the payments due from the vinedressers. Some scholars regard the messengers as representing the prophets.

12. Fenton, pp. 348 f.

13. P. Fiebig, *Die Gleichnisreden Jesu im Lichte der rabbinischen Gleichnisse des neutestamentlichen Zeitalters*, Tübingen, 1912, pp. 18 f. He points out that the metaphors in these parables are similar: King = God, servant = men, feast = eternal life. Cf. also Mt. xviii. 23 ff., xxv. 14 ff.; Lk. xvii. 10; Bill., I, pp. 878 f.; Oesterley, pp. 128 ff.

14. Cf. Isa. l. 9, li. 6; Pss. cii. 26, civ. 2, 6; Heb. i. 11, for the use of 'garment' with cosmic significance, and Mk. ii. 21 for the new garment as representing the Messianic Age.

15. A. P. Stanley, *Sinai and Palestine*, 1857, p. 350; H. B. Tristram, *Natural History of the Bible*[5], 1877, p. 79; C. Doughty, *Arabia Deserta*, Cambridge, I, 1927, pp. 337 f., 511. During the British mandate of Palestine pariah dogs were so numerous and so infected by rabies that over 15,000 were destroyed. Cf. V. Howells, *A Naturalist in Palestine*, 1956, pp. 55 f.

16. Findlay, p. 86, mentions seeing a ragged man lying under a window in Jerusalem. Dinner was being served. He was told that the beggar was placed there in the morning and removed at night. He picked up the bread which the guests used as hand-wipers and then tossed into the street. Hesychius and Julius Pollux allude to the custom among the Greeks. Shakespeare's dislike of dogs was due to their fawning for food around the table. Cf. W. Whiter, *A Specimen of a Commentary on Shakespeare*, 1794, pp. 138–141; E. Armstrong, 1963, pp. 168–171.

17. Gressmann, 1918, pp. 1–90; Bill., II, pp. 231 f.; B. T. D. Smith, p. 64; Bultmann, pp. 196, 204.

18. Jeremias (p. 60) believes that Mt. xxv. 21, 23, should be translated: 'Enter into the banquet of the Lord'—the ultimate reward of the faithful.

19. In II Enoch the Third Heaven is described as being on the southern side of a ravine and similar to that summarized in Watts' hymn: 'There everlasting spring abides and never-withering flowers' (A. and M., 536), whereas on the other side of the gulf there is darkness and gloom' and murky fire flaming aloft'. In IV Ezra vii. 36 we read:

> And then shall the pit of torment appear,
> and over against it the place of refreshment;
> The furnace of Gehenna shall be made manifest,
> and over against it the Paradise of delight.

20. *Purgatorio*, xxxi. and xxxiii.

21. J. D. M. Derrett in 'Fresh light on St. Luke xvi. II. Dives and Lazarus and the preceding sayings', *New Test. Studies*, 7 (1960–61), pp. 364–380, equates Lazarus = Lazar = Eleazar = Eliezer. Eliezer was Abraham's steward, believed to be the servant sent to look for a bride for Isaac (Gen. xv. 2; xxiv). This suggestion was made as long ago as 1868. Cf. Abrahams, II, p. 203. There is a parallel with the Rich Man's request that Abraham should send Lazarus to warn his brothers. Moreover, earlier in Lk. xvi. we hear of The Dishonest Steward. There appear to be underlying associations linking The Rich Man and Lazarus with some of the imagery and ideas in this chapter and with the raising of Lazarus (Jn. xi. 1–14, xii. 2–17).

22. *Paradiso*, xxvii. 4.

CHAPTER IV

1. The whimsical hyperbole in verse 6 is characteristic of our Lord's teaching—the picture of a deep-rooted tree such as the sycamore being whisked away into the sea (Lk. xvii. 6) and of a mountain sailing through the clouds (Mt. xi. 23). The significance of the latter illustration becomes clearer when we find that an erudite rabbi, able to expound difficult passages of scripture, was called a 'mountain-mover'. In the former we have again the extreme contrast between the tiny mustard seed and the huge tree combined with another extreme contrast—the deep-rooted tree taking to the air like a bird. These extravagant contrasts may be considered oriental hyperbole deliberately employed to lift men's thoughts out of the materialistic rut, as when Jesus pictured the camel shouldering its way through the needle's eye (Mt. xix. 24; Mk. x. 25; Lk. xviii. 25), the meticulous Pharisee gulping down a camel (Mt. xxiii. 24) and the near-blind man spotting a speck of dust in his interlocutor's eye (Mt. vii. 3 f.; Lk. vi. 41 f.). Compare the Hebrew proverb: 'If one says to one: Take the mote from between thine eyes, he would answer: Take the beam from between thy eyes.' Cf. G. Dalman, *Jesus-Jeshua*, 1929, p. 229. The appendix to this work contains a useful comparison of Gospel proverbs and maxims with others found in Jewish literature.

2. F. C. Conybeare *et al.*, *The Story of Ahikar*[2], Cambridge, 1913, p. lxiv. In connexion with the fate of Judas it may be noted that both he and Nadan were guilty of ingratitude. Cf. Zech. xi. 13 f.

3. Burney, 1925.

4. The buckled belt or girded robe, hitched up to facilitate energetic action, and the lamp, are traditional symbols of preparedness (Eph. vi. 14; I Pet. i. 13).

5. *Hymns A. and M.*, 268.

6. In Mark the divisions of the night follow Roman custom, in Matthew they are according to Jewish reckoning.

7. Fenton, pp. 24–26.

8. An historical parallel is provided by Archelaus' journey to Rome. He sought to have his inheritance confirmed, but was followed by a Jewish delegation disputing his claims. He ruthlessly suppressed opposition. Some scholars believe this parable contains an allusion to these events. Cf. S. Perowne, *The Political Background of the New Testament*, 1965, p. 22.

9. As evidence of early attempts to 'gild the lily' the version of this parable in an apocryphal gospel may be mentioned (Gospel of the

Nazarenes). In it there are three servants: 'One who devoured his master's substance with harlots and flute-girls, another who multiplied it by trading, and another who hid the talent.' The first was put in prison, the second accepted and the third rebuked. Cf. M. R. James, *The Apocryphal New Testament*, 1953, p. 3. Manson, 1949, p. 248, considers this kind of expansion arose from an attempt to get over the difficulty presented by verse 30 by a writer who failed to realize that it was not an original part of the parable.

10. An Oxyrhynchus saying (p. 1, saying 6) reads: 'A town built on the summit of a high mountain cannot fall or be concealed.' In Thomas (lxxxvii. 7 f.) we find: 'A city built on a mountain (and) fortified cannot fall and cannot remain hidden.' Grant and Freedman (p. 142) comment that cities on hills are not impregnable, but H. Montefiore in *New Test. Studies*, 7 (1960–61), pp. 240 f., thinks this objection trivial. His view that Thomas preserves an earlier tradition than the Synoptics of The City set on a Hill and The Lampstand (Lk. xi. 33) is not easy to accept.

11. Isaiah (xlix. 6) spoke of the Servant as 'a light to the Gentiles' and said, 'A clearly burning lamp will he not quench' (xliii. 3; cf. lxii. 1 f.). Outstanding rabbis were likened to lamps. Cf. Bill., I, p. 237; Abrahams, II, p. 171.

12. Bill., I, pp. 235 f. A number of allusions show that salt was recognized to have cleansing and strengthening qualities.

13. E. P. Destrick, 'Salt, soil, saviour'. *Bibl. Arch.*, 25 (1962), pp. 41–48. Salt, like leaven, can have opposing significations. In Old Testament times it was believed to cause infertility and to sow with salt was considered a means whereby the curse of infertility could be imposed. Cf. F. C. Fensham, 'Salt as curse in the Old Testament and ancient Near East', *Bibl. Arch.*, 25 (1962), pp. 48–50. Salt, like a number of other substances and objects with unaccountable potency, was regarded as possessing ambivalent qualities.

14. The suggestion by H. Montefiore in 'A comparison of the parables of the Gospel according to Thomas and of the Synoptic Gospels', *New Test. Studies*, 7 (1960–61), pp. 220–248, that Luke's version is a conflation of Mark and the tradition behind Thomas is plausible only in so far as a proverb lies behind all versions of the saying. Cf. Dalman, 1929, p. 229.

15. 'Unrighteous mammon' was not owned morally even if a man were entitled to it legally. Such a person was, in God's eyes, a thief. The steward had gained a name for dishonesty before he compounded with his master's debtors, and during the last phase of his stewardship obtained God's approbation by doing what His law required—releasing

the debtors. His master made the best of the situation by commending what would be regarded as the steward's pious behaviour. As for the steward, even if asked, as he might have been, to take an oath of honest dealing before taking office he had nothing to fear as the oath related to God's law, not man's. Cf. J. D. M. Derrett, 'Fresh light on St. Luke xvi.', *New Test. Studies*, 7 (1961), pp. 198–219. The humour which this writer detects in the parable appears in a number of our Lord's sayings— Mt. vii. 3 f.; Lk. vi. 41 f.; Mt. xxiii. 24 f.

16. G. B. Caird, 'Expounding the parables. I. The Defendant', *Expository Times*, 77 (1965), pp. 36–39.

17. In earlier times such barbarities occurred. Cf. Amos ii. 6, viii. 6; Isa. l. 1; Neh. v. 5.

18. Perrin, pp. 194–196; Jeremias, 1959–60, p. 146.

19. Our Lord's words to Peter, preceding this parable, are in direct contrast to Gen. iv. 24 and the doctrine of an eye for an eye and a tooth for a tooth. Cf. Abrahams, I, pp. 139–167; Oesterley, pp. 91–100; Dalman, 1929, pp. 223 f.

20. For evidence that Shakespeare's thought was powerfully influenced subliminally by scriptural imagery, cf. Armstrong, 1963.

21. Cf. F. A. Wright, *The Girdle of Aphrodite*[2], 1926, p. 10.

22. J. M. C. Toynbee and J. W. Perkins, *The Shrine of St. Peter*, 1956, p. 58.

23. Feldman, p. 238.

24. Bill., I, p. 469.

25. A. Bertholet, *A History of Hebrew Civilization*, 1926, p. 33.

26. Tristram, 1894, pp. 36 f.

27. V. H. Stanton, *The Gospels as Historical Documents*, Cambridge, 1903–9, II, pp. 298 f.

28. L. Cerfaux, 'Les paraboles du Royaume dans l'Évangile de Thomas', *Le Muséon*, 70 (1957), p. 314. Cit. in Jeremias, p. 32.

29. W. J. Perry, *The Children of the Sun*, 1923.

30. Cf. Grant and Freedman, p. 167. Thomas misinterprets Matthew's 'moth and rust'. He assumes *brosis* to mean 'eating' and therefore drags in 'worms'. In contrast to his preference for Thomas' version of The Pearl Jeremias (p. 198) regards his version of The Hidden Treasure as 'completely distorted'.

31. J. C. Fenton ('Expounding the parables. IV. The Parables of the Treasure and The Pearl', *Expository Times*, 77 (1966), pp. 178–180) agrees with Jeremias in preferring the version of Thomas, but if, as Fenton holds, the parables were not originally a pair and Matthew assimilated them to one another he is unlikely to have altered his source from a

general merchant to a merchant in quest of fine pearls. Our preference will be influenced by the extent to which we interpret these parables as eschatological and believe, with these two writers, that the stress is on the element of surprise.

CHAPTER V

1. After noticing a man going from one Arab passenger to another in a train in Jordan I found that he was an evangelist engaged in telling these parables to Moslems. He had found this the best method of introducing them to the Gospel.

2. For comparisons from a rather different standpoint, cf. B. Gerhardsson, 'The Good Samaritan—The Good Shepherd?', *Coniectanea Neotestamentica*, 16 (1958), Lund-Copenhagen. Manson, 1949, p. 282, regards both these parables as belonging to what he calls the Gospel of the Outcast.

3. J. D. M. Derrett, 'Law in the New Testament: Fresh light on the parable of The Good Samaritan', *New Test. Studies*, 11 (1964–65), pp. 22–37.

4. The authenticity of Luke's setting of The Prodigal Son may be queried when we notice that it is introduced: 'He said to His disciples . . .' and observe that in verse 14: 'The Pharisees, who loved money, heard all this . . .' The reference to avarice, more appropriate to the Sadducees, reinforces the probability that the Pharisees are dragged in.

5. Jeremias, pp. 202 f. H. Montefiore, 'Thou shalt love thy neighbour as thyself', *Novum. Test.*, 5 (1962), pp. 156–170.

6. As an exception, Abrahams, II, pp. 39 f., cites a Midrash story of a shipwrecked Roman who was given hospitality and financial help by a rabbi.

7. An outstanding instance of hatred of a third party causing those at daggers drawn to make common cause is provided by the joint denunciation of Archelaus in A.D. 6 by Jews and Samaritans.

8. H. H. Rowley, *Men of God*, 1963, p. 270.

9. Josephus, *Antiquities*, xv. 7; Jerome, Ep. xxvii; A. P. Stanley, *Sinai and Palestine*, 1857, pp. 314, 424.

10. F. C. Grant, *The Economic Background of the Gospels*, Oxford and London, 1926, p. 52.

11. C. V. Glines, *Doolittle's Tokyo Raiders*, 1964, pp. 374 f., 414; Cf. E. Gordon, *Miracle on the River Kwai*[2], 1965.

12. Theophrastus, *Hist. plant.*, ix. 12; Bill., I, p. 428. Oil and wine

were used sacrificially (Apoc. vi. 6) and had much traditional symbolism. An odd detail is that the bandaging is mentioned first.

It is difficult to avoid the conviction that the parable of The Good Samaritan contains reminiscences of II Chron. xxviii. 15 which tells how the naked were clothed, anointed and carried upon asses to Jericho. Then their benefactors returned to Samaria. Derrett, p. 36, regards the parable as 'a kind of midrash' on Hosea vi. 6 and adjacent or at least as a sermon hung on these verses.

13. *Jerusalem zur Zeit Jesu*[2], Göttingen, 1958, IIA, p. 38. A labourer's normal day's pay was one silver piece (denarius) (Mt. xxvii. 7). Bill., I, p. 831.

14. It has been maintained that the parables in Luke are 'literary productions' (Black, pp. 132 f.) and some writers have commented that The Prodigal Son, in common with The Good Samaritan, shows no traces of having been translated from the Aramaic. Cf. J. H. Moulton, *Grammar of New Testament Greek*, 1906-63, II, i, p. 8. But Jeremias in 'Zum Gleichnis vom verlorenen Sohn', *Th. Ztschr.*, 5 (1949), pp. 228-231, has pointed out that it contains numerous Semitisms.

15. Grant, pp. 81-87; Abrahams, I, p. 184.

16. Bill., II, p. 214.

17. C. G. Montefiore, 'Rabbinic conceptions of repentance', *Jewish Quart. Rev.*, 16 (1904), pp. 209-257.

18. H. M. Hocart, *Kingship*, 1927; E. O. James, *Christian Myth and Ritual*, 1933. Cf. Gen. xli. 42; I Macc. vi. 15. In the consecration of a Roman Catholic bishop a ring is placed on his finger.

19. Manson, 1935, pp. 89-115; Jeremias, 1965.

20. In rabbinic literature there is teaching with some points of similarity to the parable of The Prodigal Son. Abrahams, I, p. 92, mentions a parable concerning a king who had two sons, one dutiful, the other depraved, designed to illustrate the Pharisaic principle that 'the penitent sinner stands on a higher level than the completely righteous'. In Samaritan literature there is no mention of God as Father. Cf. J. Macdonald, *The Theology of the Samaritans*, 1964, p. 451.

21. Matthew reports this as referring to the doctors of the Law and Pharisees, but they were not specially noted for breaking their word. Moreover, it is hard to reconcile the advice to follow their words and reject their practice. Some scholars believe that verse 32 is secondary and that the setting among the 'chief priests and elders' may not be original (Fenton, p. 339). The parable is of such general application that there are other settings in which it would be appropriate.

22. Jeremias, 1965, p. 25.

23. Dodd, 1963, pp. 330, 380, points out that 'The truth will set you free' and 'He who commits sin is a slave' are Stoic maxims.

24. Grant, pp. 87–110. Taxation was two-fold, religious and civil, each levied without relation to the other.

25. Oesterley, pp. 182 f.; Fiebig, p. 84.

26. Isaiah (xlix. 22), describing the return of the exiles, speaks of their coming home with their sons in their bosom and their daughters on their shoulders.

27. Danger to man from wild beasts would not be great and the shepherd would seldom be called upon to 'lay down his life for the sheep' (Jn. x. 14 f.). Until less than a century ago leopards were fairly numerous in some areas of Palestine. A wounded or cornered leopard could kill a man. There seems to be no authenticated instance of a wolf attacking a human being in the Middle East though Tristram (p. 154) was followed by one. Rihbany (p. 217) speaks of a shepherd's 'battles' with hyaenas and Jeremias (p. 220) quotes an account of an attack by thirty of these animals when men were killed. Such reports should be treated with reserve. In East Africa children or persons asleep are sometimes seized by hyaenas. In one area as many as eight people were killed in a year, but there seems to be no instance of an able-bodied man being killed. Cf. F. A. Balestra, The man-eating hyaenas of Mlane, *African Wild Life*, 16 (1962), pp. 25–27. Undoubtedly straying sheep would be in jeopardy from predatory animals besides hyaenas, especially leopards and wolves.

28. B. T. D. Smith, p. 190; C. G. Montefiore, II, p. 249.

29. Cf. Trench, 1893, p. 385 for references to the literature of early Christian iconography; also W. Lowrie, *Early Christian Art*[2], New York, 1965.

30. Dodd, 1963, pp. 384 f., 423; J. A. T. Robinson, 'The parable of John x. 1–5', *Zeitschrift für die neutestamentliche Wissenschaft*, 1955, pp. 233–240, and in *Twelve New Testament Studies*, 1962.

31. Jeremias, 1965, p. 48, points out that, as recorded in Mk. xiv. 28, Jesus used shepherd language—'after I am raised again I will go on before you into Galilee'. Tristram, 1877, p. 140, wrote: 'The eastern shepherd never *drives*, but always leads, his sheep, and that without aid of a dog'. Rihbany, p. 211 f., states that 'the shepherd does not now invariably go before his flock'. This agrees with my own observations in Palestine. Breeds of sheep differ in the degree to which they flock closely. The merino is more social than the black face of our northern moors and fells and is therefore of a type more suited to conditions such as were characteristic of ancient Palestine in which straying sheep were liable to be seized by predators. From early times shepherds had dogs (Job xxx. 1) which

gave warning of and intimidated wild animals. Rihbany refers to the shepherd's dog lying near his tent at the entrance to the sheepfold. Many travellers testify that the sheep will not obey the voice of strangers (Jn. x. 5).

32. W. Tooley, 'The shepherd and sheep image in the teaching of Jesus', *Novum. Test.*, 7 (1964), pp. 15–25.

33. One traveller refers to a shepherd acting as door to the sheepfold. He rode up at dusk to a doorless sheepfold crowded with sheep. The walls were fortified with thorns. He writes: 'So I asked the shepherd, standing there, what was the use of walls and thorns when there was no door. "Oh," he said, "I sleep in the doorway. *I am the door.*" "Ya abdur Rahmon," he shouted. "Open up a stall for the guest and his horse." And to him and for me *the porter opened*' (J. van Ess, *Meet the Arab*, 1947, p. 74). The little parable, The Blind Leaders (Mt. xv. 14; Lk. v. 39), pictures a situation contrasted with that in which the wise shepherd leads his flock. I am reminded of seeing strings of six or eight blind men in single file, each with a hand on the shoulder of the man in front, led through the streets of a Chinese city by a sighted companion.

34. Jeremias, p. 209; Manson, 1949, p. 249; T. Preiss, *Life in Christ*, 1957, p. 47.

35. J. A. T. Robinson, 'The "Parable" of the sheep and the goats', *New Test. Studies*, 2 (1955–56), pp. 228 ff.

ACKNOWLEDGEMENTS

I am very grateful to the Rt. Rev. Bishop Chase for his careful reading of this book in manuscript, to Mr. J. F. Burnet of Magdalene College, Cambridge, for scrutinizing the proofs and to Mrs. T. R. Henn for her encouragement. During nearly twenty-four years as Vicar of St. Mark's Church, Cambridge, the relationship of challenge and response with those to whom I have had the privilege of ministering has contributed much to my understanding and interpretation of the parables so that I owe thanks greater than I can express to my Cambridge friends.

Cambridge   EDWARD A. ARMSTRONG
August, 1966